I HAVE ALWAYS BEEN ME

a memoir

PRECIOUS

BRADY-DAVIS

TOPPLE
BOOKS

Little

Published by TOPPLE Books & Little A, New York
www.apub.com

Amazon, the Amazon logo, TOPPLE Books, and Little A are trademarks of
Amazon.com, Inc., or its affiliates.

ISBN-13: 9781542044301 (hardcover)
ISBN-10: 1542044308 (hardcover)
ISBN-13: 9781542044318 (paperback)
ISBN-10: 1542044316 (paperback)

Cover design by Faceout Studio, Lindy Martin
Cover photograph © 2021 KORTO PHOTOGRAPHY
Cover illustration by David Cooper

Unless otherwise noted, all photos are courtesy of the author.

Printed in the United States of America

First edition

For Myles, who has shown me the most unconditional love I have ever known in this life. May we never part, not even through the passage of eons.

For Zayn, whose light shines so bright. You are the joy of my life. The spell is broken; the blessing is yours to inherit.

Contents

AUTHOR'S NOTE

Some names and identifying details relating to individuals who are part of my story have been changed.

One might say that the culmination of this experiment would leave me healed—understanding myself better and being further equipped to let go of the painful trauma and celebrate the triumphs I have experienced in my life. I would say both of those things are true. As I revisited the corridors and mirrors of my life, I found various lessons learned along the way on a journey that includes a multitude of experiences that one book cannot contain. For much of the text, I implored myself to not give direct advice, as I want individuals to pull out pieces of my story that relate to their own and collective experiences. At least that's my favorite part of memoirs and representation in itself, the ability to see we are a part of something bigger, in particular, for marginalized voices such as mine who have been cast off until recent years. Writing this book was deeply painful at times, and I often felt I didn't have the stamina to keep writing as I plunged myself underneath hot water in my bathtub filled with bubbles to find clarity and courage. I did. I hope you'll read it that way too. Sojourn with me. Myles, thank you for being my rock and for all you gave up so that I could write. Where possible

I consulted the parties written about within these pages to ensure my memory was in sync with theirs. This is my story and my experience to tell for such a moment as this. In some ways this memoir is an end, but for me this work is also a beginning and a reintroduction. I'm more than gowns and pretty pictures. I feel lighter having written it, absolutely vulnerable to my core, and could by no means have gotten through this without the support of my therapist. Thank you, June. This is my final letting go of the snares of my past. I discuss many triggering topics in this text, but it serves as my testament of truth after conquering life's fears one by one. It is my hope, by the end of this book, that you, too, find the freedom to let go of those things that have ensnared you and need to be spoken out loud. The work continues . . . in truth and love.

—P

A NOTE FROM TOPPLE BOOKS

What does it mean to be resilient? The life of Precious Brady-Davis is a towering example of how one can take charge of their life and live their truth as they have always dreamed.

Precious Brady-Davis's intimate memoir invites readers to follow her journey out of a difficult childhood in and out of the foster care system and her transition from a gender-nonconforming kid in Omaha, Nebraska, to Precious, a formidable social justice advocate and proud transgender woman of color. I am in awe of Precious's strength, courage, and sheer determination in this story of faith and survival. At TOPPLE Books, we are passionate about shining a light on stories that reveal universal truths, and I can't think of a better example than Precious's hopeful journey.

—Joey Soloway, TOPPLE Books editor-at-large

PROLOGUE

I'm filled with an almost overwhelming sense of peace. It's dawn, and my newborn daughter and husband are asleep. Looking out the bay window of our bedroom as the sun peeks its head out over Chicago, drenching Lake Michigan in light, I can't help but smile. If someone had told me that one day I'd settle into blissful family life at the age of thirty, that I would meet my soul mate, appear on a nationally syndicated TV show to choose the wedding dress of my dreams, then support my husband through a pregnancy, I would have *very theatrically* laughed in their face!

Yet in order to live my very best life now, especially as a mother, a wife, and a public figure, I need to resolve some of the lingering questions from my childhood. That is, in part, why I'm writing this book.

How much trauma can one endure as a child before subconscious survival mechanisms override our minds, and memories can't be trusted? As I reflect now on my childhood, I still don't have any definite answers. Dredging up memories brings to mind the photo albums that were a great pride of my childhood. I used to page through the images with the beaming delight of what *family* meant and could be. There were photos of us as little kids at the zoo, eating ice cream, on the swing set in the backyard. One particular image is seared in my mind, although I cannot look at the original now to cross-check my memory with reality because one of my relatives refuses to share the albums or photos with the rest of the family. She claims they are buried in storage.

This photo shows me at my first public swimming pool. I'm on the other side of a chain-link fence, staring into the camera, wearing a peculiar expression and a light pink shirt, my curly hair billowing. My enigmatic *Mona Lisa* moment. I have this feeling that if I could just see that face again, my own face as a child—if I could just look into my own eyes, all my questions would be answered. Was I happy? Was I afraid? Was I just a normal kid in a normal family? Or could it be that I was surrounded by abuse all along?

The iterations of family in my childhood were fraught and complicated, full of drama and instability and hurt, and so I didn't believe that I would ever have a family life that was any different, that was stable and loving and would allow me to be who I am, who I have always been. Now I sift through a combination of powerful visceral memories and vaguer muddied memories, along with an ugly, disjointed puzzle of family hearsay, in order to arrive at a version of the truth about my early life. Many of the details included here came to me much later in life and, rather than bringing clarity, only added to the cacophony of trauma and uncertainty around trust and family. This story is painful to construct, but I'm committed to doing the necessary excavation so that I can heal and get clarity, so that I can move forward and show up for the family I've created. And, for those who have been or are going through their own difficulties and confusions, who are feeling lost or alone or unloved, I offer my story of hardship and healing as a vision of a way through. There is love—whatever that means to you—on the other side, if you are willing to claim who you are, stand up for yourself, and do what it takes to create it.

ONE

Early Family Trouble

I was under two years old, running around the Twenty-Fourth Street projects of North Omaha in dirty diapers, when my birth mother, Tammy, lost custody of me and my two siblings. My father, Nathaniel Paul Holbert Sr., was in and out of the picture, and when he did come around, he ruled Tammy with his fists. He used to whoop her ass for being neglectful of his son, especially when she took me outside without adequately dressing me for the Nebraska cold. Right after my younger sister, Tanisha, was born, and Tammy gained a third baby daddy, the struggle of single parenting became too much for her—and she fell apart.

A five-inch scar across my stomach serves as a visual reminder of that time of neglect. From what I'm told, it was a bad burn from the door of the oven. In one version of the story, Tammy inflicted the injury, not through violence but by way of carelessness. She used to leave the oven on and open during the winter to heat our home, and she says she told me time and again to stay away, but I was "hardheaded" and went and climbed on it anyway. I was barely a year old.

My older brother, Dexter, who was around six at the time, finally worked up the nerve to tell one of our neighbors about the ongoing neglect, filth, and unsafe conditions we were subjected to, though he probably didn't use those words. That neighbor called the authorities, and we were admitted to the Child Saving Institute, an Omaha-based organization that provided emergency shelter to children in crisis, among other services.

Tammy remembers it differently. She said the burden of parenting simply overwhelmed her and eventually caused her to have a psychotic break. She was admitted to the hospital—but she wouldn't be formally diagnosed with bipolar disorder until decades later. She says she begged her father, my grandfather Clyde, to take us while she was institutionalized, but he refused at first. In the end, she dropped us off at the Child Saving Institute on her way to seek help, and it was only because she ended up being hospitalized for over a month, surpassing the crisis center's holding term, that we wound up in the foster care system.

Those few chaotic years after we were given up are blank in my mind. Of course, I was only a toddler. I have no memories of any of the homes or foster families Dexter, Tanisha, and I shuffled between. I do remember the first murmurs, after I turned four, that we would be going to live with Grandpa Clyde and Grandma Ethne, and a vague understanding that this was going to be a permanent situation. I now know that Tammy relinquished full guardianship over us one at a time, first Dexter, then me, then Tanisha. As a child who already felt unwanted, my partial understanding of that situation combined with the knowledge that Tanisha was still technically Tammy's child after I was given up, confirmed all my suspicions. I was a mistake; I was unloved. It took years for my grandfather to explain that he adopted us then, after three years in state care, because no single foster family would take all three of us, and we were about to be split up into different homes. He couldn't bear to see us separated.

~

The day he and Grandma Ethne formally adopted me was a major turning point in my life. In some ways it was my first transition, my first transformation, from being a Holbert Jr. to becoming a Davis. It was a weekday, so I had to miss school, and I remember that morning getting dressed in my nicest clothes, filled with nervous excitement. Most of the court proceedings were too boring and complicated for my young brain to take in, but I distinctly remember the judge addressing me directly at one point.

"Do you know what you are doing?" she asked. "Do you know what this all means?"

I found her intimidating, but I considered the question and realized that, without actually understanding it all logically, I somehow *did* know what it meant. I knew it was a big change, and I knew I had a choice. I felt powerful in that moment, knowing I had a say in my own fate. This would be a fresh start. A new life. A new me.

I also felt a deep sense of loss. In order to be adopted, I had to be given up first. Tears streamed down my face as the judge made the official pronouncement that I was now Nathaniel Paul Davis. It felt right, it sounded right, but it was also a farewell. An end of the short-lived Holbert dynasty. I had been a junior, after all, named after the father I never knew. Even at such a young age, I understood the power that exists in a name. Names speak to identity. Names speak to origin.

Shortly thereafter, I learned of my birth father's death. And so, with that, my surrender of his name, and the official separation from Tammy, I felt the last tether to my birth parents dissolve.

Being fully and permanently cut off from that significant piece of identity was a loss, yes, but also a liberation. My father had abandoned my mother, along with countless other women, and my mother had abandoned me. Now I was no longer part of that legacy.

I had just started kindergarten, and Clyde and Ethne had elected to enroll me in the morning class with Mrs. Kohrs. I remember rushing to the classroom with so much excitement—I couldn't wait to tell her I was a Davis now! But as we entered the room, I froze in my tracks at the sight of the kids gathered around the weather-wheel chart.

I realized suddenly that the afternoon session was not just at a different time but was attended by a different kind of kid. The afternoon class had been made up almost completely of black and brown students, but my morning class was a mix of mostly white and some brown faces. And there I was, somewhere in between, seeing faces that looked like mine in a group I was not yet part of, being escorted by my interracial grandparents. Without knowing the term, I experienced my first feeling of *otherness*. That class stared at us like we were the strangest thing they'd ever seen. I watched their eyes dart from me to my grandparents, back to me, to the teacher, to me again.

I knew that my grandparents wanted me in the morning session for a reason, but I never really understood why until that moment. Now I realized I was not like the black kids *or* the white kids. That was the major formative experience in the development of my racial self-perception. I understood that being biracial put me in a unique position, and that I would never be fully accepted unless I leaned all the way into one side. I felt truly, profoundly different.

As if my racial uncertainties weren't enough to grapple with, it was also around this time that I started playing dress-up and house, and an awareness of my gender started to emerge. I would wrap a blanket around my waist and turban-tie a bath towel onto my head and glide down the halls as if wearing a floor-length gown. Inspired by the likes of Jem and the Holograms, Carmen Sandiego, and Storm from X-Men, I was in my element. Many an afternoon was spent prancing across the picnic tables in our backyard as I holler-sang Whitney Houston's "I Will Always Love You" as loud as I could. *"And I-ee-yah-ee-yah will always loovee yoooouuuu!"* The tall trees of the ravine were my proscenium, and the neighbors' uninhabited backyards served as my audience.

Growing up in the early nineties provided no end of divas to emulate: Tina Turner, Bette Midler, Paula Abdul, Madonna, Janet Jackson, and Mariah Carey. I remember whenever Grandma Ethne would overhear me running around the house singing, "I'm a private dancer, a dancer for money. I'll do what you want me to do," she would recoil and say, "Do you know what you're singing and what that means?" I would have to admit that I didn't, and she'd follow up with, "So don't sing it, then." But I didn't care. I loved the way Tina moved in that music video. I wanted to be one of the guests at her grand Halloween party and saunter into the middle of the black-and-white checkered floor and serve high drama on the promenade at midnight.

I loved Grandpa Clyde and Grandma Ethne's little house on Sixty-Sixth Street, where I spent the best years of my childhood. It was nestled between North and Northwest Omaha, between urban ghetto and suburban sprawl. With them lived Dexter, Tanisha, and I, plus Nina and Ginger, Clyde and Ethne's biological daughters, and so technically our aunts. Through adoption they became our sisters, and our grandparents became our parents. It is much more complicated to untangle and explain now than it felt at the time. Back then, we were just a family.

Our house was the first on the block, with light blue siding and rickety double garage doors that rumbled the living room every time they opened. There was a huge spray of pink peony bushes on the side of the house and two small white pedestal planters out front, blooming in the spring with snapdragons, marigolds, and other foliage that I could peer out at from the laundry room. At the back of the laundry room, there was a tiny doorway that led into the storage space under the stairs, a forbidden entrance that was like a portal to another world. The door opened to a secret and slightly spooky type of playland, filled with the boxes and trash bags that held the Halloween and Christmas decorations I longed for all year. We loved sneaking in there, but it was imperative that we not get caught. "Don't slam that door!" was a phrase we were often admonished with. Even accidentally slamming a door was seen as flagrant disrespect and grounds for severe punishment in the Davis household, so entering an off-limits area was an enter-at-your-own-risk endeavor, which brought the promise of swift rebuke.

In fact, most areas of the Davis household were considered prohibited. The kitchen, the furniture in the living room, the garage, the basement, the cupboards, the closets and hallways were the exclusive jurisdiction of the adults—Nina, Granddad, and Grandma Ethne—and required their explicit permission to enter or use. Even if Granddad allowed us in an adult space, he made us adhere to his favorite motto: "Children are to be seen and not heard." We were never to sit on the couches in his presence. Even if the whole family was watching a movie together, the kids sat on the floor. Only on rare occasions would we be granted the privilege of sitting on the gray velvet plushness.

On the right side of the house was a crumbling concrete porch with a black iron railing, where Grandma Ethne would sit watching us play four square as the sun set. We had a big fenced-in backyard that butted up to a wooded ravine and a small creek. We had our own big wooden swing set back there too, with a yellow slide, three blue swings, and an old rocking horse that Granddad had built and rigged up as a fourth swing. To the left of our house was a public swimming pool, where Nina often took Dexter, Ginger, Tanisha, and me on hot summer days.

Nina was much older than us and felt more like another maternal figure than a sister. She was finishing high school when I started kindergarten, and I looked up to her so much, especially for her fashion and her beauty. She was my first example of true glamour. She used to spend hours in the bathroom perfecting her tightly defined, coiffed curls and beat face, and her eyeliner was always on point! To me she was a goddess; she defined femininity. Looking back now, she seemed like the perfect nineties stereotype of a girl who dreams of driving a Jeep one day and gossips in bed on a phone with a long cord.

Ginger was a different story. She was shy and socially awkward, but always managed to be outspoken when it came to her feelings about our adoption: she didn't approve. She was clearly Granddad and Grandma's favorite and was allowed to do things Dexter, Tanisha, and I couldn't. I never recall Ginger being hit, although the rest of us received our fair share of swats from a long wooden paddle, or spanks, slaps, and belt-whips, and in extreme cases, a swift lashing from a switch Grandma Ethne would make us pluck ourselves from the peony bush.

Ginger, in my opinion, reflected some symptoms of being on the autism spectrum, but when we were kids, we all just thought she was annoying. She would always have something smart-alecky to say to me and my siblings like "That's why you were given up" or "Y'all mom ain't shit," so Dexter, Tanisha, and I would often gang up and terrorize her. We had a favorite game called sandwich, where one person would lie in between two couch cushions, and the rest of us would jump on top of them. Ginger usually ended up in between the cushions, which led to her crying and calling foul, even though she could sure dish it. Tanisha and I would laugh so hard we'd fall over. We got our asses beat, but it always seemed worth it—we were simply evening out the odds.

With Granddad's gig as a deejay at local nightclubs and Ethne often working overtime at her telemarketing job, my siblings and I ended up raising ourselves a lot of the time, and even more so after Nina got married, left the house, and moved on with her life. We were alone so often in the summers and evenings after school that a kind of structure and rhythm set in over time. Yes, there was a fair bit of wildness, and we certainly wreaked havoc on the neighborhood every now and then, but we also had our own little family dynamic among us young kids—except for Ginger. Friday nights were especially memorable. Ethne would leave us a check for twenty dollars, and we'd order the family feast from Godfather's, the local pizza spot, then watch the full TGIF ("Thank God It's Friday") lineup of ABC shows. I didn't realize it then, but those shows were ahead of their time. They each featured various representations of a blended family: *Family Matters, Boy Meets World, Step by Step, Hangin' with Mr. Cooper, Full House,* and *Sabrina the Teenage Witch* all challenged the notion of what the nuclear family unit could be.

We'd still bicker and argue, and of course taunt Ginger, but we also took pleasure in parenting ourselves. Our house was like the island of Lost Boys from *Hook,* where secretly we might have yearned for a mother's embrace, but we also relished our independence and would walk the plank to keep it. We learned to be self-sufficient through the process of feeding and entertaining ourselves. Would I have preferred it if my parents were more present and participatory? Yes. But that longing manifested itself mostly when I compared myself to the other kids at school, whose parents attended every holiday program, volunteered on the PTA, and attended class parties. In the day-to-day reality of our young lives, we felt powerful and free and mature beyond our years.

Granddad Clyde Davis was a disc jockey, emcee, and concert promoter extraordinaire, commonly known around town in entertainment circles as the DJ. He was a Detroit native who came to Omaha in the early 1960s, destined to make a mark. With his slicked-back ponytail and ball cap, eyebrows darkened with black eye pencil, thick mustache, high-prescription glasses, gold chain, gold watch, and brown loafers, he had an undeniable signature style.

We saw very little of him because he was always out hustling his cat-daddy persona. For decades, he hosted wildly successful functions that brought big-name national acts to Omaha, when no one else was doing it—Cameo, ZAPP, Shalamar, Marvin Gaye, James Brown, and later, Da Brat, Brandy, Salt-N-Pepa, and TLC. I was keenly aware of Granddad's small-time "fame" within Omaha because I heard about it wherever I went. Trips to the grocery store quickly turned into meet-and-greets with fans reminiscing about his days hosting teen parties at the Omaha Civic Auditorium, playing the Warehouse Nightclub in Carter Lake and Sunday night "Soul Skate" at Skateland. Everyone knew him.

He had an entire recording studio in our basement, where he recorded commercials, blasted albums from his turntables, and housed thousands of dollars' worth of deejay equipment that included mixers, rainbow speakers, and thousands of records from the sixties, seventies, eighties, and early nineties. I grew up hearing the words "Mic check, one two" over and over and over. As his career wound down, he would later deejay weddings, school dances, and other kinds of local social events.

All that local fame and swagger is probably how he attracted his second wife, Ethne, with whom he was in a common-law marriage before I was born. Ethne was a white woman from Seward, Nebraska, a small town outside Omaha, and she was a country girl, short with shoulder-length brown hair and rail-thin. Charlesetta, Granddad's first wife and my biological grandmother, was tall, thin-framed, fair-skinned, and freckled. I've never seen her in anything but a no-fuss pixie wig as far back as I can remember. She told me stories of Granddad's philandering when they were married but never seemed particularly bothered. In her version of the story, she put up with the knowledge of Ethne's existence for a long time. I imagine the DJ in full *Super Fly* fashion, parading his white mistress around. Granddad disputes this account and maintains that he met Ethne much later, and only after divorcing Charlesetta. But I believe my soft-spoken and unbothered grandmother who tells me the story of putting her foot down the day she came home to find Ethne lounging on *her* couch in *her* living room. She packed her bags and left that day. And so, many years later, when Granddad and Ethne adopted Dexter, Tanisha, and me, it was into a mixed-race family.

I was raised with hardly any knowledge of Grandma Charlesetta's existence, and later, as an adult, I realized it was because from Ethne's perspective, *she* was the "other woman." It pains me that I had no relationship with Charlesetta growing up. But whatever critiques I may find now in the choices Granddad and Ethne made, or in their general parenting style or characters, at the time, as a child rescued from abandonment and foster care, I was simply overjoyed to have a family and parents of any kind who cared about me.

I've always called my birth mom Tammy. She was never Mom to me. I barely even regarded her as a family member, let alone a parental figure. The idea of her, a total stranger, giving birth to me was incomprehensible. My interactions with her were on supervised visits at a Nebraska Department of Health and Human Services (DHHS) building, which was tucked in the back of an industrial park on the edge of Omaha's suburbs near Elkhorn, the next town over.

I remember the afternoon so vividly, sitting between Dexter and Tanisha in the back seat of the social worker's car with its tufted maroon seats and toying with the metal seat-belt buckle, just *seething* with resentment and plotting my performance for the meeting with Tammy. I was around seven. Soon we pulled up to a row of cars marked with the DHHS logo, and I steeled myself. I was going in with the clear intention of appearing totally aloof and unbothered. I was not here to *get* anything. I was not wishing for love or trying to earn approval. This was just an appearance. Fulfilling an obligation.

We entered the room where Tammy sat waiting on an ugly old sofa. Dexter and Tanisha squealed and ran to hug her, and as she hugged them back, I walked over to the corner and settled down to play with the colorful abacus and the Fisher-Price rotary phone. Over the course of the visit, Tammy didn't say anything to me, and I didn't look over at her, not once. It was so much easier than acknowledging the reality of the situation. I believed the stories I had heard from other family members, that Tammy really didn't care, and least of all about me. I focused on the bright colors in front of me, anything to keep from looking at the stranger taking notes on the visitation session. Anything to keep from looking at Tammy, who I knew was not watching my performance.

Our family was moderately religious, the kind of family who prayed over our dinner every night. Church was a constant that I never questioned. On Sundays I relished walking up the tiled staircase of Victory Church into big hugs from glamorous greeters who stood in the foyer. Many of the greeters were the same women who performed ribbon dances in front of the altar, waving purple and gold flags and silver metallic ribbons, adorned in flowing dresses and skirts, statement jewelry, and of course high-heeled pumps. I remember especially the way the pastor's wife, Laura, would enter and stride up the aisle to her seat in the first pew. Her authoritative strut and meticulous presentation announced the arrival of the "first lady." Everything was always on point: hair, makeup, and accessories. As if to add to the air of glamour, she would always show up fashionably late, ten minutes after the service started.

But the woman I most identified with and looked up to was Nina. I idolized her and probably subconsciously hoped I would grow up to *be* her. In the summer before I entered third grade, she took me shopping with her to find a pair of shoes that would match her off-white wedding dress. She ended up finding a pair at Payless that she liked, but we had to leave them behind to be dyed the exact ivory color she needed (in the nineties, dyeable shoes were all the rage). Her wedding colors were ivory and navy blue, air force colors, in homage to her fiancé, Marshall. When the shoes were ready and we brought them back home, I couldn't wait until Nina left the house so I could sneak into her room and try them on. It was well known in my house, even that early on, that I was *obsessed* with Nina's high heels. My grandparents absolutely hated this, and so did Nina, because this meant I would routinely enter her room without permission. To me, those heels were simply irresistible. She had such *bad* taste in shoes, and when I say "bad," I mean it in the sense of *mesmerizing*!

As soon as she left to go hang out with her friends, I raced into her room to find the box and try on those gorgeous custom wedding pumps! I nervously glanced toward her large collection of wide-eyed stuffed animals piled in a hanging net, the only witnesses to my crime. But nothing could stop my mission, and soon I was strutting up and down the halls, tripping on our matted green carpet, clomping because the shoes weren't even close to fitting, but feeling so right and so fabulous. Nina eventually came home and of course immediately noticed the box wasn't how she'd left it. She was livid, and there was no denying I was the culprit because my tiny feet had bent the corners of the shoes very noticeably. I'm lucky I was still the ring bearer in her wedding.

In my defense, I didn't feel like I had a choice when it came to this kind of behavior. I engaged in brazen acts of femininity all throughout my childhood, more often than not involving women's shoes, and almost always getting me into a lot of trouble. One memorable day I risked my experimentation outside the safety of our home, and "accidentally" wore Tanisha's Mootsies Tootsies to school. These were a popular kind of loafer for girls at the time, unmistakably not a boy's shoe. When confronted by my classmates for the ill-fitting and feminine shoes, I gave the performance of a lifetime, looking down at my feet with utter shock and embarrassment at this *horrible mistake* I'd made in my morning rush!

Looking back, I wonder whether wearing those shoes was *just* an act of feminine desperation, or did a part of me *want* to get caught and questioned? Maybe subconsciously I hoped that if I let these urges play out, someone else would be able to tell me what they meant.

I did enjoy some "boy" activities, like playing kickball at Victory Church with the Royal Rangers, which was like a Christian version of the Boy Scouts. I loved those evenings spent running around the kickball field as the sun went down on Fifty-Sixth and Sorensen Parkway, surrounded by a group of people I felt fully accepted by. I also helped out with the weekly Metro Kids Bus Ministry, where we'd pick up kids from all over Omaha and bring them to church on Saturdays for programming that included watching the Gospel told through puppet skits and mentorship activities meant to foster emotional and spiritual development. I usually assisted on the route that picked up kids from a few different trailer parks, and I always felt such purpose and pride in overseeing packing the game bins, passing out snacks, and making sure each young person was accounted for. At our church gatherings, I was always the first to volunteer for any task, whether setting up tables, making copies, or passing out bulletins. I was always the one who stood beside the projector during our praise and worship, changing out the transparencies, which had the printed lyrics for each song. Later this led me down the path of assisting teaching Sunday school, singing in the kids' choir, and serving as one of the leaders of our youth praise-and-worship team.

I went on my first camping trip with the Royal Rangers as well, and that all-boys weekend took me far out of my comfort zone but was also strangely affirming. I had only a handful of close male friends, but on that camping trip, for the first time ever, I felt totally integrated and accepted by the other boys. We swam in the dirty Platte River as puffs of off-white foam scum floated by, collected wood, built fires, trounced through tall grasses to set up camp, and learned that corn could be used as bait for fish.

On the long ride to the middle of Nebraska, I rode with the pastor of Victory Church, who was my beacon throughout all the chaos with my family. Pastor Joe Laughlin knew all the intimate and ugly details of the ongoing saga because, through Ethne's orchestration, my grandparents had attended several counseling sessions under his guidance. But he never spoke with me about any of it. Pastor Joe always kept things light and fun, maybe because he knew that's what I needed most. We sang songs, drank lemonade, and marveled at the wide-open road. For that trip, and for a short period of my life, he was the father figure I never had. I used to volunteer to mop the long hallways of the church and clean the sanctuary—anything to spend my time at the church.

At the beginning of fourth grade, I made my professional theater debut on the main stage. It was a school night on which I found myself auditioning under the bright spotlight, filled with indescribable anticipation and fearlessness. I had always loved the Queen of Hearts from *Alice in Wonderland*, which was the first play I ever saw, and would often take on her bossy demeanor and shout such lines as "Don't. You. Don't you dare!" in situations that didn't apply or when I was lost in the moment during one of my backyard performances. That diva within me was so eager to escape! I had also gotten a small taste of the stage at our school Christmas program the year before, when I was chosen as the soloist for the Christmas rap. And now, I had finally found a place where I could embrace and tap into the part of me that yearned to perform. Shortly thereafter I got a phone call letting me know I'd been cast in the ensemble of *Berenstain Bears*. I was giddy all the way up to the day of the first rehearsal orientation at which I received a manila envelope containing a pink script. I blocked out countless hours fussing over the details of my role; they were all actions, no lines. This was serious business, and everything would have to be put on hold to accommodate my new calling, including my household chores. Even with three rotating casts, the play still required a demanding practice schedule. In the evenings I'd be whisked off to rehearsal, which made me feel like a real movie star being chauffeured around town.

My grandparents were almost always late picking me up, so I had ample opportunity to wander and explore every nook and cranny of the Rose Theater. I especially loved peeking in on rehearsals for other shows that weren't on the main stage, watching the adult actors with transfixed adulation in the black box theater. They were mentors to me without even knowing it, and I knew with a burning desire that I, too, would someday master this art form.

When the show opened, I was pulled from class three or four times a week to perform, and I loved that even more. While everyone else was learning multiplication and division, I was *acting*! I got to skip entire afternoons, much to the chagrin of my teachers. In my mind, I was basically already a celebrity. This preoccupation would later come back to bite me as I fell behind in schoolwork, but I didn't care because I didn't believe I'd ever need those skills. I'd found my calling in the arts!

Getting my role in *Berenstain Bears* afforded me my first experience of physical transformation as well. I got to put on orange foundation makeup, attach a prosthetic pad onto my stomach, and have an audience of strangers regard me as a character totally different from who I really was.

The top of the second act was my big moment. My heart would skip a beat in anticipation when I heard "Up in the morning and out to school," because I knew my chance to stand out in the show was coming. I would look up, take in the lights, scan the prop table for the paper bag that would be used in the scene, and look at the person next to me to make sure they were ready. My cue was "Ring, ring goes the bell," a line taken from Chuck Berry's "School Days." I would run out from stage right and pretend to catch and throw a football just as the lights came up on the schoolhouse set. My pantomime was so realistic that the crowd's eyes would follow my imaginary throw! I was a star! That throw was also Sister Bear's cue to land her line. "What's in the bag, Brother? A hand grenade?" I would go on repeating that memorable line all throughout my childhood, forever reminiscing about my importance to that scene.

On closing night, an older actor gave me a big bag of gummy bears, and for some reason, that was the moment I knew the experience was really over. I took forever getting out of my costume that Sunday afternoon; I *lingered*, savoring my last chance to play in the makeup and enjoy the feeling of being in *my* (shared) dressing room one last time. As I descended the steep flight of stairs, I watched as the crew dismantled the set, making way for something new to emerge, one of my first lessons that all good things must come to an end.

TWO

A Family Divided

I felt particularly warm and sentimental around the holidays when we had our most cherished family traditions. We'd decorate eggs for Easter together or carve jack-o'-lanterns for Halloween, but Christmas was the best. It was the time when our patched-together semidysfunctional family actually experienced what I believed was authentic happiness. The simplest habits and rituals, repeated at their yearly landmarks, make the world feel so much less frightening and so much more predictable. I loved our traditions, especially the ones that included pomp and circumstance.

Our Christmas tree lived under the stairs, and every year, Grandma Ethne would piece together our voluminous seven-foot artificial Douglas fir from its long cardboard box. It was my job to help her decorate it. Trimming that tree was probably the thing I looked forward to most each year besides my birthday. We strung our own popcorn garlands and hung blinking rainbow lights, and even the tinsel star on top blinked multiple colors.

Interspersed among the vintage and classic red, green, and gold bauble glass ornaments were all the holiday crafts we had made at school. I loved to see my creations from previous years: popsicle sticks glued together in the shapes of stars and reindeer and embellished with glitter, and construction-paper Santas complete with cotton-ball hat trim. The continuity of my collection accruing over the years was heartening. The best part of decorating was the finishing touch on the tree: adding the tinsel. I got to stand on the ladder that doubled as my chair at the dinner table to apply the sassy strands to the highest branches. I took such care and pride in the work, and then we would all stand back and admire our dazzling, shimmering masterpiece.

Before she got married, Nina helped out with Dexter, Tanisha, Ginger, and me, especially around Christmastime. Granddad was always so busy deejaying, and Ethne did a lot of double shifts at her telemarketing job, so Nina would sometimes bring me along on her errands, which I liked, and people would often think she was my mom, which I loved.

After she was married, when I was eleven, Nina took me out to eat at Long John Silver's on a day shortly before Christmas. There were posters and promotion cards at each table for the *Muppet Christmas Carol* movie. I asked if she'd take me, and she promised she would. After lunch we went to the mall to buy presents. I couldn't have known it then, but everything was about to change, and Nina would not keep her promise.

The day before Christmas Eve arrived, but the evening wasn't filled with the usual anticipation for Santa's visit. Instead, I found myself crouched on the floor in the corner of our living room, watching a terrifying scene play out before me.

Nina had come over with her husband, Marshall, for one of their periodic visits, and this time, Marshall's twin sister, Janeen, accompanied them. Nina and Marshall had been married for two years at this point, and as their newlywed bliss shifted to plans of starting a family, they had become increasingly zealous in their expression of the

Pentecostal faith. They hosted two Bible studies, one at their home on Offutt Air Force Base and another at Marshall's mother's home in North Omaha. These private sessions eventually led them to stop attending any formal church services whatsoever. I saw Nina and Marshall sink deeper and deeper into an extremist version of the Christian faith, but their fervor had never made its way into the Davis household. Although Granddad and Ethne were practicing Christians too, they observed much more loosely. Granddad especially didn't welcome Nina's growing fanaticism, as he understood it to be due to Marshall's influence. As it soon would become clear, however, Nina and Marshall's new standards of judgment did not rely on willing participation. According to them, my grandparents were living in contempt of Christ and failing to serve him as their Lord and Savior in all things.

Clyde and Ethne had been doing their best to oblige. For several years, Ethne had become increasingly more interested in Nina's Bible studies and started watching televangelists like Rod Parsley and T. D. Jakes, which probably played a part in her organizing the inaugural Davis-house prayer meeting. But for Granddad, this was a lot to take in. Although the rest of us were weekly churchgoers, he never accompanied us to any services. His being prayed *over* by his daughter was an uncomfortable reversal of power, and I knew something serious was afoot.

While Nina paced back and forth across the living room, conjuring in tongues with shouts and murmurs—*spe-ca-sha titi-she spe-ki-titi-shi!*—Ethne stood with her eyes fixed on the ground, swaying ever so slightly. From what I'd learned in church, speaking in tongues held power. She was literally calling forth and channeling the Holy Spirit, summoning down a god of judgment, wrath, and revelation into our living room. The spirit of Pentecost. I was stunned as Nina stomped her left foot repeatedly on the carpet! Marshall stood by Janeen, who contributed her own shrills, while he focused on casting out the demonic spirits that were apparently living in Clyde and Ethne. He stood tall and squinted his eyes, alternating his gaze between them.

I watched as Marshall stepped forward and joined hands with Nina. Then they, with the strength of a thousand nations, struck their palms against my grandparents' foreheads with such force they both fell back onto the plush gray couch. It was a laying on of hands with blessed oil. An exorcism. A slaying in the spirit and a rebuke of the devil within.

Clyde "the DJ" Davis, the man of the house, local Omaha celebrity, nightlife legend, concert promoter, deejay extraordinaire, possessor of a key to the city, and the largest-looming figure of my life up to that point, had essentially just been challenged to a duel in his own home. I was stunned and could see he was too, as he sat there frozen by the slap from his son-in-law. Grandma Ethne, too, sat motionless as the spirit worked through her. In that inexplicable moment, time stopped.

The next thing I knew, Nina and Marshall had grabbed me, Tanisha, Dexter, and Ginger and loaded us all into the gray family station wagon, and off we went into the night.

We pulled up in front of a small dark house that was noticeably devoid of decorations and crunched across the ice-crusted driveway to the door, where a man we'd never seen before greeted us from the large foyer. Tammy had always had a special affinity for men either in prison or fresh out, and upon first assessment, this new boyfriend seemed like her type. I saw him eye me longer than the rest, with the look so many men used to give me, something between *What's wrong with this one?* and an urge to just start hitting. I shrank back behind Nina and Marshall as we slipped inside. Tammy was waiting on the landing between the living room and kitchen with a distracted curiosity. Her thin hair was parted down the middle and frayed at the ends.

My siblings rushed to her, and I watched as they exchanged hugs and hellos. I lingered by the door, trying not to be noticed. All I could think was that this wasn't supposed to be happening, especially not right before Christmas. This felt like trouble. *Why are we here?* I wanted to shout. *Why are you doing this to us? You know this woman has never been any kind of a mother to us!* Our mother was back at that other house. My grandparents were my parents, and their house was my real home. It was nearly Christmas, and I just wanted to go home.

Nina zeroed in on Tammy right away and began laying out her accusations against their father, Clyde, and demanding corroboration in a nearby room. In somewhat vague terms that I didn't understand, she claimed Clyde had been abusive. He denied it. She and Marshall longed for a corroborating narrative from Tammy, Ginger, and even nine-year-old Tanisha—all the girl children who had ever been around Clyde. I later learned a tape recorder had been hidden in the room to capture any confessions as evidence.

Minutes passed, and no one moved in the house or dared to speak. Low voices from the TV echoed indistinctly, and my vision blurred as tears welled in my eyes. Unable to leave or fully comprehend, I felt an overwhelming sense of helplessness. Ginger finally mustered the strength to speak, but only managed to say, "Dad never hurt me."

I agreed with her. Granddad was known to have a bad temper, but at the time, I had no reason to believe he was a monster. He would often call me over, and I knew a slap in the face was about to land, but Dexter received the brunt of the discipline in our home, and it usually entailed his being locked in our room for long periods.

I didn't understand what was taking place and had to put the pieces together over the next several weeks, months, and years. I got the sense that this was a major accusation, and I simply could not—would not—believe it was true. My fifth-grade mind refused to engage.

Tammy remained silent, unperturbed, and mildly amused that this bizarre turn of events would bring the kids she had gotten rid of back to her again.

"I don't know why y'all thought to bring all this shit on down to my house right now," she said.

"These are your kids, Tammy!" Nina shouted.

A debate proceeded between the two sisters who had been at odds for many years. Nina expanded her attack, railing against Tammy and their failed sisterhood. Meanwhile, Dexter sat still, eyes glued to the floor. Tanisha was in her own world. She had always been the beloved darling at our supervised visits with Tammy before we were adopted, so she had no reason to suspect she had any part in this trouble. I felt numb at first, but then came a growing sense of anger. I was screaming on the inside. *I just want to go home!*

"Look, y'all need to get up out my house, that's all I know about." Tammy was done with this ordeal, but Nina wouldn't let it go. She persisted, jabbing, interrogating, buoyed by Marshall standing supportive at her side, but no one else would crack or offer any substantiation.

I finally drummed up the courage to speak myself. "Take me home!" Nina immediately shot back, "No one is going back to that house!"

Tammy's boyfriend also perked up at the sound of my voice, calling over to me from across the room, "Keep your mouth shut, sissy boy." He slapped the back of one hand into the palm of the other. I shrank back, terrified and embarrassed, instinctively wanting to run and cling to someone for comfort, for safety. I wanted my mom. A mom. But as I looked around the room, it sank in that no one there could be that for me.

Nina had been a maternal figure at one point, but now with Marshall's influence and this new crusade for Christ, she was becoming increasingly stranger. There was Tammy, of course, but she was no mother to me—she had literally given us away, had given us up for adoption. Still, I remember the profoundness of the disconnect solidifying that night, in that moment. Amid all the chaos and distress, watching her child abused in plain sight, she had zero inclination to protect me. That man could have crossed the room and wrung my neck, and I think she would have just shrugged.

That may have also been the precise moment when my ambivalence toward her changed to hatred. I remember thinking, *She is not my mom!*

The tension among us tightened to the point of bursting, and in the final stalemate, the question arose of what to do with us kids, for the time being at least. Since no one would corroborate Nina's narrative, she was forced to give up on getting Clyde arrested then and there, and she switched her focus to ensuring that we were not returned to his care.

Nina wouldn't take us back home, so she called the police. They loaded Tanisha, Dexter, Ginger, and me into their squad cars.

We ended up at the police station downtown, where we sat and waited for what felt like forever as total strangers debated our fate just out of earshot behind bulletproof glass. After probably three hours sitting there with no new information, I felt certain I would never go home. Soon after that an officer came over and confirmed my nightmare.

Tanisha, Dexter, and I were once again sent to the Child Saving Institute, the crisis center and a place for children in transition. Ginger was going to the Youth Emergency Services (YES) House, which also provided emergency shelter to youths as well as support for youths in crisis over the long term. A narrative was being crafted in which she had more information but was refusing to divulge. I don't remember saying goodbye to her.

We were quiet on the ride over. The stranger driving us made no attempt at small talk, so I allowed myself to become lost in the blurred scenes flashing by my window. I was filled with a terrible mix of resentment and yearning and dread. I couldn't stop thinking about home and our Christmas tree and the presents arranged there! Normally we took turns playing Santa and passing them out on Christmas morning. But what would happen to the gifts now? Even in the midst of such a chaotic night, I was still just an eleven-year-old kid, thinking about my upcoming Christmas gifts.

Of course I knew none of my gifts would be the Barbie doll or Skip-It that I yearned for. I had gotten used to receiving "boy stuff" by now and did enjoy some things, like riding my little yellow Tonka truck down the slope in our backyard and pressing the buttons that made rev-ving noises and flashing red lights on my toy fire engine. But I also knew that later on, in the secrecy of my bedroom, I'd play with my sister's presents, choosing which outfit to dress her new Barbies and Cabbage Patch dolls in first. One lucky year I'd gotten the WWF Demolition wrestler action figures *and* a plush Spider-Man, the closest thing to dolls I'd ever received. The Demolition wrestlers wore studded black leather BDSM costumes and had red, silver, black, and white makeup on their faces. I loved the drama. WWF wrestling was somewhat of a big deal in our house, and we never missed a big match. Once, Granddad even took me and Dexter to see a match in person when the WWF came to Omaha, and we sat in the front row. My favorite wrestler was Macho Man Randy Savage, but that was mostly because before a fight, he walked to the ring accompanied by the gorgeous Miss Elizabeth, stun-ning in her sequined gowns, huge hair, and jewels.

After twenty minutes of driving, we were far away from any part of town I recognized, and I was once again faced with the realization that I might never be going home. We turned into the nearly empty parking lot of the Child Saving Institute, but at the time I thought it was just another delay, another obstacle, another cruelty separating me from my real home. We hustled out of the car and marched single file through the foggy glass door.

An attendant greeted us warmly from behind the reception desk, and we were ushered to an area with a few toys in a clumsy pile on the floor. Not really in the mood to play, we just sat in the plastic chairs, refusing to engage with the other kids in the room while the adults murmured and made phone calls.

A short time later we were presented with cookies on a big plastic tray, the clean and sterile kind you see in the cafeteria of a hospital. They were sugar cookies with green and red Christmas sprinkles, arranged in tidy rows. The cookies looked perfect—too perfect. Clearly store bought. I had always loved baking with Grandma Ethne. I knew that when she was making something, one of the eggbeaters would always come to me. If I got lucky, I'd get to lick the spatula too. I'd spend hours looking through her fancy cake magazines, memorizing every page. I loved playing with the shiny metal and green plastic cookie cutters, shaped like an angel and a star.

I knew these sugar cookies were intended as a nice comforting gesture, but the overall presentation of the entire place—the factory-made cookies, the fluorescent lights, the overly genteel staff—was like a cruel, sanitized caricature of love.

I burst into tears. Everything I had ever loved about Christmas flashed through my mind as tears streamed down my face. All the pomp and circumstance. All the shining decorations. Dressing up extra nice and singing at church. Sledding. Snowmen. Hot cocoa. The Christmas program at school. Now it all seemed so far away. By then I'm sure it was past midnight, so it must have been Christmas Eve. But Christmas was nowhere in sight. Christmas would never come again. Not really. Not for me.

I was glassy-eyed and exhausted but somehow still awake as the Child Saving Institute social worker drove us across town in the early evening hours the following day. Between the police station and the institute waiting room, we hadn't slept a wink and still had no idea where we were being taken. I was disoriented at first but then started to recognize the area we drove through because Ethne's parents lived nearby. I felt trapped in the car, being hauled against my will to this mysterious destination. I wanted to speak up, to be my normal bold, inquisitive self, to demand this adult give us some answers. But my mind was hazy, as if resisting reality. I just needed to sleep so I could wake up from this never-ending nightmare and the terror of our unknown fate.

The car slowed down as we turned onto a street where the only things I could make out were the silhouettes of an auto shop and tow truck, barely distinguishable in the darkness. We continued a short way before coming to a stop in front of a small house across the street from Miller Park. I had heard of Miller Park, which had a reputation of being one of the most dangerous areas in Omaha due to violent gang activity. During our short time at this house, we were never once allowed to play there.

The social worker helped us out of the car, and we walked slowly up the long driveway, which was packed with broken-down vehicles that looked as if they had been parked there for decades. The house was white stucco, with two windows and a jagged metal fence around the perimeter, and it resembled a sort of haunted house. The chain-link gate was open, and as we approached, the side porch light came on, and a figure appeared, holding open the screen door for us to pass through. The landing was split level, with two steep tiled steps that led into the kitchen and carpeted stairs that led down into the basement.

On the stove a large stockpot of macaroni and cheese was being stirred and tszujed by a woman with her back to us. It was Tammy. She didn't turn to welcome us but just stood there stirring. Her nonchalance was nothing new, but I still felt it. This was Christmas Eve, and for the first time in our lifetimes she would actually be spending it with her children, but she couldn't even be bothered to say hello.

I was confused about where we were. Whose house was this? And why was Tammy there? There were five other children there as well. Two twin boys, Jamel and Jamal, who said they were the biological sons of Melvin, the man of the house, from his first marriage. The other three were foster kids, two white brothers, Brandon and Steven, and a light-skinned mixed boy named Tiago. Tiago and I were about the same age, and the rest were a few years younger. Dexter, Tanisha, and I played with them in the living room while Tammy worked in the kitchen. I picked up on the fact that Tiago was some kind of favorite, beloved by everyone. He certainly was a smooth talker but also a little rough around the edges.

A little later that evening, the couple of the house arrived home with arms full of plastic bags and disappeared out of sight into their bedroom, then reemerged acting very nonchalant. The woman looked much younger than Ethne, was thin, had short pixie-cut hair, and had light skin like me. The man was tall and a little intimidating, with a small Afro and a booming voice. Slowly the reality that this was not some random foster family dawned on me. This was *my* family. That explained why Tammy was here and why we'd been brought to this house. This was my grandma's house, Grandma Charlesetta, the grandma I had never met.

I'd only heard her name mentioned in derogatory terms over the years, when Ginger would lump her in with Tammy as "the family that didn't want us." Ethne just pretended she didn't exist, seeing her as the "other woman." No one had told me that Charlesetta was my actual biological grandmother, so I had never formed a clear concept of who she was, what she looked like, or where she lived. I tried to feel thankful, amid all the chaos, for this new relationship with another set of grandparents, but the sudden realization made it almost more awkward to be there. I tried to be polite and blend in, but for the most part I felt displaced and in the way.

Past the tiny kitchen was the large dining room, and beyond that, a little bedroom where the three foster brothers all slept. Our longer-term sleeping arrangements were yet to be decided—I would end up sharing that bedroom—so Charlesetta brought out a few blankets and draped them over the brown suede couch. I chose a scratchy afghan and curled up on the love seat. Everyone went to their beds, and finally the house fell quiet. It was Christmas Eve, but instead of feeling excited as usual, I just felt numb. As tired as I was, I still couldn't sleep that night.

The living room wasn't well insulated, and the afghan didn't do much to shield me from the cold draft. I lay there shivering, eyes wide open, staring at the glowing Christmas tree with its black angel topper, unable to see its beauty amid my personal tragedy.

Christmas morning arrived, and I was disappointed to find that the nightmare was ongoing. I knew what a holiday was supposed to feel like, and this wasn't it. Sorrow hung in the air, and we were far from feeling merry. I wouldn't get to play Santa and pass out all the presents as I always did at Clyde and Ethne's. Charlesetta and Melvin had their own way of doing things, and for now that was my only option. I watched as Tiago, Brandon, Steven, Jamal, and Jamel smiled wide-eyed at the presents being laid out before them, hardly containing my resentment. But then, to my surprise, a few neatly wrapped presents were placed in front of me too. All was not lost!

I learned that Charlesetta and Melvin had rushed out to Walmart the night before, just as it was closing, to make sure that each of us had some gifts. I still felt cheated and out of place, but those presents made me forget my troubles for a moment. We all opened our gifts at the same time. The most exciting gift was a tiddlywinks game, but everything else—socks and underwear, matching sweatshirts and sweatpants sets—were practical gifts since we had come with only the clothes on our backs.

As the day progressed, I gradually felt more comfortable than I had the day before, and I started to see these strangers as family. I actually felt a little excited that I now had another set of grandparents, and as we became more familiar, my natural inquisitiveness started to come out. I was especially curious about Melvin. At first I just observed him and his surroundings, watched the way he moved and how he spent most of the day reclining in his La-Z-Boy. He was very tall, with shining eyes and a short Afro, and on the living room walls there were pictures of him in cowboy hats, photographs of him and my grandmother together, and various pieces of African-styled artwork. Elephant and giraffe motifs, flashy mirrored art pieces with blasts of vibrant color that nodded to the essence of the African American spirit. Long slender floor lamps with a modern sleek design. This was all very different from the eighties-style decor I was accustomed to back at my house. Ethne had filled her home with ornate lamps with grandiose shades, faux flame bulbs that flickered to create ambience, and scroll-detail carved wooden end tables. I had grown up in the home stylings of a country white woman, and now I was in a black home, which was far more colorful and featured proud displays of culture. I had to admit I felt comfortable there. But I still missed home.

After learning all I could through observation, I proceeded with a game of twenty questions. I learned that Melvin, like Clyde, was also an Omaha music legend, nicknamed Two-Gun Pete and known for his booming baritone. He had participated in a successful music group called the Showpushers in the early 1960s. Melvin was first introduced to Charlesetta by Clyde himself through promotional work he did for the Showpushers as well as the band the New Breed of Soul, work he did on the side while attending the University of Nebraska as a journalism major. The Showpushers sold out Omaha performance venues such as the Paxton and the Carter Lake club and eventually traveled the country performing in Atlanta, Los Angeles, and San Francisco, looking for their big break. Along the way they found themselves as opening acts for the Chi-Lites, Curtis Mayfield, and the Staple Singers. Later they returned to Omaha for a reprieve from the demands of show business.

Melvin had not reconnected with Charlesetta immediately after her divorce from Clyde. She had been on her own for a few years, supporting herself by building up a steady business of cleaning houses for nearly twenty loyal customers around the city. In 1988 she married Melvin. (Their marriage would last for the twenty-three years before

Melvin died of a heart attack.) Despite my unwillingness to see Clyde as a villain and my desire for everything to go back to normal, I did notice and appreciate some differences in Melvin's parenting style. He *commanded* respect, distinct from Clyde, who *demanded* it. While Clyde wielded power through hitting, Melvin possessed a more natural gravitas. Almost like Mufasa from *The Lion King*, his robust voice and even keel set an atmosphere of calm and control throughout his home, even when, during that month of our stay, it was overrun by eight adolescents in varying states of crisis.

As the days went by, I explored their home as if it were an ancient site full of artifacts to be discovered. I spent countless hours sifting through boxes in the basement, getting most excited when I came across old baubles or necklaces that belonged to my grandmother. I would run my fingers through tangles of costume jewelry as if I had found the treasure of the lost lamp from *DuckTales*. In the shower, I was delighted to discover the bright, fragrant scents of Herbal Essences and Head and Shoulders, along with various Neutrogena products, which I liberally slathered on myself.

Before that, the only personal cosmetic product I had known was the Blue Magic hair grease that Grandma Ethne put in my hair every morning before school after ramming a hard-bristle wave brush through my tightly wound 4c curls. Our hygiene products had included plain-scented Ivory bar soap, plain white toothpaste, dish soap used as bubble bath, and Eucerin that I would constantly reapply because I had horrible eczema on the backs of my legs. By comparison, using Charlesetta and Melvin's cornucopia of products felt like a luxury spa experience. Whenever I emerged from my lengthy sessions in the bathroom there, I'd be accompanied by a cloud of comingling scents—floral, fruity, minty, and powder fresh—and Charlesetta would eye me knowingly, half-amused and half-annoyed by my snooping and product sampling.

It didn't take long before I discovered, in a corner of the basement, a box that contained heaps of old high heels. They were mostly worn-out slingbacks from the seventies, but I coveted them as if I were Dorothy and these were my ruby slippers, my only ticket home. Soon I was click-clacking and flouncing all over the concrete floor, parading with a strut that came ever so naturally. When I was caught in the act, my grandmother yelled at me to take her shoes off. Yet her reprimand felt different from the way I'd been policed about gender transgressions before. I didn't feel like she was chastising me for the act of wearing heels, but rather because I was making a lot of noise and causing a commotion. She just wanted a little peace in her chaotic home, and I could understand and appreciate that.

We lived with Charlesetta and Melvin for about a month, and in that time, I developed genuine affection for them. Charlesetta would drop us off at the downtown YMCA on weekends, where we would swim for hours. I remember thinking of her as a kind of superwoman, dropping us off at school, working a full-time job, picking us up, and then continuing to work late into the evening cleaning other people's homes. I admired her and then loved her. I regarded her as the most levelheaded of all my family. We had an immediate rapport, and I identified with her sass, which was tempered with integrity. In all the years since then, I've never heard my grandmother make a comment about my granddad, positive *or* negative, unless I pried it out of her. She is an inspiring woman, and I'd like to think I take after her. She and Melvin made the experience as positive as it possibly could have been.

Behind the scenes, the police had been conducting an investigation into the allegations against Clyde, who denied them vehemently. Although they didn't discover sufficient evidence to pursue charges, Ethne told us that our return to her custody was contingent on him being out of the home. She filed for divorce, he moved in with Uncle Tony, his and Charlesetta's youngest child, and then, one day, she came to get us.

I remember the morning so vividly. We were brought to the Division of Children and Family Services to await her arrival. I remember watching her pull up in that familiar gray station wagon and Dexter, Tanisha, and I smiling at each other, elated to be finally going home. Ginger had been notified at school that she could go home that evening, and Ethne must have picked up Ginger's belongings from the YES House earlier. We immediately went to the Baker's grocery store on North Ninetieth and Fort, the same one we went to all throughout our childhood. We always looked forward to getting a free M&M's cookie from the bakery or a piece of cheese from the deli. Visits to the grocery store were some of the best quality moments I ever spent with my Grandma Ethne. She always made it feel like an adventure and had a good sense of humor as we rambled up and down the aisles.

That evening, we were in and out quickly, just getting what we needed—ingredients to make hoagies: sandwich bread, roast beef, Colby-Jack cheese, cheddar ruffle chips, and the malt vinegar with which I doused mine. Back at home, we sat around the familiar wooden kitchen table. We'd spent so many birthdays, holidays, and nightly dinners in this exact place, but now it felt so different. I remembered all the times I'd pulled tantrums when pot roast, pot pies, or anything with peppers or onions was served. I'd get yelled at about all the starving kids in the world, and "You'll eat what I give you" was doctrine. That night, though, I had no complaints and eagerly helped put the groceries away and set the table. I was just happy to be home.

Our sassy part chow, part terrier Tiffany sat begging at our feet like always, and I sat at my customary corner of the table, on the step stool that was my special chair, admiring the vintage sunflowers with smiling faces that hung along the wall above the wooden spice racks. The table had an extra leaf we usually kept in to make room for everyone, and it was still expanded into this longest version. But now the table seemed overly large, missing the man who used to occupy the spot across from me at the other end. Ethne used to spend many meals standing and watching over us eating, but now she had moved into the seat of power. It drove home the point to me—Clyde was not going to be in our lives anymore.

We heard over and over that we had only been allowed to come back here because he was not here. I still didn't completely understand what had happened and could not bring myself to face it, so above all I pitied him. I found out that Ethne had kicked him out soon after we were taken away and had dropped all his things at my Uncle Tony's house a mile away.

After dinner, as I moved around the house, I noticed that every surface was meticulously clean. The Christmas tree and the decorations had been taken down. There was no clutter, not one speck of dust, as if Ethne had scoured the place, attempting to scrub the memory of Clyde from her life.

That first night back home, to our extreme delight, we found our unopened Christmas presents laid out on our neatly made beds. Dexter and I broke down crying. We were just so happy to be home, and to see that for the most part nothing was changed or out of place. This was still our home, and maybe we could reclaim something of our old happy life. My toys, our little TV, our bunk beds were there. Mine was the top bunk, because I used to love jumping onto the floor instead of using the ladder, and I would swing upside down like a monkey and dangle in Dexter's face. I remembered all our life-or-death laser-gun battles that had taken place there at night, ending when my granddad or grandmother demanded quiet once the rapid-fire sounds and flashing green lights got too annoying.

The tattered old quilt that had traveled with me all throughout my childhood was the most welcoming sight of all, a reprieve I so badly needed. That blanket had been with me when I watched *Doogie Howser, M.D.* and felt something tingle on the inside that I was like him too, as well as *Mr. Belvedere, Alf,* Abbott and Costello and even O. J. fleeing down an LA highway in his white Bronco on an episode of *20/20* with Barbara Walters and Hugh Downes. So many memories contained in that one raggedy piece of cloth. I cherished being able to sleep covered in my memories.

During those first days back at home, everything felt fresh, filled with an air of gratitude, love, and reunion. But I still felt a debilitating loss. I felt Granddad's absence, maybe more acutely than anyone else. I still wanted to see him, and my persistent requests caused a rift between me and Ethne, as well as between me and Nina. One day, shortly after our return home, my granddad stopped by to give us some presents he had gotten us for Christmas, and my grandma refused to let him give them to us. They exchanged words out on the porch, and Ethne finally came in with the gifts. Nina happened to stop by later and inquired where the gifts had come from. Ethne told her, and a contentious argument began. Ethne claimed she was taking them back to him, and I said we were keeping them, to which Nina replied, "Do you want to keep gifts from someone who has done what he's done?" I muttered yes under my breath, and the lines were drawn; it was them versus me. The very fact that I wanted to stay in communication with my grandfather was enough to infuriate them, and it didn't help that with Clyde out of the picture, Nina and Marshall were also becoming more and more prevalent in our lives.

Without Clyde there, Dexter, Tanisha, Ginger, and I were able to run amok around the neighborhood, unsupervised. Gone was the rule about being home before the streetlights came on. But soon, to my great annoyance, Nina and Marshall's frequent visits started to put a damper on our freedom. They lived way out at Offutt Air Force Base since Marshall was a staff sergeant in the air force, but they would drive thirty minutes from Bellevue several times a week to randomly drop in on us. Nina and Marshall would also come every weekend for the Bible studies in which I was now forced to participate. Some would be at our home, and some would be at Marshall's mother's home, but either way, I always tried to get out of them, which brought the wrath of Marshall down upon me. I can still feel his glare, his dark eyes, framed by small circular glasses, piercing through me. Aside from being excruciatingly long and drawn out and boring, the Bible studies also turned me off because they almost always ended with some sort of cognition coming through Marshall that *someone* in the room needed to get right with God. Without fail, silence ensued, all eyes turned to me, and a conversation would open about if I died, where I would spend eternity. Just like on the night of the floor-stomping intervention against Clyde, they would work themselves up into a frenzy over saving my soul.

Fervent prayers and shrieks were recounted for my salvation, for me to get back on the path that God intended for me. It was never explicitly stated that this had anything to do with my sexuality or gender play, but on some level, I knew what was being declared *wrong* with me. Sometimes it was Nina or Marshall's sister who channeled the messages directly from the Lord, but no matter who was the vessel of communication, God always seemed to need to let *me* know that I was not right in his eyes. Although I was God-fearing and deep in my own faith, I knew something was off. I felt from the beginning that those Bible studies and the indoctrination were bogus.

During those first months after returning to Ethne's, the tone of our lives became increasingly somber and more and more devoutly religious. She lost all sense of humor. She spent hours reading her Breakthrough Bible, which was filled with broken-down lessons in the columns alongside the Bible stories. She increasingly watched televangelist preachers at night, which helped her transition further into staunch Christian ideology. By October of that next school year, when I was in sixth grade, I was not allowed to celebrate Halloween. There was no dressing up, no trick-or-treating, and I couldn't even participate in the classroom party at school or the harvest party at church.

During the school Halloween party, I was forced to sit outside in the hall with Jere the Jehovah's Witness, watching through the window as our classmates played games and ate candy. It was torture.

Ever since the third grade, I had attended services every Sunday, believed in Jesus as the Son of God, confessed him as my Lord and Savior, and had even been baptized. But this new paranoid fervor of Ethne's was something I had never seen before. She threw away all the movies I had watched throughout my childhood—*The Dark Crystal*, *The Secret of NIMH*, and even *The Little Mermaid* were all now considered ungodly. Everything I watched on TV was policed.

Up until then I had been following in the legacy of my grandfather and uncle—music pumped through every part of me. I would make my own mix tapes from songs recorded off my favorite radio station, Sweet 98, and Casey Kasem's *American Top 40*. I loved following pop culture and never missed any of Kurt Loder's MTV news updates. I'd rush home to watch Carson Daly host *Total Request Live* (*TRL*) and would spend the weekends whirling to my favorite hits I'd heard on the show. Now, however, the music on the radio was labeled as demonic.

I used to spend hours every weekend at Skateland, backward skating around the rink to Aaliyah's "Back and Forth" and other R&B jams. Skating was truly the highlight of my life. And let me tell you, I was not humble out on the rink! I would always be showing off my stunts and skills. Thankfully, Skateland was one privilege that Ethne hadn't cut off, and I took full advantage. My feet would often have blisters because I skated up until the very last minute of the sessions.

Looking back, I'm sure part of Ethne's conversion was a result of the shock and trauma of learning of Clyde's alleged abuse, but it was also largely because of Marshall's and Nina's influence. Hers was such a dramatic change from the woman I grew up with, with whom I used to help decorate our house for Halloween each year. I always got to tape the witch to our screen door and the velvet skull decorations inside the living room windows. The woman who used to take me to Kmart to buy matching *Street Fighter* clothing sets and who would look me in the eyes and say, "No matter what, I will always love you" was quickly becoming a total stranger. I'm sure another part of her overzealous censorship also stemmed from her sense that I was *different*, and she was trying to prevent me from becoming gay. She often talked about a cousin of hers who was gay and died of AIDS, and I knew she saw the two things as inextricably linked.

In her attempts to steer me away from that life, she also came to rely more and more on the only available male role model around, Marshall. I know she hoped his presence and militancy would scare me straight and turn me into the man she wanted me to be. I was fussy about dirt and bugs, and she would always force me to face my fears. She'd chastise anything I did that looked too dainty. When we were in the grocery store, if I happened to walk in front of her, she would say, "Stop switching!" I didn't know that *switching* meant shifting weight from right to left and shaking your ass, so I certainly didn't know how to stop doing it. Motha can't help it that she shakes the cakes!

It was also during this time that my brother, Dexter, started running the streets, getting involved in gang activity, and coming home late at night. My grandmother would have none of it and engaged in constant battle to get him home before curfew. Prior to that, we had walkie-talkies and pagers because my grandfather was a ham-radio operator and into Morse code—so much so that a large radio tower with a periodic antenna was installed on the side of our house. That all ended when my grandfather left, with only the unused tower remaining. Coincidentally, that antenna was later struck by lightning during a thunderstorm, and pieces of it flew through the air and scattered in our backyard. I watched them spiral to the ground before my eyes, a metaphor for the way our family was falling apart with only Ethne at the helm.

I think she could feel that losing control of Dexter was the beginning of losing control of us all, and one night she finally snapped. I sat with her while she waited for Dexter to arrive home, and as it got later and later, her anger simmered and boiled. Around midnight she made up her mind. I had been preparing myself for another screaming match, but she did something I wasn't expecting. She told me to lock the door. I was confused, but there was no nonsense in her voice, and she repeated herself several times until I walked to the door and turned the dead-bolt top lock.

Eventually Dexter came home and found he was locked out. He started ringing the doorbell, knocking and banging, shaking the door handle, yelling for someone to let him in. I begged her to let me unlock the door for Dexter, but she was unflinching. We argued, but she had made up her mind. She was done with him.

Dexter eventually wound up getting a theft charge and ended up in Tarkio, a juvenile detention center. He went on to cycle in and out of the system over the next several years, later committing other, more serious crimes and repeatedly ending up in the state penitentiary. He has suffered recurring homelessness and bouts with drug addiction, and I blame my grandparents for that. For all the abuse I endured, he received ten times worse. Dexter and I never went to the same school because he was bused to a school that specialized in behavioral disorders. But I never saw any symptoms of a behavioral disorder. He was a boy with a lot of energy, and like me, he had a natural inclination to rebel against the mindless robot actions we were told to perform. I watched adults try to medicate him with Ritalin to calm down what seemed to me like normal childlike exuberance.

Losing Dexter was losing both an ally and a tether to the life we had once lived, the way things used to be. With him gone, Ethne's fanaticism further intensified, and soon she declared that no holidays, not even Christmas or Easter, would be celebrated in our home. She said they held underlying meanings tied to paganism and devil worship. I understand now that Halloween and almost all Judeo-Christian holidays like Christmas and Easter are indeed rooted in pagan belief systems, in that they honor rebirth and fertility and ward off evil spirits. More importantly, they are intended as a way to gather loved ones together and share ancient stories.

That was the night that I realized this new version of my grandmother had lost her compassion, her heart, and nearly her mind. At the time, I put up a losing fight and eventually had to accept a life without holidays. After that, I lost a bit of my sparkle. I felt empty and resentful as I tried to keep plodding along through a life absent of so many of my most cherished childhood joys.

THREE

Church Offers a Glimpse of Joy

Along with the new reality of living with Grandma Ethne, we encountered new experiences we had to learn to navigate. We'd all gone through many transitions during the previous few years, and there were more to come—for me especially in junior high school. I faced more explicit bullying at school, navigated my growing interest in boys, and happily discovered how much I enjoyed church and everything that went with it. Money was tight.

By the start of seventh grade, I was responsible for getting myself up and to and from school. I woke up before dawn to take a shower and get dressed, so that I could leave the house by six thirty in order to make the breakfast that was served at Nathan Hale Middle School at seven a.m. Most of the time I walked, but occasionally I got a ride if the weather was cold or if it was snowing. For the first time, I was going to a different school than Tanisha and Ginger.

Now it was like something had switched on in the other boys, and suddenly the teasing and jabbing became more like torment. Every day I faced a new attack. In elementary school, people would just ask me if I was gay, but in middle school "gay" turned into a taunt, a derogatory slur. I heard "You gay! He gay!" accompanied by looks of disgust as I walked down the hall, and many times I feared for my safety. I was called *faggot* constantly, and though I didn't know exactly what the word meant, it made me feel less than human. I could tell it was a term of hate. These kids weren't laughing at me for being girly anymore. They were hating me because of what I exuded and what I represented by existing. I was being authentically me, and they couldn't stand it. That was the year after Ellen DeGeneres came out on television. I was aware of the story, but I still didn't make the connection that what she was, I was too. I could relate to her, but I couldn't quite connect the dots.

With all that to deal with, I struggled to pay attention in class. I just couldn't focus. I was still wrestling with accepting that my cherished childhood family was never going to exist again. Every day that passed, my relationship with my grandmother deteriorated; she continued to tighten the reins by barring me from participating in extracurriculars that might put me in contact with kids or activities of which she disapproved. And the divorce of my grandparents weighed on me more.

I had ample time to sit and dwell on these things during my frequent in-school suspensions for being tardy. I had to report to a room in the back corner of the school and was not permitted to leave all day. A monitor oversaw these sessions and my punishment, an exercise in which I wrote "I will not be tardy for school" over and over in pencil on white lined paper for seven hours straight. I couldn't stand the scratching sound the pencil made on the paper. This punishment seemed harsh and unfitting for showing up late, a harbinger of the school-to-prison pipeline track. They weren't concerned with my learning. They wanted me to simply obey.

I also landed in in-school suspension for talking back to certain teachers who liked to call me out in front of the class and used humiliation as punishment. Little did they know that challenging authority was in my wheelhouse, *especially* in front of an audience. I was a natural at giving sass and flipping the script. For example, if a teacher refused to let me go to the restroom, I deemed that flat-out disrespect, and for revenge I would call them by their first name to undermine the power dynamic and hierarchy. I wanted them to know that neither age nor power was a substitute for respect, and ultimately there was no real difference in our standing.

Masculinity and I did not get along, and with Marshall plaguing me back home, I had no patience left for machismo displays at school. I did have respect for my math teacher, my language arts teacher, and my art teacher, who everyone thought was gay. I don't believe he actually was, but he was indeed feminine, and I was always grateful to be around someone who could draw some of the fire from the mean kids, giving me a break from being bullied. Whenever the jokes were directed my way, he would put a stop to it.

I hated gym class most of all because my trying to play sports seemed to emphasize my femininity, and the other boys always commented on it. I hated it when we had to swim because I felt exposed wearing a Speedo. Navigating the locker room was a horrifying experience. I would huddle in the corner by my locker, and I never took a shower. Many days I walked around with my stomach tied in knots because of the fear that someone would hurt me for no reason.

On my way home from school, a kid who lived nearby would chase me all the way to my front door. Eventually I found ways to avoid him, like walking behind the houses along the creek that ran straight to Sixty-Sixth Street and then slipping back on the sidewalk when near my house.

At around this same time, I had my first sexual experience with a boy. Ginger had a friend named Terrence, who was a year behind me in school and lived in the Ville de Sante public housing projects four blocks from our house. Terrence had dark chocolate skin and, at over six feet, was very tall for his age. He was also, like me, noticeably "different," meaning effeminate. Whenever he and I crossed paths, we maintained lingering eye contact.

One night when Ethne was working her late double shift, Ginger had a boy over, and he brought Terrence along. I later learned that Terrence was there to occupy me while Ginger and Ray made out in her room in the basement. Neither Terrence nor I had ever met someone else like us before, and even though we didn't identify as gay, we'd both been teased and called *faggot* and faced religious censorship from our families.

Terrence was even more afraid and repressed than me. My natural flamboyance pushed the boundaries of what was allowed, especially in black spaces, long before I knew I was defying the rules of masculinity. Meanwhile, he thought he was a mistake by God, totally alone in this world. To Terrence, he later told me, my femininity was comforting after so many years living in fear, isolation, and self-loathing.

That first night, all we did was kiss. As Terrence remembers it, I was very dominant. He says I told him to just relax, to be still, and then, when we kissed, my lips just kind of sucked his in. He wondered whether that was considered french-kissing and whether such an exciting experience would land him directly in Hell. Even though I knew what we were doing was not allowed by the church, I don't remember feeling fear of God over it. The urge to explore felt stronger.

A few weeks later, Ginger and I stayed home from school, and Ginger called Terrence's school pretending to be his mother signing him out for the day. He came over, and we started messing around in my bedroom. That was our first time playing "show and tell." We touched each other's private parts, not knowing what to do or how to do it. Right smack in the middle of the exploration, Ginger came barging into the room and said, "Terrence, your mom is on the phone." He got in trouble for skipping school, but thankfully we weren't caught for our deeper sin.

We started hanging out around the neighborhood, and I was always fiercely protective whenever other kids picked on him. When he finally asked me where my real mom was and why I lived with my grandma, I told him point-blank that my mom didn't want me.

"I don't think my mom wants me either," he said.

After that moment of unexpected camaraderie, Terrence and I fumbled around on the floor of my bedroom one more time, and that was that.

~

As seventh grade was ending, Ethne decided to transfer me, Ginger, and Tanisha to a faraway school called Sword of the Spirit Christian School, where she believed we could get a godly education the next year.

In the middle of the summer, we attended an informational meeting. I had no idea what to expect as I walked down a flight of brick stairs into an enclosed gymnasium. The founding matriarch of the school stood at a podium and with an impassioned rallying cry proclaimed the urgency of the school's great undertaking: saving the souls of children. She laid out the basic tenets of the institution, emphasizing the community and cooperative aspects. It was technically a private school but ran on the same principles as homeschooling and had a curriculum rooted in Christian theology, messianic tradition, and prayer. Sword of the Spirit received no local or federal money and had no official accreditation. She appealed to the parents for their support since the entire operation depended on donations and volunteering. In fact, none of the teachers were paid at all. They were volunteers. Most of them were not trained educators, and many taught more than one grade level. Tuition was based on what a family could afford to pay, and if you didn't have financial resources to contribute, you could make it up by volunteering. That's ultimately why Ethne chose to send us there.

It was humid and hot in the airless gym, and I could tell that every point that sounded terrible to me sounded like music to Ethne's ears, especially the part about the school's dress code. I had not yet become very expressive with my personal style and still wore Dexter's hand-me-downs or whatever Ethne picked out for me from Goodwill. Still, conforming to a standard of dress felt like a violation of my independence. In the end, however, my feelings on the matter weren't relevant. Ethne was sold.

A few weeks later, I arrived at Sword of the Spirit with a small 'fro, a grimace, and my brand-new uniform—navy pants and a clean white polo. I was envious that the girls had way more outfit options than I did. They could wear red, white, blue, or green blouses underneath their plaid jumpers. I, too, wanted to express myself in color and style.

I used to think my mile-long walk to Nathan Hale during seventh grade was arduous, but it was nothing compared to my new two-hour round-trip commute. Sword of the Spirit was in downtown Omaha on Twenty-Seventh and Leavenworth, housed inside an old school that belonged to the Saint Peter Catholic Church next door, in a seedy neighborhood where drug use was rampant. To get there, we had to catch one bus, then transfer to another and ride it a little over an hour. Sometimes Ethne would drop us off at the first bus stop, but most of the time we had to walk. I came to enjoy the bus rides because they gave me a passing knowledge of various Omaha neighborhoods and businesses.

I slowly adjusted to my new, simpler, stricter life. I learned to find joy in the small things, like wearing my favorite shoes, burgundy penny loafers, because they made the strong click-clack sound I liked. I would click-clack up a storm down those tiled hallways. The shoes were hand-me-downs from a couple from Victory Church whom I had stayed the night with one weekend, and they were a form of self-expression before I could articulate my need for fabulous footwear. They allowed me to be feminine without crossing a line. At least for a while. Eventually, Ethne caught on to what those shoes evoked in me, and she took them away and threw them in the trash, then bought me a pair of black wing-tip shoes that were soft heeled and noiseless. I was determined to create sound from those sanctioned shoes, so I learned to slap my feet down in such a way as to at least hear a muffled stomp.

My eighth-grade classroom was another place where I was ridiculed, and my sexual orientation was called into question. I often felt unsafe and uncomfortable in that class, which included seventh and eighth graders. Both boys and girls would make fun of me, but I stubbornly refused to submit to their taunting. I had a sassy comeback to just about everything, but when they called me gay, I could never come up with anything to say. Instead, eye rolls had to suffice. Inside, I would ask myself why I was always the brunt of other people's jokes. I knew I was a good person, no matter what those stupid kids said about me. And in the end, it didn't matter because I was blessed with an inner resilience, a natural defense that warded off their daggers.

While I didn't feel like I was a part of the class community, I was fully engaged in learning about theology and in particular the movement of the Protestant Reformation, including preachers like John Wesley, the founder of the Methodist faith, Martin Luther, the founder of the Lutheran faith, and John Calvin, the founder of Calvinism. I was intrigued by these men who had made an impact in the world, particularly because they reshaped tenets of faith and belief that had existed for so long before them. They took what seemed to be fixed and unchangeable and changed it. That inspired me.

I was also deeply present and participatory during our chapel time, where we learned about messianic principles and tenets of Jewish culture. During these chapels we would sing "We Are Standing on Holy Ground" a cappella and dance the hora. As I whirled and took each step, I felt connected to myself. I loved learning about a culture that was not my own. Our principal, the school's founder, often said, "We are all engrafted into the vine," a mantra on how, in essence, we were all Jewish. Her controversial teaching undergirded Jesus as both the Christian Messiah *and* the Jewish conception of a prophet born through the same Jewish bloodline as Abraham, and therefore one of the elect.

By that interpretation, when we receive Jesus, we receive the inheritance of being in the tribe of the chosen as well.

She also taught Deuteronomy 7:6 from the Old Testament of the Bible: "For you are a people holy to the Lord your God. The Lord your God has chosen you out of all the peoples on the face of the earth to be his people, his treasured possession" (New International Version). She ended her chapel sermons with a recitation from Numbers 6:24–25 (A Faithful Version), "May the Lord bless you and keep you. May the Lord make his face shine upon you and be gracious to you." It was a beautiful piece of poetic verse.

This was a whole new take on religion for me. Being a "chosen" people was very different from being born into original and continuous sin and having to constantly atone and pray for forgiveness. I wove this new perspective into my earlier understanding of faith from Victory Church, and together they set me on a sojourn toward a spirituality that combines elements and tenets from many diverse faiths and walks of life.

One good thing about the long commute home from Sword of the Spirit and Ethne's second job that kept her away from home until close to midnight was that I was able to take full advantage of my after-school freedom. I could jump off the bus and explore, and I often made long, leisurely stops at Crossroads Mall, where the second bus transfer was. Ginger, Tanisha, and I liked to visit my Uncle Tony who worked at Dillard's. I looked up to my uncle. He was basically my hero on account of his good attitude and successful career in retail sales and as a deejay. He was the one person in my family that seemed to play a *normal* role in society, and he always treated me well.

I could easily spend hours at the mall browsing women's clothing or listening to music, but before catching the bus, I would scan the periodicals at Barnes & Noble. It was there that I accidentally discovered that gay magazines were a thing. I always took the time to thumb through every page of *Out* and *Instinct Magazine*, but I was also cautious to make sure no one noticed what I was reading. I would go squat in a corner and hover over the magazines, marveling at a world both so enticing and so foreign to me. I browsed the human sexuality section and discovered *The Joy of Gay Sex*, where for the first time, I saw what homosexual intercourse actually looked like via sketches of men in intimate poses. I would later return to that book on several visits to the Milton R. Abrahams branch of the Omaha Public Library on days off from school. My curiosity had been piqued, and for the first time in my life I actually started to ask myself, *Am I gay?* Aside from seeing RuPaul on the Ricki Lake show once in 1996, this was my first official introduction to gay culture at large. I knew these emerging questions about my sexual identity wouldn't make it any easier to fit in at Sword of the Spirit.

Even as I was becoming immersed in the new religious teachings and community at school, I was still attending services and participating in youth activities with Victory Church. That provided a familiar comfort in a world that had become increasingly unfamiliar, the one form of continuity that hadn't been ripped from my grasp in my grandparents' separation.

More and more I began to get rides to Victory from neighbors, because my grandma began attending services less and less. She now preferred to join Marshall and Nina's Bible studies instead. She had still been attending therapy sessions with my grandfather with Pastor Joe, but I heard grumblings about him not being accountable in those sessions, especially when Marshall and Nina were around. Shortly after this, Ethne stopped involving Pastor Joe in our family problems.

During the Sunday services, I unashamedly clapped and raised my hands in exaltation during praise and worship. That was my favorite part about going to church and being in "big church" services. Songs like "Cornerstone" and "Great is the Lord Almighty" were my favorites because they were arranged in minor keys. Singing in that intonation struck a deep place in my spirit. I think it's because they were both performed jubilantly and with fanfare and also evoked a feeling of sorrow in triumph, a complexity of emotions that greatly appealed to me.

As much as I enjoyed the jubilee energy of praise, my sensitive soul also savored the quieter moments. I was deeply affected by the gentle piano melodies and moments of stillness in worship led by our pianist after the praise section. A holy hush came over the congregation. Tears would often flow down my face and the faces of those around me as everyone fell silent to the presence of the Lord and everyone in one accord. Individuals stood with hands raised high toward the heavens, and some lay prostrate before the altar, as the music built up on chords of dissonance. Ushers rushed around, throwing gray cloths over any women who had been splayed out, slain in the spirit, a standard holiness protocol in Pentecostal culture to preserve their modesty and protect them from lust as God worked through them.

Most of the time after praise and worship, kids were dismissed to attend the youth church program called Power Blast. Occasionally, when we did have to stay in adult church the whole service, my stomach would grumble in disappointment, because at Power Blast we always got candy and some kind of snack. After worship, two large doors would slide open across the hall from the sanctuary and Audio Adrenaline's "Big House" or Carman's "Who's in the House?" would blare from two TVs. Red chairs were set up on two sides, one side for boys and one side for girls, and there was a small platform covered in a black Astroturf for ministering. Black curtains thrown over pipes served as a small theater for puppet shows. There were gestures that went along with "Big House," and I loved pantomiming throwing a football and eating a lot of food. In "Who's in the House?" a call and response was initiated, and we would all yell "J. C." for Jesus Christ.

Carman, a Christian emcee, would later perform at the first concert I attended at the Omaha Civic Auditorium. It's strange that I hadn't gone to more concerts since Granddad's promoting work made us proximate to the industry, but Ethne had always tried to keep us separate from that part of his world. That is, except on Thursday and Friday nights (before the divorce), when I was responsible for loading the milk crates full of records into the back of his blue Chevy Corsica.

In the escalation of Ethne's war of righteousness, Christian movies and Trinity Broadcasting Network's Christian programming had become the only mainstay in our home, and after losing cable, I latched on to the host and founder of the network. With her pink hair and lipstick and thick mascara-clad eyelashes, Jan Crouch was one piece of glamour I could cling to in a world in which all things secular were strictly forbidden. She would often cry when asking for donations to put satellites up, to bring the Gospel of Jesus Christ to all nations. I also enjoyed her show for its featured talking, singing, and theatrical productions. On days off from school, I would sneak and watch the original iteration of *The View* with Barbara Walters, Star Jones, Joy Behar, Meredith Vieira, and Debbie Matenopoulos. I also watched Sally Jessy Raphael with her signature red eyeglasses and, only when I knew that Ethne was far away at work, Jerry Springer. Once I heard Sally reference a voodoo witch doctor and added it into my rotation of words whose meanings I did not know!

Every day before and after work Ethne watched her favorite televangelists Rod Parsley, T. D. Jakes, Joyce Meyer, and Benny Hinn. She had ordered countless tapes of Parsley's and Jakes's sermons. Rod Parsley was a fiery preacher whose megachurch in Columbus, Ohio, was a different kind of church from Victory Church. Countless individuals would be slain in the spirit from him laying hands on them, and they would be falling all over the choir pews. Rod Parsley came from an old school of Pentecost that drew on the tenet of laying hands on people to heal them and cast out demonic spirits, in the lineage of Smith Wigglesworth and Dr. Lester Sumrall, both great fire-and-brimstone preachers of the twentieth century. The choir wore long blue robes, and the praise-and-worship team wore matching colored suits and had a front line of super-high-energy singers. I would often sing along with

"The Sound of Jubilee," another concert tape that Ethne had ordered. There was also Jakes's "Woman, Thou Art Loosed." Both concerts were more distinctly "urban" and featured women singers with long nails, big hair, and executive suits with matching pumps, who just wailed. I wanted so badly to be up there with them.

Ethne just had to experience a revival in the flesh, and she took us with her when Benny Hinn came to town. He was a modern iteration of early twentieth-century preacher Kathryn Kuhlman, who was the protégé of Aimee Semple McPherson, the evangelist behind the Angelus Temple in Los Angeles. Benny Hinn, like McPherson, built a ministry that was personality based and focused on healing the sick without medical treatment. The energy in the room was magnetic as thousands of people came to be healed. I watched from the rafters as people threw down their canes, jumped out of wheelchairs, and fell to the ground when Benny touched them or came close to them. This was all decidedly different from Victory Church. Pastor Joe was a country boy at heart, schooled at Rhema Bible College in Broken Arrow, Oklahoma, twenty minutes from the legendary Oral Roberts University, an institution with extremely conservative principles that was documented in the Netflix movie *Come Sunday*, which explored the experiences of the great spiritual teacher and bishop Carlton Pearson.

I soon acclimated myself to this more limited range of entertainment options and even came to look forward to them. Carman had his own show, and I never missed it. One of his music videos, "We Need God in America Again," depicted various cultural and political topics relevant in the early nineties—teen pregnancy, abortion, gay rights, and prayer in school. I was intrigued by the images of two men holding hands, but something stopped me from prying deeper into my own mind about why.

Most followers of nondenominational Christian faith can pinpoint the exact moment when they gave their life to Jesus. Usually this involves choosing to come forward during an altar call after the pastor gives an emotional plea about standing in the gap between heaven and hell unless you make a direct choice regarding your salvation. Romans 10:9 (King James Bible) reads "That if thou shalt confess with thy mouth the Lord Jesus, and shalt believe in thine heart that God hath raised him from the dead, thou shalt be saved."

I know for sure that the moment I accepted Jesus as Lord was on a Sunday at a Power Blast service at Victory Church, because after I did, I was gifted my own paperback NIV Bible with a green-and-blue cover jacket. Later, I was baptized by Pastor Joe at a ceremony in Carter Lake, Iowa.

Soon after, I had my first official evangelizing moment from the pulpit at Victory when a movement called Youthquake came to town. Youthquake focused on reaching inner-city kids by the power of Christ, and specifically targeted those who were involved in drugs, gangs, homosexuality, promiscuity, eating disorders, and other kinds of behavioral health issues. Given their youth-centric approach, they also recruited youths to oversee outreach and to serve in various leadership roles for their three-night engagements.

I'd gone to a Youthquake event at another church and was a part of a group that convinced them to hold their last night in town at Victory. The youth band was awesome and hard-rocking, full of heavy drums, mega guitar, and keyboard. I had joined the youth praise team and was on the platform clutching and singing into the mic, "I'm desperate for you." The air was so charged that by forty-five minutes into the service, the guest pastor took the platform and shared that he felt God was moving him to break bondages over people's lives. As he paced the platform, I, too, was moved to speak. I went to the mic and testified about how God was doing work in my life and that I had to continue heeding the call of God. People were captivated, and the spirit began moving. I walked around the room laying hands on people, praying that God would intervene on their behalf and show up in their lives. After the service, people told me how moved they were by my words and showing of the Holy Spirit. I had found a new stage—ministry.

During that year, Ethne stopped attending Victory Church altogether and fully committed to attending only the Bible studies led by Marshall. He and Nina had concocted some kind of conspiracy theory about Victory Church, and a prophecy that there was a man who was preying on me there came forth from Nina. Once again, a term I had never heard before was being flung at me. Even though I denied it, Ethne assumed Nina's prophecy must be referring to a couple whose house I had first begged to stay at and who now welcomed me anytime. They were youth leaders in Power Blast and had a son with whom I loved to run around the church. The insinuation was that they had lured me there, but nothing could have been further from the truth. At that point, I regularly stayed with friends' families and married couples from church on the weekends, and almost always I had invited myself. It was a way to escape Ethne's increasingly authoritarian rule at home.

Nina's prophecy had absolutely no legitimacy. She and the rest of my family seemed to suddenly forget that I had been staying over at friends' and church families' houses for practically my whole childhood. Nothing new was happening, except for the change in their perspective. Still, that one prophecy was enough to poison Victory Church in Ethne's already paranoid mind, and from then on even my churchgoing was considered demonic.

I was no longer allowed anywhere near Victory Church and was forced to attend only Nina and Marshall's Bible studies, which typically had a small group of participants, all relatives. Usually it was just Marshall's mom, his two sisters, one of their daughters, Ethne, Nina, Ginger, Tanisha, Nina and Marshall's young sons, and me. It was a far cry from the massive communal spirit I was accustomed to.

I was devastated to be cut off from the community that I loved so much. In an attempt to find a substitute, I started watching the Crystal Cathedral, Dr. Robert Schuller's *Hour of Power* services that were broadcast on ABC every Sunday morning. He, like Pastor Joe, preached in monotone, but the beautiful architecture, large glass windows, swaying palm leaves, and energized throng took on the grandeur of big-church worship and served as a symbol of God manifest in the world.

Watching yet another preacher do his work, I had a recurring thought—*I could do that.* At the same time, the constant barrage of conspiracy theories from Nina and Marshall and on the Christian radio stations strained my relationship with religion. On car rides with Marshall and Nina, I was forced to listen to Jay Sekulow, an extremely conservative lawyer who would later represent Donald Trump in the Russian collusion probe, and Bob Larson, who calls himself "the foremost expert on cults, the occult, and supernatural phenomena."

The theology regarding satanic masonic programming being hidden everywhere is a never-ending rabbit hole. Once Ethne started looking at the world that way, she spiraled ever deeper into obsession over what kind of content and activities we could engage with. She truly believed the end-time and the rapture were imminent. She, Marshall, and Nina were obsessed with a Y2K conspiracy theory proclaiming that society would collapse and the Antichrist would arise in the midst of an economic crash as soon as the clock struck midnight in the year 2000. They started hoarding water, investing in gold coins, and collecting canned food. I called it out as a farce and was ridiculed for not going along with or assisting in the doomsday preparations.

There were so many times either Marshall, Ethne, or Nina would look me in my face and tell me that when the rapture came, I would be left behind and would have to fend for myself. I was ready for such a challenge. Anyway, I couldn't stand being in the room with a group of paranoid fools who believed something just because there was a conference and videotapes about it.

Then one day, Ethne got her wish. Marshall and Nina would be moving in with us. I truly questioned if I'd be able to survive. With all of us under one roof, the stage was set for war.

FOUR

Which House Is a Home?

For four years, Nina and Marshall had lived on Offutt Air Force Base adjacent to Bellevue, Nebraska, a thirty-minute drive from our house via US Highway 75 and Interstate 480. During the early years of their marriage they would often host family get-togethers, happily entertaining in their modest home. A sliding door opened onto the small concrete slab that marked their backyard, which was on a slope, in close proximity to the neighbors, and didn't have a fence. I fondly remember playing in that backyard as the entire Davis clan celebrated the birth of Nina and Marshall's first child, Little Marshall. In those days, Nina chose which one of us kids got the privilege of staying the night at her house. It was usually me who kept Nina company before and after she had Little Marshall and soon thereafter Baby Marshall. Their father spent long hours as a staff sergeant working underground in Strategic Air Command.

Their house was often in disarray, littered with bottles with remnants of milk and high chairs filled with the crumbs of stale cereal and french fries. Little Marshall, Marshall IV, had been born when I was in fourth grade, and Baby Marshall, Marshall V, when I was in fifth grade. At first, Nina cared for her boys in a lenient manner that differed completely from Ethne and Clyde's preferred parenting style. Nina was present and nurturing, always clearing a space for me on their dingy brown couch so I could sleep in the living room, which was an island of baby toys, dirty laundry, and leftover fast-food bags. There were many things I loved about spending the night at Nina and Marshall's, from getting to choose my favorite ice cream at Baskin-Robbins to visiting Divine Truth Christian Store.

Marshall would later recruit me for Civil Air Patrol meetings on the weekends. While I had a slight interest in planning future banquets and ensuring that rice pilaf was on the menu, I didn't want to be involved after a visit to basic training on a cold, rainy Saturday at Camp Ashland, which operated as an Army National Guard training facility. One glance at the barracks and I knew being on the receiving end of a drill sergeant's yelling wouldn't work for me. I was called and chosen for ministry and the stage! I have the utmost respect for those who serve in the military, but I wasn't up for all that grit. It was obvious that Marshall wanted to push me toward a more disciplined life.

Those occasional sleepovers served as a welcome distraction—until they ended. Marshall had broken his leg during Officer Candidates School basic training for the marines, which led to his unceremonious ejection back into civilian life. This left his ego bruised beyond repair and made moving back home with us the only option for their little family. I was infuriated! Not only would four extra bodies in our small home encroach on my personal space, but Marshall's increasing surveillance would surely stifle the essence of who I was and who I was becoming.

Marshall was the only man besides her boss whom Grandma Ethne respected after the divorce, and she informally appointed him the new "father figure." I felt I had something to prove to Marshall, and he thought of me as the perfect "project" for him to take on. I'm sure my queerness and penchant for performance had something to do with it and that Marshall believed old-school discipline might inspire his version of black masculinity within me.

Marshall's demeanor changed as he and Nina literally ascended and took over the master bedroom. Ethne moved down into Granddad's old recording studio in the basement, and Little Marshall and Baby Marshall were given my and Dexter's room. It was clear I had no choice in the matter, and I was forced out into the living room to sleep on a pullout bed from a couch given to us by Marshall's mother, Brenda. I no longer had any privacy or the sole rights to my beloved possessions—all my toys were passed on to my nephews without my permission. From the outset, this new dynamic felt unfair to me, and I didn't keep that opinion a secret.

At church people saw me as eager to help and eager to please. I was respected, encouraged, praised, and even loved for my enthusiasm and voice, which made me want to give in return. At home, the opposite was true. My family considered me disobedient and full of back talk. I began making my complaints known at every opportunity, and Marshall and Ethne took turns responding. A two-against-one scenario brought forth a bolder me who refused to be berated.

"You're not my father!" I'd yell at Marshall.

"I don't want to be," he would calmly retort.

Yet he certainly didn't mind being my disciplinarian. Marshall would wake me up at around five in the morning and force me to run several miles with him outside my middle school. He forced me to walk up and down stairs as a punishment or stand with my nose to the wall for hours while being chastised. Sometimes I was made to sleep on the landing of the entryway, where a constant draft ensured I was sleepless and shivering.

Suddenly, my minor misbehaving and mumblings were considered serious infractions. If I ever said no to doing anything Ethne asked or got caught disrespecting Marshall in her presence, she would slap me across the face. I'd been slapped and spanked my whole life, with hands and belts, switches from the peony bush on the side of our house, and a wooden paddle that was kept in the back of the closet in the master bedroom. But now the frequency increased and so did the range of punishable offenses. What once seemed to be coming from a place of love or an attempt to "train up a child in the way he should go," in the Proverbs 22:6 way, now morphed into hitting, fueled by rage and a desire to break my spirit.

They increased other attacks against me as well. At almost every Bible study in our home and at Marshall's mom's house, someone would call me out, saying, "Someone needs to get right. Right with the Lord. Hell is real," and all eyes would look to me.

At every possible turn, they stomped on my voice and my authenticity. I was hushed, dismissed, silenced, and stifled, which forced me to stick up for myself on a daily basis.

I knew what this was really about: I had chosen not to distance myself from my grandfather. In fact, I dreamed of what living with Clyde would be like; at least he did not tolerate religious fanaticism.

Whatever their reason, I was sick of being the punching bag at home. Whenever I felt overwhelmed by the attacks, I would say, "I'll go live with my granddad!" which would make matters worse. Nina was already extremely upset that I wasn't "on her side" and wanted my full cooperation in the takedown of my grandfather. This only fueled the fire that was consuming our family, except Tanisha and Ginger weren't forced into such rabid debate on the topic, only me. I think another thing that got them so mad was that they saw a bit of my granddad in me: I, too, was an entertainer, a natural people person, and the possessor of a certain magnetism. My unwillingness to condemn him was equal to his unwillingness to take responsibility. We were coupled together as the villain in their eyes.

For years, I had stayed silent, as the pain of this situation festered. I had examined it from every angle, trying to figure out how to reconcile the part I played with all the unknowns. I was just a kid, after all, caught within the family's crossfire. In the age of #MeToo, I think Savannah Guthrie summed it up when speaking about the accusations against her former colleague Matt Lauer: "How do you reconcile your love for someone with the revelation that they have behaved badly?" My grandfather's approach to the accusations was problematic, to say the least. He admitted to doing some things that could have been, as he says, *misinterpreted*. If that is the case, then his first reaction should have been a simple apology, not a rambling defense.

One night, the tension hit a fever pitch. We were sitting at the kitchen table after one of Marshall's Bible studies. Ethne was going on and on about giving Marshall jurisdiction over me for ninety days and that he needed to talk to me about my erections. I had a habit of putting my knees inside my sweatshirts because I was cold, and this was interpreted as my trying to conceal a hard-on. I felt both embarrassed and insulted, like I was surrounded by a gang letting me know I was no longer on my own turf. Ethne kept pressing me to submit to Marshall's command, as if I were enlisting in his boot camp.

"No," I said.

With that, Ethne stood up and got in my face. I could smell her breath as she rested her arms on the sides of my leather chair. But I was through hearing her foolishness. Firmly and clearly, I told her, *"No."* She looked at me as if I were the devil incarnate, then pulled a long wooden spoon from the kitchen drawer and hit me so hard on the back of the hand that the spoon split in two. My knuckles seized from the pain. My first instinct was to freeze. But she continued yelling in my face, and a straight-up brawl ensued. Then her weight was on me, and I was kicking and screaming and punching every which way I could. Several minutes later we reached a stalemate, and I retired to my bed in the living room.

The following day Ethne returned from work clutching her eye, which had started to swell and turn purple. Marshall and Nina freaked out and started testifying that I was some kind of abusive monster. They demanded she press charges, which was also the recommendation of her coworkers. Of course, her coworkers had not heard the entire story. Over the next few days, Ethne held that prospect over my head. I was surprised by her black eye but stood strong in the fact that she shouldn't have hit me in the first place. After years of getting hit, I had reached my breaking point.

Life resumed. I took out the trash when asked, mowed the lawn, and even accompanied her to our regular trips to ALDI's. There was no further mention of charges being pressed against me—until, a few weeks later, Ethne informed me that I had to go to court.

She drove me there herself. During the ride, she said she was considering dropping the charges. I could sense she was just using this as leverage. She didn't seem to feel guilty for instigating this violent episode, or for turning me in. What if I ended up getting shipped off to a juvenile detention facility like my brother?

As we entered the courthouse, I was struck by the familiarity of the setting. The mural of Nebraska Native American history on the rotunda reminded me of the day I was adopted, but now I was here to face charges made by the woman who had adopted me.

In juvenile hall, a public defender and a judge joined me and Ethne. The judge asked me questions first and then followed up with her. I explained about the wooden spoon incident and that I'd acted in self-defense, and the judge immediately dismissed the case. I later solicited the police report, which stated, "Davis, Ethne advised officer W. Sherman that on Saturday, January 8, 2000, at approximately nineteen hundred hours she had an argument with her son suspect Davis, Nathaniel over some item he had stolen. Davis, Ethne stated that she slapped Nathaniel because he started cussing at her." That was a lie. She knew what would get me locked up, what would get me the same fate as my biological mother and brother. The truth was, after a lifetime of violence, I was simply sick and tired of being hit.

~

At least the horror of Marshall and Nina living in our house would be coming to an end, as he had earned his bachelor's degree and secured a job at a bank downtown. I was relieved that they were leaving, but that relief would be short-lived.

A few weeks after the family of four had moved out, Cathy, the school secretary, informed me in hushed tones that all my belongings had been dropped off in the foyer of the school. I walked around the corner and saw my whole life piled up there like garbage. I couldn't formulate a response as I contemplated those white trash bags. I was overwhelmed by hurt, sadness, and above all, confusion. I imagined Ethne soliciting Marshall's and Nina's help to collect my things. To make matters worse, atop the heap sat a single CD, still in its wrapping. It was Avalon's *In a Different Light* album. Avalon was a contemporary Christian group whose number-one song at the time was "Can't Live a Day," which served as a kind of goodbye note, since apparently Ethne couldn't muster the courage to say goodbye to me in person. The message was clear. Kicking me out was what God was calling her to do.

There I was again. Abandoned in a single second. Yet another "mother" had reached her limit and was just *done* with me. Ethne had simply quit her job as mother, abdicated all responsibility. The ultimate betrayal. There had been no last supper, no warning, and no ultimatum. Just dropped into the lap of Pontius Pilate.

In fact, recently we'd walked in the March for Jesus in downtown Omaha. We'd stood side by side amid the people holding signs that declared that Jesus was Lord, and we'd joined in the proverbial chant, "I have decided to follow Jesus, no turning back . . ." I'd thought we were in a good place. But now I, too, was an enemy to be defeated, a chore that needed crossing off the list. Tossed out like a used ironing board onto the curb.

~

I moved in with my Uncle Tony, just as Clyde had when Ethne kicked him out. Being separated from my siblings and put out from my childhood home felt strange at first. Many times I had threatened to go live with my granddad, and now I had.

Tony sold men's Polo for Ralph Lauren at Dillard's for years and on the side was a deejay for Complete Music and one of their most frequently requested emcees. He had been a constant source of joy throughout my tumultuous childhood, dropping into our world and lighting it up when no one else could. He always came by on holidays and checked on us when he was out and on his way home from running errands. He made sure we did fun activities and that we had special experiences outside the house. Anytime I got into trouble, not spending time with him was always the first punishment my grandparents had threatened.

When I was with Tony, trouble didn't exist. It didn't hit me until I was much older, but Granddad and Ethne were actually his parents too—he lived in between Granddad Clyde and Ethne's house and Charlesetta's house during his youth—so he understood what it was like growing up under such authoritarian rule. Whenever we'd get the treat of a sleepover at his house, he'd make popcorn from a cast-iron skillet over the stove top. From the living room we could hear him pouring in the seeds and oil, followed by the popping. Then we'd sit under the portraits of Malcolm X and Dr. Martin Luther King Jr. in Tony's big leather recliners, watching movies and eating pizza. Time with Tony always felt special and celebratory.

I was under the impression that all my troubles would melt away once I was living under his guidance, and in many ways, they did. He made sure I had a home-cooked meal and walking-around money to catch the bus to school and buy lunch, and to cover any other small expenses that came up. He treated me like his own son.

He didn't give any indication of feeling put out or annoyed by my presence, but as time passed, I could tell he felt inconvenienced by having first his dad and now his nephew cramping his bachelor lifestyle. His fridge was stocked with forties for the taking after a long day on his feet. Tony, who had natural curls and was well over six feet tall, possessed an entirely different swag from my grandfather, and the waterbed to go along with it. He was calm, cool, and collected, and the ladies couldn't get enough of him, which meant he always had girlfriends around.

Tony was deejaying and emceeing under the name Tony D, carrying on the legacy of the family business of entertainment. He was known locally as the mixtape and CD king. He traveled all around town, but especially to barbershops and beauty shops, to sell his mixes. I'd sometimes make mixtapes, too, by recording songs off the radio. I was interested in the entertainment business but not in being an emcee.

During those first weeks at Tony's, I would still see Tanisha at Sword of the Spirit Christian School. Ginger had started doing correspondence homeschooling a little before I left and working at Easy Spirit, a shoe store at Crossroads Mall.

To me it was another example of Ginger getting to do whatever she wanted, but at least I got to see her on a regular basis. It was only through Tanisha and Ginger that I found out about the death of Ethne's father, Leroy, and Ethne losing the house.

Leroy was one of the kindest, gentlest people I have ever known. A calming, stable force; a veteran; and a bus driver. Ethne was the apple of his eye. In our backyard on Sixty-Sixth, he commissioned a full patio renovation so we could host family get-togethers. He also gifted us two picnic tables that served as my catwalks and stages for many years. He often brought potato salad, marshmallow fluff, spinach dip, and grasshopper pies on his visits to our house.

Darlene, Leroy's second wife and Ethne's stepmother, was another matter completely. She was a real redheaded bitch. For one thing, Motha's hair was coiffed. And I mean beehive coiffed. So coiffed that if it were raining, she would cover her head with a plastic shawl. She walked with a cane and wore orthopedic shoes. Whenever we visited her and Leroy, Darlene was always yelling about something in a piercing tone. Ethne sometimes mentioned her strained relationship with Darlene, which began after her biological mother, Phyllis, died from alcoholism. Darlene was pretty much perfectly cast for the role of wicked stepmother.

I learned that Leroy had bought the house and given it to Ethne and Clyde as a wedding present when they married in the early nineties, and that our visits to Darlene and Leroy's weren't just for family time but to pay him back. The moment Leroy passed, Darlene looked over at Ethne and said, "I want you out of the house. You have twenty-four hours." Ginger cussed her out like only a black girl can. But Darlene was unfazed. Since the house had never been officially transferred from Leroy's name to Ethne's and Clyde's, it automatically went to Darlene upon his death. Darlene had never been supportive of Ethne's interracial marriage, and this was her chance to do something about it.

Instead of fighting, Ethne decided to walk away. She went to stay with Nina and Marshall for a short while; Ginger ended up moving in with Tammy; and later Ethne decided to move to Las Vegas with Tanisha. I was puzzled about her choice. Sin City didn't seem like a good fit for a woman of God. Ultimately, I believe her telemarketing job gave her an opportunity to move to a different market.

Looking back, I think on some level I saw Ethne's breaking point coming. How could anyone deal with the realization that her life partner was a serial cheater and had allegedly harmed their firstborn in a way that she never thought possible? My resistance to disavowing Clyde created an untenable rift in her and my relationship. To her, I was like Tammy 2.0, a wild child that wasn't *really* hers in the first place. Her only hope was to turn to Jesus to free her from the damnation that circled her.

~

When Granddad and Tony were working on the weekends, I had many hours to watch whatever I wanted on TV and browse the nascent World Wide Web. One night, I came across a show with a nasty name on a pay-per-view channel, and on a whim, I decided to buy it. Although I was initially timid, I was also eager. I watched it for a few minutes—it made me feel giddy—but soon changed the channel. After that I pretty much forgot about it until one afternoon when Tony nonchalantly mentioned that if I wanted to purchase something on TV, I should simply let him know.

My granddad wasn't as open-minded. On another day when I was home alone, I got online and typed something like "gay naked" into the search bar. I had no idea what would happen. Of course, the page filled with websites that offered XXX gay content. I clicked on one of the results, and a man with an erect penis appeared. Blood rushed to my nether regions; periodically glancing toward the front door, I browsed for several minutes, then exited out of the screen, closed out all the tabs, and turned off the computer. I was left with a feeling of new awakening and spent the rest of the night pondering what I had just seen.

The *very next day*, my granddad turned on his computer and was immediately inundated by gay-porn pop-ups. I was in the living room when I heard him shout, "What the hell is this!"

I rushed in to deny responsibility. "What is this?" I said, playing up my innocence. "Wow!" Of course it was me, but I couldn't let Granddad know that. He looked at me, looked at the monitor, and sat back in his chair as if I were insulting his intelligence.

After that, my granddad put a password on his computer. For weeks, images of naked gay men greeted him anytime he went online. But he never mentioned it again.

Since perusing the internet was no longer an option, I returned to my casual browsing of gay magazines at Barnes & Noble. I came across a leaflet to order a free subscription to International Male and jumped at the chance. International Male was my first introduction to the world of soft-core porn—men in banana hammocks and lace, opera coats, two-piece double-breasted white and colored suits fitted tight to muscled torsos; men with sensual, smoldering gazes posing in sexy destinations. I was inspired by the way the line combined the masculine and feminine aesthetic.

For the first time in my life, I saw gay culture outside of David Alan Grier as Antoine Merriweather and Damon Wayans as Blaine Edwards in the "Men on Film" sketch on the TV show *In Living Color*. While I could relate to the attitude of those men, that sketch didn't show much by way of the gay fashion continuum, and International Male did. If Tony were the one to pick up the mail, he'd hand International Male to me with no fanfare. My young queer heart clutched it as if it were a bible, a guide to be studied. I *loved* that catalog, though I never did order anything from it.

Around this time, I had my second sexual experience, this time with James, a boy at school. Since living at Tony's had been generally fulfilling and ridicule-free, I felt emboldened to explore and experiment. We'd noticed each other in the neighborhood and at school, and so I eventually invited James to the house. Within minutes, we were lying down on my cot, kissing and bumping bodies. His skin was clammy, and I felt a rush as my Jheri curl met his. It was a brief but enlivening encounter.

I continued to see James in the neighborhood, but we both agreed we couldn't do what we had done ever again because it was ungodly. James was more concerned than I was. The extra independence I'd gained living with Granddad and Tony allowed me to finally address what was inside me, yearning to be free. As a Christian I was conflicted, but I believed in a forgiving God, so I was less worried about the sin part. I would simply ask for forgiveness later.

At that point, I didn't register those few intimate experiences as anything more than exploration or as an indication about my sexual identity. Instead, I saw myself as a young person figuring out the messages from my head and heart.

I worked a few hours a week at a package express business that leased office space from Victory Church. Living off Sixtieth and Ames, an entertainment thoroughfare, was very different from living across from a school. Ames Avenue runs from Thirteenth Street downtown to Seventy-Second leading into North Central Omaha, the epicenter of black life in the city. With record stores, churches, bars, restaurants, and barbershops all within walking distance, I knew I had found the life I wanted. I relished going to Uptop barbershop and getting a slick, tight, clean fade. It was the first time I got to choose when and how I got my hair cut.

Around that time, my granddad was producing shows for public access TV, and he started to take me along to help out and to teach me how to man the cameras. For the first time ever, I felt like he was taking an active interest in me and actually treating me like his grandson. He taught me to pan right, pan left, how to zoom in and create the perfect tight shot, and how to create a clean fade. The only other up-close and personal view of his work I had had before then was the couple of times he brought me along to Backstreet Lounge, the club he deejayed at, to retrieve his records. I had a solid relationship with those records because I was the one loading them into his trunk every weekend. But now, he was investing in me by sharing his passion and showing me the ropes in broadcasting. It was the most quality time we had ever spent together.

One of the shows Granddad produced was hosted by a woman named Ella Mae. It was called *Giving God the Praise* and featured her singing "Jesus Is Coming Soon" in an old songbird style over chords and backing tracks from her electric keyboard. I was secretly thrilled when Ella Mae came in to record—her gold tooth would be shining for Jesus, and her blue sequined beret added sparkle to her already eccentric performances. My granddad would run back and forth between the cameras and the control room—it was a real production!

After an extended stint of long evenings at the studio with Granddad, I had heard all the preaching I could take. On top of that, some of the shine had worn off, and often my granddad and I would arrive midargument. I started to avoid him and instead hang out with the studio manager, Chris Kraddock, who, without fail, would deescalate the situation by encouraging my granddad to give me a break.

At the end of a night of running errands, I'd sneak off to the break room down the hall to get full cable access on the studio TV. It was there one Monday night that I stumbled onto *Queer as Folk*, one of the first shows on television to graphically depict gay sexuality and culture. I was instantly entranced by Club Babylon and hunky Randy Harrison who played Justin, whose father was struggling to accept his homosexuality. I, too, longed to be freed by the music of the night and dance around with cute boys. From that point on I was eager for Mondays.

Queer as Folk fed me as an emotional battle continued to wage on within me. Chris is the first person I remember talking to about the fact that I might be gay. He reassured me, saying that the right thing was to "just be you." He would come into the break room and fill up his coffee cup while I watched TV, a silent ally who provided cover. At home, Tony also encouraged me to be myself. Meanwhile, Granddad was becoming more and more vocal about his disapproval.

~

I was still involved in church and youth-group activities and didn't feel the need to ask for permission or share my whereabouts with my granddad. I carried on as if I were grown and no longer required supervision. Anyway, I wasn't doing drugs like Dexter was, or getting involved in gangs. I was a good kid. I was only going to church, after all.

Granddad didn't take too kindly to that and interpreted it as a challenge to his parental authority. Of course, I believed he'd lost that authority long ago. After all, whom could I trust after so many people in my family had failed me? Nina, Marshall, and Ethne had given me parenting that felt more like punishment than guidance. People at church gave me the recognition for my individuality and creativity that I craved, along with tending to my physical, spiritual, and mental needs.

I went on frequent church and youth-group outings, including horseback riding, boating, and tubing, as well as gatherings at our youth pastors Matt and Tonya Morris's house in Irvington. I was grateful to tag along for restaurant meals with Pastor Joe, Laura, and the church leadership, especially since I could order anything that I wanted. I took quality time where I could get it.

I would frequently walk the mile and a half to Victory Church, imagining what my brother and sisters might be doing. Pastor Joe would often see me and pick me up on his way in, and Nancy from the praise team would usually give me rides home. Nancy was a divorced mom of two, and we found solace in each other as we played the hands life dealt us. Her smudged eyeliner and beseeching worship enthralled me. She would kick her shoes off and drop to her knees, crying out to God to intervene in her life. I usually did the same. The seats that used to be occupied by Ethne and Ginger were empty.

I knew I had something more to give. It just so happened that, soon thereafter, I heard about our youth group going on a mission trip to Mexico City. I thought it would be the perfect thing. How could I not take advantage of the opportunity to experience a place that was so far away from everything I had ever known? I had heard of the missionaries from our church globetrotting in places like Nepal and Botswana, preaching the Gospel and representing our church. My favorite Sunday-school teachers, Daron and Angie, were missionaries, and if Daron and Angie could do it, I thought, so could I. I had a feeling that greater things were waiting beyond the borders of Nebraska.

I'd always believed that my life trajectory was headed toward ministry—I'd helped out teaching Sunday school, sung in the choir, led youth praise and worship—so this mission trip felt like the next logical step. It would allow me to both experience the outside world and begin my own calling.

Not once did I ask my granddad for permission. Instead, I simply *told* him I would be going to Mexico. It's not like he was the one who made sure I got to school and ate every day. My Uncle Tony did that. I think there was a bit of paperwork he needed to sign, and I needed his help in securing my passport, though I had managed to arrange everything else myself. The youth group had already held multiple fundraisers, and I had participated in the basic Spanish lessons offered at church. I was working hard to learn basic lines of evangelism that included phrases like *todo lo puedo* or "Through Him, I can do all things." I even crafted the layout for the bulletin board that hung in the church entryway announcing our upcoming trip.

But then Granddad told me I wasn't going because I hadn't directly asked for his permission. We argued about it for several days until my Uncle Tony intervened on my behalf, laying out in staccato why my request for the experience of a lifetime was reasonable. Surprisingly, Granddad obliged.

~

At the beginning of August, Pastor Joe bid us goodbye in prayer, and away we went. I was glad to be surrounded by so many familiar faces as I embarked on a major first in my life: my first airline flight. Before this, my only trip out of state was to a summer camp in Iowa, and now I was taking an international flight to a place unknown, where fresh wonders awaited me, to minister to the people of Mexico and share the love of God that was running through me.

We landed in a sunlit Mexico City. Green VW Bug taxis swirled around the circular streets. As we drove from the airport through the city to the hotel, I was enthralled by the colors of peach, cyan, and brick red, the buildings stacked high into the distance. I had the perception that Mexico was a poor, undeveloped country that needed saving and that I was there to contribute to the effort, but with every detail I observed, I was overwhelmed by the richness of a history that was both alive and thousands of years old.

The next day, we set out early with our tour guide to travel to the outskirts of Mexico City. En route, we saw a poor community living near a garbage dump. Sheets hung from tin ceilings to form walls. Brown gutter water sloshed and seeped through open front doorways. Trash was everywhere, flat underfoot or piled high in the corners, and the smell was unbearable.

I was shocked and humbled to see the extreme poverty there. That hardship contributed to my growing awareness of my own family's socioeconomic standing. What was it like to live next to a landfill? The children ran around with smiles on their faces and welcomed us as visitors. What was it like to be them?

I walked up countless cliffs and down as many alleys, crying out, "Muppets! *Payasos!*" to lure viewers to our evangelical puppet show. Once enough people had gathered, we served rice and passed out candy to the children. After everyone had something to eat, the puppet show began, presenting a simple message to the people—"Jesus loves you."

I felt so at home in that servant role, in building fellowship across cultural and lingual barriers. It came naturally to me. I felt like I was stepping into my calling and claiming my destiny, even when I didn't know what was on the other side.

Later in the week we went to a local church service so packed that we were nearly standing outside. The spirit of God began moving, and instantly I saw similarities in how we worshipped the same God in the spirit of praise. I once heard a prophetess say that the spirit of God lives in the timbre of music, and I believe that is true. Music has a universal ability to transcend language and borders, and even walls.

On the last day we visited the Plaza de la Constitución and the Palacio Nacional. I remember walking in and seeing Diego Rivera's *The History of Mexico* in the main stairwell and looking up to observe the storied history that I had never been taught. When we left, out front in the plaza there were Aztec warriors with big colorful headdresses stomping, blowing smoke out of skulls, and waving feathers. I immediately passed judgment, thinking *demonic* as their feet hit the ground.

How, I wonder, was I not overcome with appreciation for the radiant and mystical spirits that they were embodying and evoking? How was this any different from us catching the Holy Ghost and speaking in tongues?

I'll never forget standing on the roof of our hotel with another church member. We had just gotten back from buying big jugs of water at a little market nearby. We could see millions of tiny lights flickering in tenement windows far beyond, sprawling endlessly as the pink sun disappeared below the horizon. I felt small and humbled to experience such a vast world so different from my own.

FIVE

Churches, Drama, and More Houses

I had always wanted to follow in Nina's footsteps by attending Northwest High School. And I would, at least for a little while. But Northwest would end up being the first of several high schools I'd attend over four years, as my relationships with family, friends, and church community expanded and contracted and influenced my identity in ways I never could have imagined.

Victory Church and Christian principles remained guiding forces in my life, but at Northwest I also began to explore new facets through Youth for Christ, JROTC, and junior choir. I became a committed attendee of the Youth for Christ morning prayer meetings before school and took the instruction of its leaders seriously. They laid out a path of youth righteousness that included no sex before marriage, no smoking, and no pornography. I struggled with the latter as I dabbled in viewing images of naked gay men on the internet and asked the group leader to help me fight what I had been taught was a perversion. He created a new email for me, transformedbyjah@yahoo.com, to serve as a technological reminder that God had made me anew and that I should flee from the wicked temptation.

Junior choir provided something a little different. The choir was led by an effeminate music teacher who was also one of the ministers of music at Christ Community Church in Omaha. Though there was rampant speculation that he was gay, he never publicly identified as such. Nonetheless, I found his effeminate manner and Christian beliefs comforting. His laugh was haughty, dramatic, and his knack for carrying himself in whimsical theatricality gave me permission to do the same. Singing in that choir gave me a space to disappear but also to be seen. It was a space in which I felt truly included and that my contribution mattered. This led me to explore my interests more comfortably in music and theater.

My music teacher was also the director for the yearly school musical, and when they announced that the fall production would be a revue of songs in tribute to Andrew Lloyd Webber, I knew I had to audition. I sang a rendition of "Shout to the Lord," which must've been moving because a few days later I learned I would be a part of the chorus. I was thrilled. Just as I was basking in the happy news, heartthrob and drama-club officer Justin Whitney looked at me and said, "Congrats." I couldn't believe it. His frosted hair, bright gleaming smile, and Abercrombie style made my heart palpitate. I already saw my crush frequently in drama club, but now I would get to see him every day and up close. Roderick, another one of the leads and a drama-club officer, was someone I'd known growing up. His was the last house I passed on my daily walk to Nathan Hale in seventh grade. We were friendly but not exactly friends.

Rehearsals began, and I noticed with delight that there were at least five people who I suspected were gay. During the staging of numbers from *Evita*, *Jesus Christ Superstar*, and *Cats*, I watched Justin and Roderick shine and couldn't help but wonder if I, too, had what it took to stand onstage in all my glory. Something inside told me I did.

Roderick was the reigning femme queen of the school. And when I say *femme queen*, I mean it as a term of endearment that bestows nobility on queers who put the fresh in fierce and the pomp in circumstance. As captain of the Highsteppers drill team, a member of JROTC, and one of the school's most talented singers, he was certainly a force of nature. His kicks, quick steps, and flanking-arms combos wowed the children into submission and gave them everything they weren't ready for and more. I had the attitude but not the moves. (Even when I became a full-time performer, I always referred to myself as a "strut queen" and called what I was doing "twirling.")

In JROTC, I became good friends with Adrienne, with whom I shared easy laughs, a bond over our love of punk fashion, and common histories of being in foster care and the juvenile justice system. I often wore shiny pleather button-up shirts paired with a stainless-steel ball-chain necklace, and glitter gel in my caramel texturized hair. My fashion choices reflected how I felt on the inside: dark, rebellious, and desperate for attention. Adrienne lined her eyes with dark black eyeliner and often wore a gray shirt with Mickey Mouse on it along with the same pair of jeans, black shoes, and black-rimmed eyeglasses. Her shiny midlength black hair, a gift from her Native American roots, caught the breeze whenever she walked across the room. Her eyes were piercing, beautiful, and warm.

Our teacher, Sergeant Van, often spoke to me conversationally about issues we disagreed on; mainly he wanted to understand my challenging and boundary pushing. I learned the drills and appreciated the uniformity, the pageantry, and being a part of something that engaged my social intelligence. He openly shared that he was Muslim, and I was fascinated as he was the first person I had ever met who identified with that faith.

Then I announced that I was going to wear a dress to the military ball at the end of the year. Sergeant Van told me I couldn't, plain and simple.

"Why?" I asked.

"You just can't" was all he said.

Still, I had a feeling I should wear a dress to the event. I'd gotten a job working at McDonald's as a cashier, and with the money I'd earned, I purchased a floor-length powder-blue evening gown and matching light blue heeled sandals from Payless.

I felt at home in those heels and looked forward to the moment when I could unzip my backpack, take them out, and then pound the pavement with authority as I walked to the bus stop. By riding the bus wearing heels, I was acknowledging a piece of my truth to myself and the world around me. A public coming out of sorts without any labels. The next emergence would be my public debut in a dress.

The very next day I huddled at my locker, which was in the basement down the hall from JROTC, and showed off my outfit to Adrienne, who had always encouraged me to be myself. But when I sat down next to her in class, she looked over at me and said, *"You need to get saved!"* I was stunned that the supportive friend I had thought to be down with all things alternative was now preaching Gospel to me. It was through her that I met Pastor Brian Gallardo. I was struck by his captivating energy. He invited me to Eagle's Nest Worship Center where he was the youth pastor and oversaw a youth group called Youth Xplosion. It sounded cool, and I agreed to visit.

I was determined to do so, even after Adrienne's admonition. I didn't question her friendship; instead, I felt emotionally vulnerable and desperate for approval. I didn't consider my desire to wear a dress to be in spiritual misalignment. The military ball was months away, so for the moment, I pushed the controversy to the back of my mind.

Before what I call my "second abandonment," Ethne had imposed her moratorium on all things not Christian, and I'd made do with videotapes of Rod Parsley laying hands. The choir, slain in the spirit, would literally fall from the rafters after he touched them on their foreheads. All of the great Pentecostal legends preached every year at Parsley's annual Dominion Camp Meeting, including Prophetess Juanita Bynum, Bishop Iona Locke, Bishop Jackie McCullough, and even Bishop T. D. Jakes.

Gospel greats were not just great preachers but magnificent orators and public speakers. Most people don't realize it, but preaching is a skill that requires studied gesture, stance, and elocution. Especially in the Pentecostal world. *Ev-ry. Singull. Word-ah. Meeeannsss. Sum-thing.*

Fashion is a big deal too. Women come in *done!* At Eagle's Nest I saw women in lime-green and red skirt suits that touched my soul more than the word that was being preached. I had royal blue, powder blue, and teal suits that were *cleannnnnn.* I knew I was the flyest. Thank you, Burlington Coat Factory!

It was its own kind of theater. I loved the way sermons were delivered and the way talking points were articulated based on the preacher's personality.

I envisioned myself becoming a great preacher or a minister of music and joining the praise-and-worship front line at World Harvest Church. The frontline singers were the ones who led the praise and worship instead of just being in the choir. The idea of sharing my faith in a way that demonstrated my theatricality excited me.

To this day, my public-speaking style most resembles that of a pastor, transforming my audience into my congregants. Something similar can be said of my style. Anywhere I go, I imagine myself as the first lady of a church, the representative of the entire congregation.

Eagle's Nest Worship Center was based in a commercial property space in a strip mall behind the Long John Silver's where Nina used to take me. It was completely different from the style of church I was used to. The youth group was run out of a bay next to the church, a long rectangular room that featured a banner on the wall that said "Ezekiel 37,"

referencing the biblical prophet who had a divine vision about seeing dry bones revived to life. What an interesting metaphor to describe young people. It assumes that all young people are lost and dead inside. I was far from dead and actually very much alive and searching for stability, authenticity, and truth.

Pastor Brian assumed that I was unchurched and needed to get saved, based solely on the fact that I was a boy whose demeanor and appearance was feminine. His message of mending brokenness spoke to me. He shared that he had grown up fatherless and in poverty, and he later found out that his dad committed suicide.

I was enthralled by Pastor Brian's charismatic preaching. I wanted to be a part of the movement of God he was curating, inspiring youths to walk the halls of their high schools full of dominion, discernment, and deliverance while preaching the Gospel and slinging their Bibles. He preached about overcoming abandonment and rejection and about how we could ultimately empower ourselves through Jesus Christ. The message resonated with me so much that I rededicated my life to the Lord. I was hoping to find who I truly was on the inside.

That moment began a four-year battle in which I found myself before countless altar calls begging God to remove the sin of homosexuality from my life. Forget that an anger consumed me because my biological mother never wanted me. Forget that I grew up in a house of seven where I was the middle child and nothing I did would ever be good enough, that I would never be as important as my brother. Forget that I was just on the other side of seeing all my things in garbage bags, as if my life had no meaning and Ethne weren't listed as "mother" on my birth certificate. I needed help and felt Pastor Brian's ministry would be the salve that would heal all my wounds.

I was thrilled to be invited to the Firepower retreat the following weekend at Faith Tabernacle Church in Aurora, Illinois. I joined the group of youths for the nine-hour drive to what they were calling "Chicago." (Now, as a decade-long resident of Chicago, I scoff at the idea that Aurora could be considered a part of the Windy City.) That was my introduction to urban life outside the city of Omaha. On that trip, I reconnected with Alicia Jones, with whom I had participated in Bible study, and China Love, who had gone to school with me at Sword of the Spirit. Connecting with people I had previously known was reassuring.

I believe that the Pentecostal faith is not only divinely inspired by the resurrection of Jesus Christ but operates off the energy of people who come together and pour out their hearts, vulnerabilities, and desires. At the same time, assembly in faith can lead to groupthink, which can, in turn, discourage individuals from challenging or critiquing key pieces of doctrine that seek to control people's lives.

Such was the case on the first day of the Firepower retreat. As the worship began to build, one of the pastors began praying for people and prophetically speaking words of encouragement. Then, unexpectedly, he called me from the back of the church where I was busy having my own worship experience. I walked forward as he pointed at me and screamed into the microphone, "I bind the foul spirit of homosexuality out of you. You are not a woman, you are a *man*." It was the first time I had ever heard anyone refer to me as a woman. I was shocked but in a state of holy contemplation as he lunged and laid hands on me to "cast out the devil." I felt the weight of force on me as several reinforcement spiritual warriors assisted in the exorcism, and everyone in the room stretched their hands toward me. I fell out in the spirit, as many Pentecostals do when overwhelmed by the experience.

I woke up a short time later to find several women praying over me as I lay prostrate on a kitchen floor. I stared up toward the ceiling, with no idea how I'd gotten from the carpeted basement floor to the white tile. The women helped me up, and I walked out of the room.

There is a place in my heart that still feels the pain of this moment, when someone prescribed to me who and what I was at fifteen years old. Christian doctrine that demands unquestioning obedience does not serve to empower young people, and it can do a lot of damage. People like myself, who fall outside conservative definitions of Christian acceptability, often end up sidelined and marginalized rather than loved as Jesus loves each and every one of us. The pastor who called me out in front of the congregation was not doing his job; creating a sacred space of inclusion is every Christian leader's responsibility.

I have carried this trauma with me for years. At the time, I was in pursuit of divine alignment in hopes that God would change me and make me righteous in his eyes. I believed that deliverance was real. In every other space of my life I attempted to dictate the rules of engagement, yet when it came to church, I grinned and bore it for the sake of my salvation.

However off-putting that experience had been, I was still committed to the church. Now, however, I had to choose which church to attend full-time. Victory Church represented my childhood and coming of age. Pastor Joe was a great teacher. But Eagle's Nest had Pastor Brian, who was the kind of great preacher I aspired to be. He preached about stepping into your purpose and out of shame and regret, messages that made me feel like I could do anything. The church's motto, "A place for refuge, restoration, and celebration," spoke to me too.

After a brief deliberation, I chose Eagle's Nest. It would be a new season, with a new spiritual father, in a new place where I could find some direction.

I divided my time between church, work, and school. Even so, the quarrels between my granddad and me about my coming and going as I pleased continued to rage. I didn't see a reason to ask permission or have discussions about my choices—that included my choice to wear a dress to the military ball.

As the event neared, I mentioned to several people that Roderick was my desired date for the dress's debut. It got back to Roderick, and he showed up to my locker to express his dismay that I had insinuated that I, as a lowly freshman, was even on his radar. My tactic of grabbing his attention worked! Sure, it was a stupid tactic, but I had officially committed my first bitchy high school act and let Roderick know there was a new queen on campus. After that, Roderick and I became mortal enemies. I walked into JROTC after our exchange and decided that I would be the belle of the ball.

Before the social part of the event, all the schools gathered to enact a military tradition. I assumed my position among the saber team. With the stern command "Present saber" from Sergeant Van, I raised my sword in the air along with my comrades to form a saber arch. I held my sword with pride. As soon as the rank and file entered from all the schools, we were dismissed.

I slipped out of the hall and went to change in the restroom. I'd weighed the fact of Sergeant Van's disapproval of my wearing a dress and decided to wear something else. Not to appease him, but to show him that I was my own person and I could find a way around his rule. I would follow the letter of his law but not the spirit.

Jocelyn, one of my classmates, showed up dressed in business attire, a gray suit dress with a long overlay that nearly hit the floor. As soon as she came around the corner, the tails caught the wind, my head turned, and I was hypnotized. I immediately told Jocelyn that I had to wear it; I was so moved by the sartorial dress and suit combination. Jocelyn agreed and *loant* it me. Having learned a lesson the last time, now I didn't tell anyone that I had chosen a new piece for my debut.

Minutes later, I reemerged, liberated and unstoppable with tails flailing behind me, wearing a pair of strappy black heels. Sergeant Van stopped in his tracks, and I moved to lose myself in the crowd jiving on the dance floor. It just so happened that my Uncle Tony and Granddad were deejaying the event. Sergeant Van walked up to my grandfather to let him know of "my disturbance" after I had been explicitly told that wearing a dress was unacceptable and dishonorable. I didn't care, of course, and I became the first male-identified person in Nebraska history to wear a dress to the JROTC ball.

I was happy to end my freshman year with a bang. At the beginning of my sophomore year, Granddad and I moved out of Uncle Tony's house and into a Section 8 rental across town. The trek to school became yet another arduous commute. After keeping it up for a while, I lost the initiative to make the long journey each morning and started skipping, instead focusing on working more at McDonald's and enjoying the late-night buffet at Harrah's Casino, the ultimate dad version of dinner, with my granddad.

One morning, when I should have been on my way to school, I turned on the TV in my bedroom and caught breaking news that the World Trade Center had been hit by a plane. It didn't seem real. I was stunned by the images of smoke and debris as the twin towers collapsed. I, like so many people across the world, witnessed a moment of history, a next-level catastrophe. This was my introduction to the word *terrorism*.

Later that evening it came out that President George W. Bush had been flown to a bunker at Strategic Air Command at Offutt Air Force Base while Al-Qaeda terrorist activity continued to unfold at the Pentagon. I realized with some pride that I had been on the same air force base as the president of the United States.

Shortly after 9/11, I transferred to Westside High School since I was now residing in its school district, and the long commute to Northwest High School had been a disincentive to attend school at all. This was not ideal given the fact that most of the kids who attended Westside were middle to upper class, and I was poor. The people of District 66 seemed to have a certain amount of elitism, class, privilege, and access. Parental donations to the school bought show-choir placements, and the cafeteria boasted an Arby's and a Pizza Hut. At Westside, I had no friends. I ate lunch alone and walked the halls alone. I was altogether tired of being the new kid, so despite no longer having a long commute, I just stopped going. I much preferred to go to Youth Xplosion at Eagle's Nest anyway.

With so much change on a personal and national level, I became more anxious, constantly worrying about what new calamity would happen next. I didn't know if I could take any more, and I was sure my life would completely fall apart and soon. I was still reeling from Ethne's rejection, and I was depressed about the fact that my family would never reunite because of the allegations against my granddad.

My grandfather, meanwhile, continued to start fights about where I was when not at home and whether I should have to ask permission to go to work, church, and youth group. He was unaware of or didn't understand half of what I was going through, nor would he engage me on an emotional level. I think he was powerless in other aspects of his life and relied on disciplining others to find some sense of control.

I once told Nina that our entire family needed therapy and that we should come together in one room to hash out our differences.

"The main person responsible for quite a bit of the issues is still unwilling to be honest," she told me. On that opinion, she and I actually agreed.

Later, I discovered that Granddad had demons of his own to deal with. His parents divorced when he was seven years old; his mom died when he was fourteen, followed six years later by the death of his dad. His brother, like mine, had issues with drugs, and he died of an overdose.

I didn't find out much of this information from him until I was an adult—he refused to discuss it. He refused to connect the dots between his experience, his behavior, and his impact on others. "People don't talk about the bad things that have happened to them," he told me. As much as I feel for him, I have to ask: What kind of example does that set for the next generation? He created so much havoc in our family, always denying responsibility and blaming others. He hurt the people he was meant to love.

It was during this time that I learned from Tammy that my biological father had been receiving social security disability benefits after his brain injury, and once he died, those benefits rolled over to me. She made me aware that I had a right to that social security check.

I stood up to Granddad and told him that I knew about the check that was coming every month for me. It became an ongoing argument between us: he claimed that he was using the money for my care, and I wanted a part in making sure that money was actually going toward my needs. I wanted a new bunk bed, a new desk, and new church clothes. I wanted money to get to church and for social activities like going out to eat after church, hanging out at the mall, and going to the movies.

One night, Granddad and I got into a serious row when I returned from church. He claimed to not know the people who had picked me up, and he also expressed anger at my fashion choices as he felt they evoked defiance. He didn't like the idea that I might be gay. It was the most embarrassing thing to him.

I was so angry that he was trying to impede the only lifelines I had left—my clothes and church. In the heat of the moment, I pushed him. My indignation had reached a crescendo, a culmination of hurt from his actions: his sending my brother away, cheating on Ethne, hurting his daughters, and now this. It was a final claiming of my voice, of my life. Why was it that my being slapped, hit, pushed, and locked in my room was deemed as appropriate discipline? Did my grandparents expect me to take it forever, for me to never hit back?

The Davis stronghold had to come to an end. I wanted out. I couldn't take any more.

~

After my granddad and I got in what would be our last altercation, a police officer asked me if there was somewhere I could go to cool off. I immediately thought of Ron and Valerie Love, youth-group leaders with whom I had developed a strong relationship. They often held cookouts and BBQs at their house, homey events that featured the trampoline in their backyard. They also chaperoned many of the youth activities, like going out to eat at Applebee's or going to see a Sunday-night movie. Often they would welcome me to spend the night after these events. I had developed a friendship with their kids, particularly Chelci, Alex, and China.

Ron and Valerie were affirming and believed in the act of service. They served as youth pastors for ten years. Valerie worked as a lunch lady at Sword of the Spirit. Ron was one of Pastor Hart's armor bearers, someone who, in the Pentecostal faith, is appointed by a pastor or bishop to create a barrier between the leader and the congregation, help protect their integrity, serve as their personal assistant, ensure that the pulpit is treated like a monument and altar and is ready at all times for the proper deliverance of the word of God, and deliver sermons in their absence. It was understood that Alex would carry on his dad's legacy. Ron and Valerie's support of him was a key signifier of their Proverbs 22:6 "train up a child" parenting style.

They used that same mentality when parenting the many, many kids who came into their care. (I asked them how many people had lived with them over the years, and they said around sixty.) From the very beginning of their marriage, they were foster parents and did emergency placement for at-risk adolescents. They also hosted foreign-exchange students from Mexico and always housed at least one kid from their youth group who was struggling with family discord. Behavioral issues didn't faze them, including when their daughter Chelci rebelled. You could see in their eyes how their love for her never wavered, even while she was caught up in drug abuse and other destructive behaviors. They would never abandon her.

I had no clue of this when I started hanging around their house; it simply felt youth friendly. Shortly after the police officer took me to their place, I went back into the foster care system, and shortly after that, Ron and Valerie agreed to become my foster parents, taking guardianship over me by recommendation of the county attorney. I was also given probation and appointed a guardian ad litem for truancy, threatening my grandfather, and disturbing the peace. The judge ordered me to participate in counseling, psychological testing, and a psychiatric evaluation, and to attend three PFLAG group sessions to assist with my "sexual identity issues."

After the Loves took guardianship of me, they adopted two more children and fostered another six kids. Living with others who were very different from me was certainly an experience. I didn't mind dealing with all the personalities. I was free from the Davis family and was starting a new life. I had chosen them as my parents.

My guardianship became permanent, and the Loves seemed like the perfect family. A mom. A dad. The freedom to attend every church service and activity on Wednesdays and Sundays. I jumped at the chance to help Valerie around the house. I vacuumed, did laundry, and ran errands with her—happily.

On the side, Valerie ran a home-cleaning service, and before enrolling in yet another high school, I assisted her in cleaning the weekly rotation of houses in West Omaha. That was another introduction to a world outside my own as I vacuumed lines into carpets, dusted shelves, and cleaned other people's bathrooms. I marveled at the walk-in closets full of designer clothing, the deep soaking tubs, and the pools in the backyard. This is perhaps when I developed my preference for deep soaking tubs—don't bother booking me a hotel room if it doesn't have one!

Ron had been invited to speak at the US Army military base Fort Leonard Wood in the Missouri Ozarks, and he took me along to serve as an armor bearer. Ron motioned to me as the service wrapped and instructed me to start laying hands on the thirty to forty men and women who knelt before God in camo fatigues, praying for his guidance, support, and wisdom through the journey they were facing in basic training and beyond. I felt useful and needed, and the experience made me consider my potential future in the ministry—I thought I could perhaps end up as a military chaplain. I appreciated taking to the open road with Ron on the drive back to Omaha as I thought of him as a true positive male influence. When he wasn't in the pulpit, he offered all kinds of dry dad jokes and tended to a never-ending to-do list of projects.

I also started working at Culver's as a cashier. Chelci was a shift manager and functioned as a different kind of older sister figure from Nina. Chelci would peel out of the driveway in her Toyota Camry, whirling the wheel while shifting the stick shift and smoking a cigarette at the same time. *Badassery.* Her car always smelled like Lucky You perfume and nicotine. Both of us had one foot in the youth group and one in the world, and so our rides together to work were always "real talk moments." She reminded me that in this life we shouldn't have to put up with the expectations of others, no matter who they are. I agreed.

With Chelci, I let my guard down. She was the one who encouraged me to work at Culver's. I think she knew I needed to see someone who identified as lesbian or gay. Betty, the manager, ran a tight ship and was the first black lesbian woman I had ever met. Her presence was inspiring, and being around her brought out the radiant shine in me. In my experience, queer people can walk past other queer folks and feel the magnetism they are channeling. *Yup,* we might say to ourselves, *she's one of us.* I use *she* respectfully, in the way of reclaiming femme terms like *Mary, Nelly,* and *girl.* Betty's visibility made me think about lesbian and gay people as working career professionals with partners and families, and as contributing members of society, not just racy images in magazines.

At the same time, I was receiving ample messaging that homosexuality was a sin. I soaked up all Betty's energy to pull from at a later date. I appreciated the extra income, but I ultimately got fired. One day Justin Whitney walked through the door, looking like Zack Morris from *Saved by the Bell*. I rang him up and gave him a senior discount on his meal. The owner watched my flirtation and picked up the receipt to find the words *senior discount*. I was called to the back several minutes later and fired. I didn't care. Justin Whitney was my first high school crush, and I had to show him that I was still infatuated with him.

It was shortly thereafter that Ron and Valerie and I began a conversation about picking up my education. They were clear that going back to Northwest was not an option. Burke High School was ten minutes from their house and thus the only viable option. We decided independent study would be a perfect transition, and then I would return to public school in the fall. After basically flunking my freshman year, I now got As and Bs in math and physical science. I flourished in independent study because I was able to work at my own pace and didn't have to deal with the issues that came along with the traditional school setting. We had rarely discussed academics at Ethne and Clyde's house, and I'd never considered the need to prep for college. In fact, I had no expectations around higher education.

That summer the Loves piled us all into their green Astro van, and we'd go out to a nearby Sonic Drive-In to enjoy ice cream Blasts and mozzarella sticks while music boomed from the speakers above. One evening I observed someone in roller skates carrying a tray of food whiz by and knew how I wanted to spend the rest of my summer. Roller-skating was the absolute joy of my childhood and is still something I love to do when I get a chance. Put on anything by Aaliyah, and I will backward-skate like my life depends on it.

I got hired and soon became a star carhop who worked quickly, taking orders, whirling drinks with ease, and delivering food with a smile. I worked late nights on the weekends, serving countless jocks who came to flex and show off their Trixie girlfriends and muscle cars. People had talked about my derriere being ever so pronounced, and in khaki shorts and roller skates, it was further positioned to catch glances from the gays as well as jeers from folks who disapproved of my unabashed feminine nature.

It was at Sonic that I encountered a transgender woman for the first time. There was talk that Tiffany, a manager from another store, would be coming over to fill in for a shift. I didn't understand what the chatter was about until she opened the door and I saw her, with her distinct blue contacts, long corn-chip nails, and gelled hair sticking out of her Sonic khaki hat like a cornucopia. She was a calm presence, and a tingly feeling reverberated through me; I felt like I'd discovered someone with the power to reveal all that was going on in my head. I intentionally asked her work-related questions so that I could observe her and say her name aloud, which gave me space to ruminate over what her presence in the world meant to me as a young Pentecostal boy who was often told how to style my hair, what wrist I should wear my watch on, and what clothes were appropriate for a man of God.

Summer turned to fall, and I walked up the stairs to Burke High School ready to make the most of a new environment. I'd signed up for drama, music, and yearbook, along with the required classes. I'd mimicked Alex Love's style, building a wardrobe with pieces from American Eagle and Hollister, so that Valerie and Ron wouldn't suspect that I was returning to a homosexual lifestyle.

I stormed the halls of Burke High, sure in my commanding presence that allowed me to exist without labels. Of course others called my sexuality into question. But my classmates showed me a particular kind of respect because I was walking in my truth.

In yearbook I carved out a space to flourish in journalism. I wrote several articles, helped with layouts, and pitched stories. Ms. Watzke, who supervised the yearbook, connected with us like young adults, not teenagers. Her classroom was a place where I could say what I was feeling, unlike at church. Ms. Watzke was an ally, and I often spoke in detail with her about the struggles I was facing between my sexuality and my faith. She always listened and supported me.

I joined concert choir and took a position as section leader of the baritones. I found singing choral music to be therapeutic. It was a world where my soul lifted from the intergenerational trauma that followed me. I relished the soaring, the lifting, and the kneading of the various tempos and melodies. My voice, in harmony with others, was another instrument to articulate more of the inner me. My voice was robust and unique. I sat on the edge of my chair fully engaged, determined to learn sight reading, and belted a range of music from Japanese folklore, Jewish culture, and Broadway classics.

In drama class, I excelled in improv exercises and realized that spontaneity, the ability to make anything happen with a moment's notice, was a talent and a skill. I hated anything scripted and refused to memorize lines. My drama comrades provided the kind of audience that pulled out my natural talents of comedic timing, improvisation, and theatricality. For me, acting was just being a larger version of myself. This was when I first remember feeling free to be me. Instead of being policed, my identity was embraced, and for the first time, I didn't care about fitting into any one group.

I met Corey through Brie, a mutual friend. Corey was a cute, blue-eyed, blond boy who would mix and match contemporary wear with vintage T-shirts and hoodies. He and I both participated in drama club—and I couldn't take my eyes off him.

Drama club was a space that welcomed camaraderie and talent, and I always proudly wore the T-shirts we had designed with our names on the back. We'd gather for ice cream at TCBY, white elephant gift exchanges, and a yearly themed drama club banquet. I donned a form-fitting sequined red dress I'd borrowed from Chelci and a long blond wispy wig with great poise and assurance; in this setting, I felt confident presenting as female.

The balcony platform outside the auditorium overlooked the entrance of the school and, to me, was just another stage. I would step out onto the platform and shout at the top of my lungs whatever word or expression came to mind. The most common word that I yelled was *wench* (in reference to my Spanish teacher, of whom I wasn't fond). Corey would laugh at my outburst. One day, I emerged for my routine exit, but this time Corey beat me to my own punch line. *"Wench!"* he yelled at the top of his lungs.

My experience at Burke was in stark contrast to my experience in music and drama at Westside. In my first semester at Burke, I was cast in the chorus for the musical *Grease*. I loved the rehearsals, loved how immersed I felt in artistic excellence and how bonded I became to folks from across the program. The cast was its own class and family. Despite most of us not being publicly out, there was still an unspoken camaraderie.

After *Grease*, Corey and I became inseparable. It didn't take long for us to realize we were each other's safe zone. Corey was also questioning his sexual orientation, which was in conflict with his religious beliefs, and we promised to work through the confusion together.

Corey drove a white Honda Accord he aptly named Beulah and would often give me rides home from school and on the weekends. Shortly thereafter I took driver's ed in order to get my driver's license— and the freedom that it promised.

Ron challenged me to save a thousand dollars for a car and enough for six months of auto insurance. He promised he would go out and find me a car only after I'd accomplished that. I appreciated the challenge of saving, and it didn't take long as I was working twenty hours a week at Sonic. Seeing my commitment and wanting to support and encourage it, my caseworker even kindly agreed to pay the first installment on my car insurance.

After saving the money, Ron went and found me a car as promised. There was no discussion about what kind of car I wanted. I just figured he would get me something modern like he had for Chelci. I just wanted wheels so that I could go to and fro as I pleased.

One Friday night, as I was zipping around taking and delivering orders on my roller skates, I noticed what looked to be a classic eighties-looking Cadillac pulling into the lot. Out of the corner of my eye, I watched it park at the nearest car stall. Skating closer, I saw that it was a 1985 Oldsmobile Cutlass Supreme, with a silver top and sangria glitter panels on the sides, and that Ron and Valerie were sitting in the front seat, smiling big. Immediately dread came over me. I skated up to the car and Ron called out, "This is your car! It's a pimp car!"

Ron taught me practical skills like how to change the oil and spark plugs and how to put sandbags in the back to balance out the rear-wheel drive in the winter. It was pretty 'hood, but I drove the car with pride because I'd paid for it. And it gave me the freedom I'd long been looking for.

Though my grades had improved from failing to average at the end of my sophomore year, I refused to put any effort into core subjects going into my junior year. I truly only cared about music, drama, working part-time, and being involved in church, and my grades reflected that, as soon I was failing half my classes again.

I auditioned for show choir and was cast as an alternate. I was called in to sub when one of the boys suffered an injury and couldn't participate in ensemble, but Ron immediately put a stop to my participation. Ron called Merlin, the show-choir teacher, and told him that my grades needed to improve before I would be allowed to join in any extracurricular activities. I was stunned and sad that I couldn't do something I had dreamed of doing since seeing "Scarlet and Crimson" perform at Northwest High School, but my teacher agreed with Ron's assessment that my grades needed to be top priority. With some reluctance, I admitted that Ron was right, and I worked hard to catch up. Ultimately I was grateful to him for challenging me to apply myself equally in all subjects, not just in classes that aligned with my passions.

Being in a theatrical production will quickly show you that not all things are meant to last forever. Yet all your sweat and tears and the sweat and tears of your drama comrades can combine into a moment or moments of excellence, and along the way you learn new things about yourself, new things about working with others, and new things about the craft to take with you for the next project. That's why I loved theater so much. I had long identified with the notion of letting things I love go. That call for surrender hits you the moment you take the final bow and the curtain drops. It is a reincarnation of sorts.

Those endings also brought to me a stark realization. I would feel happy, like I was shining and achieving something great, but then no one from my biological or foster family would be there to greet me. I saw other families fawning over their kids, giving them hugs and kisses and flowers and cards. At least those kids knew their families were proud of them. Often I ran into the arms of other families who appreciated the energy I brought to each program and who knew that I was a good kid from the time I spent hanging out at their houses on the weekends. Many of those families had huge houses with heated pools and basements with large entertainment centers. We, the drama kids, didn't drink and smoke regularly; that wasn't fun to us, so the parents were fine with leaving us to entertain ourselves.

Even though I felt sad that I didn't have any family cheering for me, I still held on to the attitude that I was doing something great, no matter who was watching. I feel the same way about my work today. In a parade of show ponies, you will still find me in the back, the working horse wearing golden horseshoes.

As the auditorium emptied out, I would take off the makeup that I was always so excited to wear, wet my hair so that my curls looked freshly sprung, and don my favorite blue-and-maroon raglan-sleeve T-shirt that felt like a home unto itself. I'd jump into my Oldsmobile, pull out of the parking lot, and head off to the cast party, a beloved ritual I could see myself doing for years to come. Until I got the invite to Anytown.

SIX

Breakthroughs

A guidance counselor sent a pass for me and several friends to come to the counseling center. Usually, a pass to the counseling center meant either it was time to register for classes, you were being scouted by a college recruiter, or you were in trouble. But this time, the counselor explained to us that we had been recommended by our teachers to attend a weekend-long, locally based leadership camp called Anytown. I was excited to be picked but even more excited to see that Corey and our friends Rachel and Amelia had also been selected. I truly didn't know what to expect.

We pulled up to the Anytown camp in our yellow school bus to find the retreat counselors standing in the roundabout. They welcomed us, then helped bring our belongings up to a large room with a high vaulted ceiling, which served as the locale for the weekend's activities. We were in for a series of in-depth, meticulously facilitated discussions about the structural forces that shaped our lives.

Once settled, we started with an opening activity that explored the concept of community, during which we came up with the theme for the entire retreat. After several rounds, we settled on the mission of "Believe. Unite. Change . . . It's not just a camp thing." We memorialized our charge on large banner paper and taped it to the wall to serve as a reminder of why we were there for all the high school students from around the city of Omaha.

That evening, we discussed power and privilege. Tensions were high, and as we moved on to discuss sexism, emotions flared even more. It was uncomfortable, but we were encouraged to "trust the process," and we did. An exercise on sexism that was meant to highlight the misogyny women face on a daily basis resonated with me, but I didn't have the language to articulate why I sympathized with those who identified as female more than those who identified as male. I had been catcalled, called out of my name, and made to feel unsafe because of my gender and sexual identity. Some of the male facilitators felt passionately about holding space for individuals who were female identified and didn't consider the multiple complexities that existed within the continuum of gender.

That same year, President George W. Bush announced his support for a constitutional amendment to ban same-sex marriage, while Massachusetts became the first state to perform same-sex marriages. The latter was a huge step forward in the fight for marriage equality, though in 2004, we weren't yet having national conversations about gender itself. Justice work is complex and imperfect and incremental, built on past victories and by seeing the best intentions in one another. Every step counts.

I naturally connected to the social justice curriculum that explored issues on ability, faith, appearance, class, sexual orientation, and racism. I was particularly moved that weekend by several exercises. The first was a section on hate crimes that showed forensic video of where James Byrd Jr. had been dragged for three miles behind a pickup truck driven by a white supremacist in Jasper, Texas. The video highlighted markings of where Byrd's remains had been found in pieces after the brutal attack. We also watched video footage that chronicled the murder of Matthew Shepard, who had been beaten and robbed, then tied to a fence and left to die in a field for being gay in Laramie, Wyoming. Wyoming and Texas were not that far off in terms of both culture and distance from the state of Nebraska, which left me terrified. I was further stirred by a walk through a gallery that held the accounts of various individuals whose lives had been lost to hate, violence, and oppression while the theme music of *Schindler's List* played in the background. It felt like a spiritual awakening was happening in my soul and that the fight for diversity and social justice was my ultimate calling. I had tapped into a deeper compassion and an understanding that I could play a part in moving the moral, ethical, and social issues of the world forward.

On the last day, we were separated into groups and given various labels based on our own self-identification. We were then lined up and told we could only eat with individuals whose labels matched our own. Looking at the layout of the room once everyone was seated, you could see African Americans students were in the back, and white students were in the front of the room. I was one table ahead of the African American students, at a table of biracial and multiracial folks. The awkwardness played out for some time before the facilitators broke the process, and we lamented what the division felt like.

"Why did no one speak up or try to break the exercise?" one facilitator asked.

After a moment's hesitation, I decided to chime in. "I was simply listening to what I had been told to do," I insisted. That's when it hit me. I had followed the rules without question, simply doing what I'd been told, even though I could see the unfairness of it. That understanding was what the exercise was meant to provoke! I learned a life-long lesson in that moment about the power of speaking out and speaking up, even when it's uncomfortable.

I was deeply moved by the diversity I encountered at Anytown, and so many of the people I met there would become dear friends. I was incredibly inspired by the different narratives and the way everyone embodied their *own* diversity. It helped me to understand myself as being on a spectrum.

When it was time to leave, we came together to form a wagon wheel. It was a beautiful ceremony in which goodbyes were not exchanged via words but by holding the hands of each participant for a few seconds and looking straight into their eyes while music played in the background. I sobbed as I witnessed the beauty of the souls that I had connected with, on a whole different level from what I did at church. I cried all the way home as I processed the experience.

Anytown created a new crew of allyship at our school and in my life. That weekend I met a contingent of folks who inspired me to love deeper than I ever had. They were among some of the first people to truly see me, *fully* realized and present. They affirmed my belief in the humanity of others and my robust optimism in the face of adversity. Nkiru Nnawulezi, a beautiful Nigerian goddess of a woman, commanded me with the words "go forth and be fierce." She remains one of my best friends to this day and was the maid of honor in my wedding. David LeFebvre, a dedicated Catholic, showed me that you could be spiritual and that the work of justice was truly tied to Christ's work. Umang Talati, a larger-than-life Indian man, provided an ear to help me process my adolescent fears. Tylena, who came from a single-parent home, reminded me that humor was the best medicine for the soul. We would laugh so hard it hurt. Hillary Nather-Detisch and Todd Savage were the lead facilitators on my first Anytown weekend, and I will be forever grateful to them and executive director Barb Angelillo. Collectively, they are the reason I and so many others are still doing the work of advancing justice today.

We returned to our schools bonded by a common purpose and the promise to remain a safe space for each other and to create a welcoming and inclusive community for diversity at Burke High School. And we did. It became my mission to bring people together. Though I remained in my youth group, I began to understand the violence that existed within my own faith community. The countless public rebukes and healings were profoundly harmful, I finally saw. It was at this moment that I allowed myself to be more than just one version of myself. I refused to uphold tenets of faith that prescribed bigotry.

～

I was determined to make the most of my senior year and raised my grades so that I could participate in ensemble (show choir). I attended show-choir camp, which widened my network of local gays, and I choreographed several numbers with Corey, Jenna, and Mallory, some of my closest friends. We danced and twirled to "I've Got the Music in Me," "Pinball Wizard," and "You're the One That I Want." I continued to be a leader in concert choir and demonstrated to a host of underclassmen that hard work and dedication yielded results. I had compiled a full network of friends that I hung out with on the weekends, outside of school, and when I was off work.

I also became the Burke High School mascot, donning the large inflatable golden bulldog costume and jumping around, yelling all kinds of things that, fortunately, no one could hear. I performed at the junior varsity and varsity basketball and football games. When I wasn't being a golden bulldog, I was singing the national anthem. Sometimes I did both.

I appreciated a full schedule and a long to-do list, a habit that began then and continues to this day. Using my experience and unique talents in multiple ways makes me feel accomplished and affirmed.

Each year, Burke High School hosted a powder-puff game as a part of spirit week. During this game, the football team and cheerleaders switched roles. Cheerleaders played flag football, and football players cheered. And let me tell you: the football team was into it. They wore padded bras stuffed with toilet paper and walked around school the day of the game showing off their brawny legs in miniskirts, with smug looks on their faces. As the mascot, I got to participate too. Of course, I was grateful for any excuse to wear a dress. I donned a vintage Burke High cheerleading uniform with a matching headband and got lost in the thrill of reciting the signature "dominate and devastate" cheer while attempting to do front kicks that barely made it halfway off the ground. On my cheeks I proudly displayed the 05 I'd drawn with a black eyeliner pencil, showing strong upperclassman spirit as I posed for pictures to document the moment for our yearbook.

Beyond the guise of the large bulldog costume, I was a mascot unto myself. Several times a week I gave school-wide announcements over the intercom, and I would leave for lunch at my discretion, returning to school with a pizza for my friends and a strawberry Frappuccino in tow. I used cast parties as an opportunity to wear heels and a dress and to tie something in my hair. Many times the shoes and clothes were borrowed from Chelci and China. I felt uninhibited in those spaces and leaned into that feeling. I'm so thankful for the parents who affirmed me and let me prance around their living rooms and frolic in their basements. That everyone was accepted and embraced was the standard in those homes. In turn, I took every opportunity to create iconic moments of visibility and coming out: I wore a pair of stiletto boots under my choir robe and, during spirit week, a skintight Geordi La Forge *Star Trek* costume, complete with eye visor. I played the role of Franklin in *You're a Good Man, Charlie Brown* with gusto. All these covert and overt measures uplifted the different facets of who I was becoming. Over the years, so many of my former peers have written to tell me that my bravery in high school encouraged them to be their authentic selves too.

The authenticity I was able to showcase in school stood in contrast to the strict pursuit of holiness that was part of my charismatic youth group and church. I was somewhat able to compartmentalize what I was taught at church versus what I was learning from my theater friends. During my time at Eagle's Nest, the church outgrew its bay sanctuary and purchased a new building on the lot of Victory Church. It was a strange twist of fate when I found out that I would remain close to the place where I had originally discovered my faith in God.

In my free time, I liked to help Pastor Brian with preparing the new building for services. Pastor Brian had many strengths, among them his sense of humor, but most of all, it was his ability to build a ministry that was naturally youth friendly that drew me to him. I served on the leadership team that assisted in coordinating details for each service, which included overseeing sound, singing on the praise-and-worship team, and assisting with outreach. I quickly learned what it took to run a successful media ministry.

Pastor Brian's expressive arched eyebrows added to his thunderous delivery of scripture, which focused on seeing God's glory manifest through signs and wonders, healings, casting out devils through the laying on of hands, and belief in the power of the Holy Ghost. There were many times when Pastor Brian laid hands on me in prayer and said, "You ready for this thang to come up off you?" By "this thang" he meant my homosexuality. I wanted very badly to be righteous in the eyes of God and for Pastor Brian to view me as an heir apparent to the ministerial throne.

Jamison, another youth leader and our church keyboard player, was also adopted, grew up in a ministerial family, and attended Northwest High School when I did. He offered me space to talk about issues that concerned me, but the majority of our time was spent laughing and hanging out at his mom's house. He provided a respite for me when I felt overworked and underappreciated at the Loves. Jamison and I became close brothers, and he never called into question any kind of issue I was dealing with during the entirety of our friendship. He had a young son from a high school relationship that I helped babysit from time to time, and Jamison knew if he ever needed help with any task, I would be there. As a man, he was far less concerned with the state of my masculinity and sexual orientation than my well-being as a person.

Jamison's mom, Bea, stood up on the platform in the sanctuary, behind the microphone. Bea's chic power suits, tall pumps, and short red hair were striking. As church began she would walk up to me and, in a soft yet elegant tone, say, "Hello, glorious jewel! Hello, precious gem!" then gesture to me with the lift of her hand, inviting me closer and disarming me at the same time. I was drawn to her Southern gentility and soft femininity as she pulled me in for a hug. Bea's embrace made me feel welcome, and at school I attempted to mimic her accent. To my theater friends I shouted with a sizzling vibrato, "Aah! Glorrr . . . eeeeeooouuuussss jewelllll!" and "A-bunnndant *life*!" The adults and teachers who overheard couldn't figure out what was going on.

"Are you doing an impersonation of Katharine Hepburn or SpongeBob?" they asked.

It was neither; instead, it was a voice that I had created, intending to be elegant. Intending to be like Bea.

∽

Meanwhile, the illusion of the Loves as the perfect family began to disappear. I'd been growing frustrated at what I considered to be Valerie's unfair treatment of me. Out of all the foster and biological kids, I had the fullest list of cleaning responsibilities, on top of my work and school obligations.

Valerie spent much of her days running errands for her big family and driving various foster kids between therapy, caseworker appointments, and school, using her cell phone as a command station all the while. The moment I got home from school or rehearsal, the phone would ring, and on the line, she would rattle off a barrage of domestic assignments.

"Can you wash the dishes?" she'd say. "Did you wipe the baseboards? Did you pick up all of the dirty clothes from around the house? Is everything ready to go for church?" Once she was satisfied, I could hear her click the end button with her fingernail, signaling that the tasks were to be started immediately and completed by the time she pulled into the driveway.

One of my main tasks was doing laundry for the family. I fluffed freshly washed clothes in the dryer for several minutes, then grabbed each item of clothing, hung the damp shirts and pants on hangers, and placed them on the metal fence in the backyard to dry. Once the clothes were dry, I ran back and forth from outside to inside, upstairs to downstairs, putting the clothes away. I was happy to iron clothes before church several times a week, along with choosing and gathering outfits for the boys to wear. It was a somewhat tedious chore, but it signified that I was a part of the family.

I didn't mind helping out. I wanted to show my gratitude for living at the Loves'. At the same time, it was plain to see that the distribution of domestic responsibilities wasn't equal. Often I would be hanging up or ironing the family's shirts when Alex walked through the door after basketball practice. He'd peel off his sweat-soaked uniform and toss it on the floor in the laundry room. I would then pick it up and throw it and any other dirty laundry in the washer without hesitation.

China and McKinzie, the girls of the house, were also responsible for these kinds of chores, much more so than the boys. In one respect, my inclusion in domesticity affirmed my femininity, and indeed I labeled myself Cinderella. Of course, this traditional division of labor—of the girls having to take on "women's work" while the boys came and went as they pleased, leaving sweaty socks and jerseys on the floor in their wake—wasn't exactly the best marker of womanhood. It wasn't fair—I knew it, and China and McKinzie knew it. But, I figured, as a foster child, I should be grateful for the privilege of living in a stable home, so I would make the most of the constant demands. If Valerie needed me, I reasoned, then she was less likely to reject me in the future.

Valerie never commented on the imbalance—maybe she truly didn't see it as such. But I saw it, and it agitated me, especially since the consideration given for Alex's various engagements was not given to my choir concerts, musical rehearsals, or Anytown activities. When Corey came to pick me up on the weekends, he would often have to wait for me while I finished my chores.

Even my obligations at work weren't considered a priority. I remember one Saturday afternoon when the phone rang at Sonic. I was surprised to hear Valerie's voice on the line. "I'm coming to pick you up," she told me.

"What? Why?" I asked.

"You didn't finish your chores," she said.

I knew there was no use in arguing. Stunned, I looked at my manager and then out the window. "I . . . uh . . . I have to go," I said. I had no idea how to justify myself, so I simply added, "It's kind of a family emergency."

Minutes later, Valerie pulled up in the green Astro van. She was seething. I hopped in, listened to her rant all the way home, then completed the task as quickly as possible so that she could take me back to work.

Another afternoon, I was getting ready for work in the kitchen when Valerie began rattling off a list of things she wanted me to do. I could tell that she was in a mood. "Laundry," she said, holding up a new bottle of detergent. "There's lots of laundry to get done."

I was already doing a litany of other chores, and it just felt so unfair. I was getting ready for work! I looked up at her and said, "No."

Valerie immediately took a few steps into the kitchen and hurled the bottle of laundry detergent at me. The cap flew off, and detergent oozed all over the tile floor.

"Clean it up!" she yelled.

Which I did. I had gone through this kind of thing too many times before, and I was trying my best to pick my battles. Later, I vented to Bea and Jamison, who encouraged me to keep my eye on the prize: graduation.

~

But first, there was the senior prom, to be held at Milo Bail Student Center at the University of Nebraska at Omaha.

I donned my signature S curls and paired them with the tuxedo with tails I had picked out from the mall. My date, Jocelyn Olney, the most talented soprano in concert choir, was on my arm as I swaggered into the dance. She, like the other girls I took to school dances, was a good friend, with a spirit I resonated with. I was nominated for prom king but didn't win; I didn't mind, though, because I was voted Most Unforgettable for senior superlatives. I was just happy to be recognized for my contribution of authenticity and school spirit.

Then, finally, came graduation. The ceremony began with the school band playing a rendition of "Pomp and Circumstance" while the graduating class of 2005 filed in. Members of the school board gave welcomes and commendations, followed by remarks from our principal, the valedictorian, and other students who had been selected to speak. I was among those chosen to sing.

As the violinist struck the opening orchestration, she went sharp and hit a wrong note. I looked back at Corey, who was standing behind me. Our gazes connected, and he smiled.

Stepping forward with my head held high, I gestured with pride as the concert choir sang the "oooos" and "ahhhs" of accompaniment. I clutched my hands, lifted my chin, shook off my nerves, and let my robust baritone voice swell from my diaphragm, filling the space in the auditorium. "When I am down and, oh, my soul, so weary," I sang. "When troubles come and my heart burdened be." The golden tassel on my cap swung back and forth in front of my face as I gestured, tilting my head up and down. At the end, I knew I had delivered the solo with panache.

Then the procession began. Since I was a part of the program, I was one of the first to walk across the stage. Cheers of support rang out from the audience as my name was called. I vivaciously shook each of the faculty's hands, clutched my diploma with gratitude, and strutted off to find the Loves.

As I pushed my way through the various families that had gathered to celebrate their loved ones, I spotted my sister Nina standing mere feet from me. Shocked, I ran into her arms and burst into tears. Our disagreements faded away for a moment as I laid my cheek on her shoulder, my ugly cry going into full effect. Her hug felt like the true mother's touch I had been longing for my entire life. I was overjoyed that she showed up to one of the most important milestones in my life.

I was getting ready as though I were headed for a routine hangout with Corey. Usually he and I would walk around the Old Market, visit Gene Leahy Mall, eat at Spaghetti Works, visit the water fountain at Heartland of America Park, or get ice cream from Ted and Wally's. This evening, however, would be far from routine.

I jumped out of the shower with my curly shoulder-length hair dripping wet and applied the clear gooey activator that made my hair glossy and gave it my signature S curl. I left my hair to air-dry as I put on distressed light wash American Eagle jeans, a button-down shirt with green, pink, and blue stripes, a kelly-green men's blazer from Goodwill, and a pair of black-and-brown oxford shoes that Ron had brought me from a mission trip to São Paulo, Brazil. I took my time getting ready.

Once done, I slipped out and pulled the front door shut. I opened the gargantuan Oldsmobile door as quietly as I could, then jumped into my car, which was parked on the slope of the hill in front of our house. I looked up to make sure no one was watching from Ron and Valerie's bedroom window that faced the driveway. I immediately threw the gear into neutral so that the roar of the ignition would not create a time stamp on when I was leaving the house. As I rolled to the bottom of the hill, I started the ignition, then drove up the incline behind our house and pulled out of our neighborhood subdivision marked by power lines, an elementary school, a gas station, and two nearby on-ramps to the interstate.

There were butterflies in my stomach as I merged onto Interstate 80 downtown. I passed the Eighty-Fourth Street exit where I had lived with my grandfather in the Westgate neighborhood. Images of *Queer as Folk*'s Babylon, with its towering columns and throbbing techno beats, swirled around in my head as I pulled off the exit onto Twenty-Seventh and Leavenworth, near where I had attended Sword of the Spirit Christian School in seventh grade. Driving past these markers, I felt like I was beginning to discover my true independence. I didn't know what kind of experience awaited me as I headed down Leavenworth past the 11-Worth Café and the Four Aces convenience store, where I had purchased Little Debbie snacks and Fruitopias after school with Ginger and Tanisha.

After circling around the block, I pulled into the gravel lot of the after-hours and youth gay club known as the Run. Many times I had flipped through the yellow pages to search for whatever I could find under the words *gay* and *lesbian*, becoming familiar with what existed around town for gay people. Under a short list of bars I saw DC's Saloon, the Max, and Omaha Mining Company, which also served as the Omaha Rainbow Outreach Center. Although I didn't know what an outreach center did, I called the number and talked hastily, getting all the information I could about the Run.

Throughout high school Alex and I would visit the Christian teen club "The Rock" and Corey and I would hang out at Caffeine Dreams and the Shelterbelt Theatre. These were safe, brief forays into the worlds of Christian and theater kids. Those experiences couldn't get me into trouble like this outing could.

Getting out of my car, I noticed broken glass on the ground. Boys milled around chugging liquor straight out of the bottle. Walking out of the parking lot and toward the long line, I noticed boys of all kinds. All alone, I took the last spot in line, feeling out of place and insecure, but I wanted to experience the thrill of nightlife for myself. After all, I had grown up in a family that was supported by deejaying, but never once had I been inside a bar at night. I'd been outside a bar when I accompanied my grandfather to pick up his records from Backstreet—that was the full extent of my bar experience.

I waited shyly as regulars cut ahead of me and flirted with the doorman to skip the line entirely. I observed everything from the rattling of the windows, to the booming bass, to the rainbow flag banner affixed atop the storefront. The Department of Corrections jail loomed across the street.

At the front of the line, an obese black man in a yellow T-shirt checked my ID and then began patting me forcefully on my crotch, feeling me up from front to back in a caressing motion. I felt violated and uneasy as he motioned me inside, where an old man with heavy bags under bloodshot eyes and bad teeth took my five dollars. This was the first gay bar I had ever stepped foot into.

The stale stench of cigarette smoke hit me as I made my way along the brass-railed bar past boys wearing black eyeliner, Von Dutch hats, Hollister T-shirts, Abercrombie polos, and spritzed and frosted hairdos. Turning around, I noticed an open dance floor with a small platform stage that jutted out from the wall, along with mirrors that reflected the flickering disco ball hung from the ceiling and a sign that said "The Run." A cool blue light lit the room. Two pool tables stood next to a long staircase that led up to the second level, which overlooked the dance floor. From that perch, I watched people crowd the floor and bounce and shake to Cascada's "Everytime We Touch," Lindsay Lohan's "Rumors," and Ciara's "1, 2 Step." I was happy to just watch, to play the role of voyeur—until Britney Spears's "Do Somethin'" came bumping through the speakers.

The music compelled me to walk down the stairs, find a spot in the corner of the dance floor, and let go of my shyness in a bouncy two-step. It was humid and hot AF, but that didn't stop me from having a kind of divine encounter as I yelled Britney Spears lyrics, first to "Do Somethin'" and then "My Prerogative." I loved how the lyrics were fiercely unapologetic, declaring the freedom and empowerment I was feeling in the wee hours of the morning.

The music unleashed a freedom and a piece of my identity that night, which I couldn't fully articulate in the light of day. I didn't need anyone's permission to live my truth. Being among other queer teenagers in that social setting confirmed it. I had finally come face-to-face with other local gays whose reputations preceded them at show-choir competitions and all-city music festivals. It was truly cathartic. It felt like another shift.

At five a.m. I returned home, lightly pressing the code on the keyless entry to unlock the deadbolt. I slipped through the front door, made a quick dash over the landing into the kitchen, through the door to the family room in the basement, and down the hall to the bedroom I shared with the other boys. Jumping into my bed on the bottom bunk, I listened for footsteps.

Satisfied that no one was awake, I tried to get some rest before church. I fell asleep thinking about the clothes hanging behind the door that I'd promised Valerie I would iron. A couple hours later, I jumped out of bed, set up the ironing board in the family room, and began pressing and creasing dress shirts and pants as Valerie came down the stairs to turn on her coffeepot, a routine occurrence at about six thirty. Carrying her cup of coffee to the kitchen landing, she asked, "Which church service are you planning to go to?"

"I'm going to miss the nine o'clock service, but I'll go to the second service at eleven," I told her.

She nodded and walked up the stairs to begin her morning routine before the weekly battle over the bathroom commenced. As the blow dryer blared from upstairs, I finished the ironing and retreated for a little more sleep.

A few hours later, I put on the clothes I had worn to the Run and got in my car. On this particular Sunday I wasn't on the schedule to teach the kids' program, Honeybees, or run the multimedia slides from the back of the church for Pastor Hart's sermon. I pulled into the parking lot at eleven o'clock sharp.

I usually parked behind the row with the Reserved for Pastors signs on Wednesdays and Sundays, but my tardiness on this day forced me to the far end of the lot. Inside the entrance to the church, the usual middle-aged women greeted me and engulfed me in hugs as the music swelled with the sound of drums, cymbals, and keyboard. Making my way to the youth section on the right side of the sanctuary, I was conscious that several hours prior I had made my debut in the world of gay nightlife, that I was wearing the same clothing I'd danced in to the pulsing songs of Britney Spears. Now I was walking into God's house, and I knew for sure that somehow my sin would be recognized, and I would be disciplined immediately.

I took my usual seat behind Pastor Brian, who preferred to have everyone in our youth group sit in the same section so that our exuberant praise was on full display. He encouraged us to come to the front of the sanctuary to clap, jump, and move when the spirit moved us. I began to clap but refused to go to my normal spot down in front or take up the tambourine that I usually pounded in high moments of praise.

To my surprise, nothing happened. No one called me out; God did not strike me down.

Several weeks later, Pastor Hart preached a fiery message condemning homosexuality in a screed of offenses individuals needed to get free from. I ran to the altar to ask God one last time to free me from my sin, but this time, no one laid hands on me, and I felt . . . nothing. The spiritual covering and inheritance that once was guaranteed me was now null and void. I got up and walked away, feeling the same way I did when I had knelt: gay.

I admitted to my transgressions in correction meetings, and soon Pastor Brian ran out of patience. My behavior was far outside the lines of his strict standard of holiness, and now his warnings turned to discipline. At one correction meeting, Pastor Hart sat back in his chair and said, "Change is a process, but commitment to it is voluntary."

Pastor Brian added, "This is your last chance."

I'd felt like a failure for a long, long time. I'd done everything I could, hadn't I? And yet I'd just kept failing.

In that moment, I decided that their expectations of me no longer mattered. I had had enough.

Eventually, I started regularly going to the Run with a group of Westside High School boys who freely cut the line. Andrew Tatreu wore skinny jeans and a long messy mane; thin Zev Eisenberg had soft dishwater curls and a chiseled face; and David Ryan, who was the tallest of the group, had long relaxed hair and distinct supermodel hazel eyes. We were all foolishly putting chemicals in our hair in the early 2000s.

I'd met Andrew and Zev at the Run, but David and I had met through our mutual friend Nkiru at Anytown. Andrew would swing by my house and pick me up in his beige Chevrolet Tahoe for our Saturday-night hangs. As a regular, he showed me the ropes, including how to take shots of Barton vodka in the parking lot and how to cut the line, though we still had to suffer through the invasive pat down to ensure we weren't bringing in liquor or drugs. He also drove me out to Valley, a small city on the outskirts of Omaha, where I could see we had come from two different worlds as we pulled into a fortress of a home. There, Andrew had his own bedroom, a large swimming pool, and a pristine landscaped backyard. I marveled at his life of privilege and the freedom he had to be himself as he slipped into his signature look—a plain white T-shirt.

I had the same feeling when we went to pick up Zev, whose dad was an early investor in the Berkshire Hathaway empire and whose mom was a sex therapist. Zev's mom welcomed us as she sipped a glass of wine and held court with the trio of boys who had gathered in her living room before migrating out to the Run late at night. Zev and his parents seemed to be best friends. I looked on and wondered what it would feel like to be best friends with your biological mom.

David was adopted like me. He would often pull into a stall at Sonic in his gray 1993 Dodge Caravan when I was working. It was always a joy to see a familiar face as I queened out and spun around on my roller skates to music that blared from the speakers overhead. He laughed in a way that was like Mufasa laughing at Simba, the young, naive cub. Our friendship helped me step out of the closet I kept backing myself into. He later moved to Chicago and became a successful art dealer in the Caribbean and started going by the name Milan. Of course he named himself after one of the major hubs of fashion and culture in the world. He was very that way.

I love it when queer folks claim space and name themselves after legendary things to ensure we will never be forgotten. I was naturally drawn to hang out with people who dared to be different and told the world what to call them instead of letting the world decide.

I also started hanging out with Josh Mischo, a classmate from yearbook, on weekends and evenings. Josh had long been pressuring me to come completely out of the closet to the Loves. His mom was totally accepting, and after a brief introduction to her the first night I'd gone to his house, he and I had taken a turn in the hot tub in his backyard. We developed a sexual relationship in a series of overnight sleepovers, and my encounters with Josh pushed me toward a state of sexual liberation. Each and every time I drove away from his house, however, it was guaranteed that I would get pulled over by the police in Papillion,

Nebraska. It was a clear reminder that I had ventured into the wrong part of Omaha and that my poor black ass wasn't welcome.

That summer, Corey and I attended Omaha Pride. Perusing the vendor booths of various LGBT community-based organizations, I came across a tall black man with big lips, a swimmer's build, and a cute smile. After brief introductions, I could tell Dallas saw me as a fish fresh out of water. We exchanged numbers and soon started hanging out. My heart fluttered as we bonded over our shared background in the Pentecostal faith, and I marveled at his ability to reconcile his spirituality and life as an out gay black man. It didn't take long for Dallas and me to start dating and hooking up on the regular. Long walks on the University of Nebraska at Omaha campus late at night and long phone conversations built a comfort between us that led me to extend him an invitation to the Loves'.

I figured that since I was on my way to college, I might as well start acting grown, leaving hints that I would be gay after I moved out. When he arrived, I nearly leaped off the porch into his arms. The Loves surprised me by welcoming him without much questioning or judgment as I introduced my new "friend."

Dallas and I headed down to the basement. In the family room, he sat on the couch and spread his legs so that I could see his raging hard-on through his jeans. I closed the door and approached. "I'm not wearing underwear," he teased. It took no time for me to unzip his pants and begin to engage in a fully courageous exploration. But then, in the middle of our pleasure, he stopped me. It was almost as if he wanted to savor the moment. And, I believe, he wanted to respect me under my foster parents' roof.

Given that music and theater had such a profound impact on my high school journey, I applied to the University of Nebraska–Lincoln, which had many stellar performance arts programs. I received a letter saying I would be admitted if I went to community college for a year to prove my academic merit, since my grades had fluctuated so much the past few years.

I decided to go to Iowa Western Community College, a nontraditional school in Council Bluffs, Iowa, that had the feel and amenities of a four-year college. The brochure showed a beautiful campus and on-site housing and revealed the fact that they put on a big musical each year. I had won a music and theater scholarship, and in my excitement, I began to prematurely pack my things. Soon enough I would be moving out of the Loves' house and going to live on my own in the dorms.

My eagerness increased when Valerie invited a woman to move in who had recently started attending our church and was living out of her car with her two kids. Her children ran around the house unsupervised and often in dirty clothes, while she disappeared during the day and fled into the upstairs bedroom at night. That made me think she, like my biological mother, Tammy, didn't care about the well-being of her kids. I scoffed at the fact that she had joined our household but refused to take on any of the work that the rest of us were expected to do.

Things got worse when she made accusations about my spirit. "God has told me that you need to get right and are possessed by a demon," she said. Every day there was a prophecy, a vision, or a dream that came forth and forecast hell and damnation for my future. Once again, a person with their own troubles had taken it upon themselves to judge me. Never mind that she had little control over her life. She was just like Marshall when he came back injured from Marine Officer Candidates School and tried to force his controlling nonsense on me. I didn't hold my tongue then, and I wouldn't hold my tongue now.

"You're delusional," I told her. "I don't know who you think you are, but I'm not listening to you." I looked her dead in the eye as she prayed under her breath. Looking back, I think she probably had an undiagnosed mental health issue. But I was only eighteen and had no idea what I was dealing with. Sadly, many in the Christian faith refuse to seek out proper psychological support from a licensed clinical professional. In this way, I believe the church often actively feeds or simply turns a blind eye to trauma and gives folks a false sense of security.

Ron and Valerie often watched and, for whatever reason, failed to intervene when I received these accusations, which fueled my frustration with them. After my high school graduation, I was to be confronted with yet another incident that deeply hurt me and felt like an unforgivable act of betrayal. It cut me to the core. I wrestled with whether to say something or to let it go.

With my idea of the perfect family shattered, I began feeling resentment for anything Valerie asked me to do. In fact, I started doing chores on my own timeline, and Valerie and Ron noticed. They became furious and agitated the evening I muttered, "It's not fair." One day Ron came home amid the squabble, and Valerie yelled for her usual backup support. "Ron! Go talk to him! He's not listening." Ron ran down the stairs and saw me sitting on the top bunk and stormed into the bedroom and grabbed my shoulders. "You listen to Valerie or find somewhere else to live." It was the first time I had ever seen Ron mad at me. I was shocked. In his defense, every night, he came home after work and had to put out a different fire between Valerie and one of the kids.

I was visibly shaken as Ron retreated upstairs and eventually to his office in the backyard after he slammed the door at the top of the stairs. Valerie was just sitting there rocking in her favorite beige love seat. I walked up the stairs, opened the door, and presented her with information that was extremely painful to me; I was devastated that the perfect family wasn't as perfect as I had thought. How could this happen to me again? After I tearfully confronted Valerie with the information I had in my hands, I immediately headed to Ron's office out back with Valerie right on my heels. When I entered the office, Ron turned in his chair and looked over his glasses sitting slightly at the tip of his nose as I then explained to him the injustice I had discovered. He was angry and even shocked at this impropriety by someone in his family. Having heard the information I had presented, Ron scratched some words on a white piece of paper he pulled from a nearby printer, slid it across the desk folded, and asked me to sign it. The paper said I wouldn't seek legal recourse from the incident. To remedy the situation, Ron offered to give me the 1999 hunter green Chevy Cavalier he had just purchased. I agreed, signed the paper, and ran back into the house to continue packing my things into boxes in anticipation of the first day of college that was in a few weeks. It was an easy deal for me as the transmission in my Oldsmobile Cutlass Supreme had blown, and I had just taken it to the junkyard, where I was paid several hundred dollars for its worth in metal. I felt it was a fair deal, but that didn't heal my broken heart.

Corey's mom, Sandy McKenna, had been witness to the drama at the Love household and wanted to see me removed from the chaos, especially after Valerie's betrayal. Sandy became a new kind of maternal figure. Corey's dad, Gene, was gentle, quiet, and often could be seen sitting in a rocking swing overlooking the koi pond he'd built in their backyard. Since Corey and I were best friends, and I hung out at their house practically every weekend, I was already a part of the family.

Sandy and Gene invited me to stay with them, and I took them up on their offer. Despite everything that had happened, I didn't exactly leave the Loves on bad terms. But I knew that, in order to heal, I had to distance myself.

Corey and I explicitly vowed to navigate our feelings together. We would sit on the couch late at night watching *Degrassi: The Next Generation*, *Queer Eye for the Straight Guy*, and *Queer as Folk* DVDs, which I had ordered on eBay and Corey kept hidden under his bed. Gene would often swing downstairs for a midnight snack in the kitchen, and Corey and I prayed he wouldn't notice the queer content we were watching in the living room. If he did, he never said anything. He and Sandy were nothing but kind to me, offering their home to me when I really needed one.

A few weeks later, I was excited and nervous as I drove alongside charging semitrucks and past cornfields toward my new life. The rolling hills, yellow valleys, and sprawling trees signaled that I was entering a rural existence, just twenty minutes outside Omaha, in Council Bluffs, Iowa. Neither my biological family nor my adopted families were there to see me off. I would be exploring a new world alone.

SEVEN

An Education

At Iowa Western Community College, I settled into a suite with three other roommates. I had my own room and shared a bathroom with just one other person, a highly luxurious state of affairs. A few days after I moved in, who should arrive but the highest stepper of all Highsteppers, Roderick Cotton. It seemed improbable that my archnemesis from Northwest High School would be assigned to my suite, but there he was, in the flesh. *This can't be happening,* I thought to myself, lamenting that the new chapter I intended to start might be marred by my past. I peered out from my room to confirm that it was in fact him; he refused to even acknowledge my presence.

After several weeks of cold stares, circling gossip, and awkward exchanges, in a bold act of maturity, I decided to nip the Roderick problem in the bud. I knocked on his door and braced myself for confrontation. When he opened the door, I looked at him for several seconds, then finally uttered, "If there is anything that I have ever done to offend you, I'm sorry."

Roderick looked taken aback. "Thank you," he said, then closed the door. In choir the next day, Roderick let me know that he was "cool" with me. And so, with that turning over of a new leaf, my next chapter could officially begin.

Once our sisterhood was in full swing, Roderick and I would sit in the computer lab scrolling over our Myspace pages, looking for our closest friends to chat with. We browsed gay hookup sites like MegaMates, Adam for Adam, Manhunt, and gay.com, which ended up being quite fruitful, for me, at least. Adam for Adam was specifically for African American men, and I preferred chatting with the men I met there rather than taking a gamble on MegaMates and Manhunt. It was on gay.com, however, that I met a man who worked for the University of Nebraska–Lincoln and who drove over an hour for us to have a fifteen-minute sexual encounter in my dorm. I also hooked up with a married man early in the mornings. Don't judge me! I was nineteen and looking for love in all the *wrong* places. I briefly dated an adorable theater nerd on campus who wielded a rolling book bag, which was wack in hindsight. But that fling didn't last long, as I couldn't put up with his whining diva tendencies, especially in the dark. I have always known that if there is going to be a diva in the relationship, it's going to be me.

During my first semester, Roderick introduced me to Thirsty Thursdays at Thunder Bowl, a local bowling alley where the drinks were cheap, and there was karaoke. He encouraged me to live a little instead of always doing homework in my dorm while most of the performing arts students were out partying. I reluctantly agreed to hang out. I knew I couldn't mess college up—I had no safety net to fall back onto. Still, I lacquered my curls up with activator gel as Roderick painted his face and glossed his lips, blasting music and pregaming with shots of Jack Daniel's that burned as they went down.

The bowling alley provided a bit of welcome respite from campus. It reeked of cigarettes. Initially I hung back in the corner with several girlfriends from theater who were sharing pitchers of beer. When a cup filled to the brim was inevitably handed to me and I took my first sip, I realized the bitter taste of beer along with blasting instrumental karaoke tracks was not for me. Despite that, I went back week after week to hear Roderick sing. He was a standout vocalist who always received thunderous applause for singing the Fugees' rendition of "Killing Me Softly."

Back on campus, whenever Roderick and I walked through the cafeteria, we were a force to be reckoned with. If anyone had anything negative to say about us, we never knew it. We had a little crew of gay guys: Brandon, Steve, Ryan, Jesse, Topher, Jayson, and Ramone. We may not have always liked each other, but our numbers and our visibility were strong.

In theater, I shone. I was a natural performer who understood the basics. At orientation, I had approached Kat Bagby Coate, an earthy woman with frizzy hair and the theater chair, who had graciously granted me a theater scholarship on the spot. In exchange, I worked in the scene shop several days a week under the guidance of Carl Dumicich. I also found unlikely refuge in organizing the costume closet.

Kat helped me deepen my understanding of the core tenets of acting and character development. Her teaching style was frank but patient. She pushed me out of my comfort zone and encouraged me to pursue roles onstage and backstage.

I was cast as First Fairy in the fall play, *A Midsummer Night's Dream*. Kat and Moira, the director of the production, had composed and added in a lullaby, which I sang at the top of act 2. From upstage left, I glided up the ramp covered in foliage, large branches, and oversized leaves to enter a forest of flowers. There, costumed in a black floor-length floral frock, a picked-out glistening Afro, and a sunflower tucked behind my ear as the finishing touch, I looked down at the audience while several other fairies circled me, the regal earth mother. I sang the lullaby softly, newly empowered by Moira and Kat to completely embody another character while still being myself.

During the final performance, I looked out and saw Valerie sitting in the audience along with the rest of the Love clan. I was glad that they were seeing me in my new, hyperfeminine form, and that night I thought for the first time that I could possibly make a career out of this, out of just being myself. I would search for roles that allowed me to present as a woman, like Angel Dumott Schunard in *Rent* and Mary Sunshine in *Chicago*.

I went on to perform regularly at Iowa Western. I was cast in *Joseph and the Amazing Technicolor Dreamcoat* as the brother who performs the number "Benjamin's Calypso." Though I didn't get the lead, that play gave me the opportunity to sharpen my craft and deepen my commitment.

I continued my streak of performances and decided that I wanted to spend my time in musicals. The director of the production of *The Best Little Whorehouse in Texas* at Chanticleer Community Theater in Council Bluffs begged me to audition because there were way more women than guys. I auditioned but made it abundantly clear that I planned on auditioning for the Omaha Community Playhouse's production of *Ragtime*, and if I were cast in that, I would accept the role.

I was confident in my singing abilities as I walked into the basement of the playhouse to audition for the director and choreographer, who sat in the back of the room. I greeted the music director, who spread my sheet music across the piano and began to play. This was my first audition as an adult in the real world, and it felt amazing. My sixteen bars went by quickly, and I was sure that my swelling baritone had secured me a spot in the show.

The same could not be said for my dancing. I struggled to pick up the audition choreography, and I was mediocre at best—which is not something you want to be in a world full of triple threats. Though the choreography was difficult, I pushed through the audition, and each time I was called to the floor to perform the group choreography, I showed out fully with high claps and kick ball changes. While I may not be a natural in technique, movement and performance are in my blood, and if you give me material, believe me, I'm going to sell it so that even the children in the cheap seats can feel what I'm giving.

I was elated to be cast as one of the four African American men as part of the Harlem ensemble. I would appear alongside Omaha native and Broadway actor Kevyn Morrow, an original cast member in *Dreamgirls* on Broadway and an actor in another one of my favorite Broadway musicals, *Smokey Joe's Cafe*. We worked well together, and at rehearsal, we both understood the significance of the task before us: to tell a story about American capitalism and greed, segregation, racism, sexism, and the plight of immigrants in America at the turn of the century. Our winning of a Theatre Arts Guild Award for Outstanding Ensemble for our performance of *Prologue: Ragtime* was one of my proudest moments. In that opening number, an upper-class Caucasian family, a community of Harlem beatniks, and a throng of immigrants moved around the stage, singing in a swirling trifecta.

With the assistance of the TRiO program center on campus, where I went several times a week for tutoring and support for developing good study habits, I flourished academically with a full college workload. I was especially involved in my sociology classes. Usually I was one of the first students to raise my hand to offer a response to the readings. Slowly, and building on what I'd learned at Anytown, I began to understand the methodology for interventions involving complex social issues. I even contemplated a career in social work. I briefly had an internship at the Sierra Club, but I quit after a few weeks, once I realized that the job's primary duties involved data entry. I didn't want to sit behind a computer all day—I wanted to interact with people.

I managed to get straight As in English, environmental science, and sociology, and with a feeling of accomplishment, I returned to Omaha to live with the McKennas. With my newfound freedom of expression, I openly wore women's graphic T-shirts and even purchased a black strappy dress from a boutique that didn't place number sizes on clothing, instead identifying the items with dots. I also had my hair professionally pressed out for the first time at Sonia's, the salon where Ginger and Tanisha got their hair done the day of Nina's wedding. I wanted to experience what it was like to get my hair done at the salon instead of at the barbershop. As I made changes on the outside and on the inside, I realized that the time had come for me to make a difficult decision. That summer, I left the church for good, vowing never to return. The days of shame and blame, repression and suppression were over.

After successfully completing a year of community college in Council Bluffs, Iowa, I had satisfied the academic merit requirements for my admission to the University of Nebraska–Lincoln. I was a new transfer student eager to continue my studies in music and theater education when Corey and I fulfilled our best friends' dream of becoming college roommates in Harper Hall.

It didn't take long for us to integrate ourselves into the campus community. Just a few days into the semester, at a "weeks of welcome" ice cream social put on by the Queer Student Alliance (QSA), we met a handful of people who would become dear friends. Allen Ratliff invited us to his apartment, and within seconds I blurted out with conviction, "Why would any group ever form under the name *queer*? What a hateful word!"

The word *queer* had always been hurled at me as a way to degrade or embarrass me, my gender expression, how I walked, and how I talked, long before I ever had a chance to self-identify as gay or anything else. The word triggered memories of people looking at me with disgust and yelling "queer!" and "faggot!" in my direction as I walked down the hall of my middle school, of people waiting along the path home from school in order to fight me just because I was, in their words, "fruity." When I was in middle school, there was no respite from the hateful shouts and whispers. To me, those words meant erasure, pain, and danger. They had been used to make me feel unsafe, to signal that I shouldn't be allowed to exist comfortably, that I should be seen as the ultimate disgrace: a black boy proudly bearing feminine characteristics, a faggot. I stared Allen down in defiance, awaiting his reasoning.

"Reappropriation," he said simply, like the social scientist he was. He went on to explain that people who don't easily fit within the label of LGBT often choose to identify as queer to signify that their identities were undefinable and couldn't be represented in a normative sense of sexual orientation or gender. I understood the sexual orientation piece but couldn't wrap my head around the gender piece. I hadn't encountered anyone who identified as queer during the entire year I had spent at Iowa Western, or anywhere else for that matter. But I quickly realized that, according to Allen's definition, *I* was the very definition of queer, and so were many of my friends. This was the first of many conversations with Allen that added to my burgeoning interest in queer activism and LGBTQ history. I began to participate in QSA meetings and activities, where I was exposed to a plethora of predominantly trans men for the first time.

The University of Nebraska was vastly different from Iowa Western with its secluded bluffs and student body of five thousand. Now twenty-two thousand students were my peers, and walks across campus were several football fields long. Fraternity and sorority houses with big Greek letters proudly affixed above door posts lined the streets, and sheets hung from windows advertising on-campus parties. The Nebraska Union was filled with fast-food joints, a bookstore, a computer lab, and a gallery space that showcased student art.

My first meeting with my general studies advisor marked a turning point in my life. I was eager for academic advising, but the older white woman didn't seem up for the task. She seemed slightly confused by my skintight T-shirt, and from the way she looked at me, I felt like I wasn't worth her time.

"How can I help you?" she said.

"I'm interested in becoming a theater teacher," I said. She looked uncomfortable. Did she think someone like me couldn't be an educator? I continued, "I had a phenomenal experience in my music and drama program in high school, and I want to have the same kind of impact on someone in the future."

"If that is your goal," she finally said, "then you are going to have to triple major in English, education, and theater. A theater education major doesn't exist here at the university."

It was almost as if she knew exactly what to say to scare me right out of her office. I contemplated her suggestion, realizing that I wasn't scared at all. I was up for the challenge.

But around this time, I found myself spending many nights in the back room of an apartment complex off campus gazing at the iTunes visualizer for hours listening to Damien Rice's "Eskimo," high as hell. Whenever some folks who worked at the front desk of our dorm invited Corey and me to smoke weed, we usually obliged. This, of course, caused more problems for me academically.

A few months later I found out I was failing American History after 1877 and philosophy. The lecturers felt far too abstract and irrelevant to my life at the time. I couldn't force myself to care about something I just didn't care about.

Lincoln's many social entertainment options didn't help matters any. Especially after Corey and I discovered the small-town gay bar housed in a long brick building reminiscent of a firehouse on Ninth Street, walking distance from campus. At first, integrating into a new social scene felt daunting, until I began to bump into many of the people I knew from the Run after hours in Omaha. The doorman was an actual gentleman who respectfully took my cover and gazed extra closely at my ID to check that I was over the age of eighteen, the required age for entry. Although I was twenty years old at the time, I looked much younger. My short height, thin frame, and curly hair made me look like a pubescent teen boy. I was just glad I didn't have to experience another weekly feeling up by the doorman at the Run. Corey had begun dating our high school friend Kenny, and one evening we smoked weed outside his dorm. When I exhaled, the stadium lights on the tennis courts glowed brighter than before. On my walk back to Harper Hall, I could swear that the leaves bristled extra loudly in the cool breeze, and I began to mumble about being the king of Nadiobladium. Images of the royal ruler Cairon, the mystical caped god who commissioned Atreyu with AURYN to save the childlike princess from the Nothing in *The Neverending Story*, swirled around in my head and filled my eyes. I was still something of a mystical preacher, living in a fantasy world of my own creation, my dorm looming in the distance like a castle. It felt similar to what speaking in tongues in church felt like. High as hell, I conjured Nadiobladium a few other times, before my experiences with weed became filled with paranoia and anxiety. When it was no longer an enjoyable activity, I stopped smoking.

Corey continued to date our high school friend Kenny on and off, and the three of us signed up for concert choir and walked to class together every day. If one of us went to the dining hall, we all went and kept each other company. We were a trio of tightly knit friends, except at night, when groans, moans, whimpers, and the sounds of kissing emanated from beneath the sheets on the top bunk bed across from mine. I got frustrated that my friends would disrespect me in this way. "I can't believe this," I would say to myself, then more loudly, "Hello?" They'd stop for a few moments, giving me enough quiet to fall asleep. But soon enough I'd wake to sounds of their encounters in the dark.

It wasn't that I didn't have fulfilling romantic and sexual experiences myself. I had encounters with all types of men. But there was something about the audacity of my best friends hooking up in my presence that bothered me.

To keep myself occupied outside of the trio and to make some money, I went and got a serving job at Magnolia, a new contemporary fine-dining restaurant in the Haymarket District. Dressed in a pressed, starched white shirt and black slacks, I served many of the faculty from the university during lunch, along with fancy dinner clubs of elderly white women and walk-ins who came in before and after the Husker games. I often extended over-the-top greetings to diners in my section, like "Welcome! We count you all as honored guests," which was actually a line I borrowed from Pastor Hart's greeting of first-time guests at Eagle's Nest. It felt like another extension of performance, and I didn't care in the slightest if anyone winced—and some did.

Several times a week, I walked into concert-choir rehearsal, clutching the handles of my caramel Aldo tote, having donned sky-high red velvet heels and silk scarves, which I had started wearing in my daily life. I would join Corey, Kenny, and new friends Jay and Adam in the baritone section. I had bonded quickly with Jay, a thin redhead, over our similar robust vibratos, and Adam, a talented pianist who often accompanied my recitals. Adam was a tall, quiet, shy kid with black curly hair from Papillion, Nebraska.

Later that fall, Allen Ratliff invited me to a fundraiser at the Q, hosted by the QSA, on National Coming Out Day. I had no clue that by *fundraiser* he meant *drag show*.

At the Q, I took a seat on a bar stool as a tan curtain went up on the stage and fog began to billow over the audience. Bright strobes of green, pink, and blue filled the room. Someone I knew from my work

A happy moment in the backyard on Sixty-Sixth Street before Nina's high school graduation. I'm far right.

Sitting on the front stoop of my Sixty-Sixth Street house. From top to bottom: Dexter, Ginger, me, Tanisha.

My biological grandmother Charlesetta and my stepgrandfather Melvin. I like to think that I inherited her fair complexion and smile.

I'm pictured here wearing Payless sneakers that I hated and wishing to escape from the family Bible study. How quickly the conversation usually turned to me "getting right with the Lord."

Here I am, center, clapping my hands at Firepower camp and feeling passionate and reverent for the spirit of the Lord.

Powder-puff game, Burke High School. I couldn't wait to put on the cheerleading outfit!

Show choir, my high school happy place.

Stargazing near Gene Leahy Mall in downtown Omaha with Corey, my first true love. I thought we'd end up together as life partners.

Me wearing my signature staple, a raglan baseball tee, in my 2005 senior picture.

Burke High School graduation, 2005. Completing night school gave me enough credits to walk across the stage.

Unbeknownst to me, Nina attended my graduation, and she surprised me outside after. For mere minutes, the world stopped. Marshall looks on.

Banjee Girl in downtown Lincoln, Nebraska, otherwise known as "coming out number 5,474," in 2007 at the University of Nebraska–Lincoln, but this time making it queer. (Photo by Kan Seidel)

The "ankles of excellence" themselves. When life gives you trials, find a heel to express yourself. (Photo by Kan Seidel)

Left: Performing "When You Believe" at the Q with Alexus Rayeé, my Miss City Sweetheart sister.
Right: Saying goodbye to Nebraska in 2008. I knew I had to go. The world was calling.

Soaking up the rays with a fresh haircut in Millennium Park
after officially becoming a Chicagoan.

Left: On one of the nights of our Glam Rock New Divas of Halsted show, Phi Phi O'Hara painted me for the back row. Right: Channeling my inner Dominique Deveraux in homage to my idol Diahann Carroll at Chicago's Lincoln Park. (Photo by Foto by Mateo)

A young Precious Jewel parading midriff along with the ability to pull together outfits out of nothing for a show. (Photo by Jed Dulanas)

Performing Rihanna's "Fire Bomb" in Thursday-night shows at Spin. The song became an anthem of standing on my own two feet.

Performing at Chicago Pride Parade for the first time, in 2010. (Photo by Joe Carlson)

Legs for days! Performing Whitney Houston's "How Will I Know" at the opening of Chicago Pride Parade in 2010 as a pride flag waves in the distance. (Photo by Joe Carlson)

I used to refuse to wear coats in drag even when it was cold to showcase my look. A fellow classmate, Tessa Konkol, began documenting my forays into gender bending and took this pic on a stroll where they dressed up in drag in my honor for Halloween. (Photo by Tessa Konkol)

Above: My graduation from Columbia College in Chicago, 2013. I'm celebrating the completion of what I had truly come to Chicago to do. I'm sporting an Akira dress. Left: Angelica Ross and me at the Women's March in Chicago on January 21, 2017, the day after Donald J. Trump was inaugurated as the forty-fifth president of the United States. (Photo by Myles Brady-Davis)

Above Left: A career woman is born as I transitioned on the job while working at the Center on Halsted. Power suits and heels became the norm. These braids still give me chills. Above Right: I participated in my first ad campaign with the Chicago Community Trust in 2014, "On the Table". (Photo by Tim Musho for Chicago Community Trust, 2014)

Above: Speaking at Loyola University Chicago for the Inaugural Black Lives Matter Conference in 2016. I have had the pleasure of speaking at many colleges and universities across the country and count it as my ministry. (Photo by Mark Patton) Right: My first kiss with Myles.

Left: My love and I had the great pleasure of hosting the Trans 100 in 2015 as a newly engaged couple. (Photo by C. Grost Photography) Right: I never thought I would be on the Video Music Awards stage, but in 2015 Miley Cyrus gifted me and the rest of the Happy Hippie Presents #InstaPride crew the honor of introducing her closing number. I stood next to Taylor Swift and Selena Gomez before walking onstage, and it felt so surreal. (Photo by Jeff Kravitz/MTV1415/FilmMagic/Getty Images)

On set with Miley Cyrus for the #InstaPride shoot in 2015 at Milk Studios. (Painted by Pati Dubroff)

Because you understand me better than anyone else does. Myles and I were engaged in 2016. (Photo by Korto Photography)

One of our wedding photographers caught the moment Myles saw me in my dress for the first time. (Photo by Korto Photography)

All smiles as I walk down the aisle after becoming Mrs. Brady-Davis. (Photo by Korto Photography)

Left: Philanthropy is forever close to our hearts as we support issues of social justice and equality. Seen here at the Equality Illinois Gala in 2019 wearing my favorite color. (Photo by Mystic Images Photography) Below: Lady of the Lake. (Photo by Annie Flanagan)

A Scorpio love story seen at the Japanese garden in Jackson Park on the South Side of Chicago as Myles flaunts his baby bump at six months along. (Photo by Mystic Images Photography)

Like the love of Akhenaten and Nefertiti, our love is for all of time. Myles and I took this shot mere hours before we welcomed our little wonder, Zayn, into the world. (Photo by Korto Photography)

A new family of my own. I never expected to be called Mother. (Photo by Baby Bella Photography)

Zayn Yemaya Echelle. Our beautiful goddess of the water, the moon, and the rainbow. (Photo by Baby Bella Photography)

Me and my loves. (Photo by Baby Bella Photography)

as a camp counselor with Anytown had recently ventured into drag and opened the show by performing a Faith Hill number. Felicity Slayter followed by lip-synching a number by the Dixie Chicks, wearing tall white laced-up boots. Then thick calves and clear slide heels were all I could see as Dominique Divamoore casually walked to the middle of the stage, capturing my full attention in an off-the-shoulder black-and-bronze shimmering gown tightly cinched at her waist with a soft leather black belt. She remained planted, turning ever so slightly so that the top of her torso and her face were completely captured by the spotlight from the back of the room, and she began lip-synching a Whitney Houston medley. Twinkling her fingers with french-tipped nails in front of her face, she reached for the moon and pulled back the stars over the black hair that framed her sharp brows and cat eyes made with thick black eyeliner. Smoky maroon eyeshadow blended to create a cut crease above her plum-painted pout. I could see she was an audience favorite, and as folks lined up and extended dollar bills in respect to her form, I thought to myself, *Ha! I can do that . . . maybe even better.* As the veteran drag performer exited the stage clutching a black feather boa, I could see she was catching her breath after her sport, as the emcee slowly and dramatically yelled into the mic, *"Give it up for Dominique Divamoore!"* The room thunderously cheered in appreciation of her excellent performance and precise emoting.

As the tan curtain went back down, I felt like I was in the midst of a revelation: I had dreamed of this scene as a child. The emcee went on to announce that a yearly competition known as the Beauty and the Beast Pageant, a contest for first-time performers, would be taking place in a few weeks. As he made the announcement, Allen looked at me from across the table and said, "You should do it!" I knew I would be a natural, but I refused to let on that I was even going to give it serious consideration.

I returned to campus thinking to myself, *"I'm not a drag queen!"* and told my friends as much. I couldn't fully free myself from the thought that a drag queen was the clearest example of an abomination, based on everything that I had been taught. I recalled being reprimanded for "switching" and for walking in Nina's high heels, and Pastor Brian's continual request that I "act like a man." I was scared to take a leap into the world of drag and truly feared my soul would be damned to hell, but I also believed that Angel Dumott Schunard in *Rent* was fierce, and so was I. The memory of seeing the show in high school never left me, nor did the line "I'm more of a man than you'll ever be; I'm more of a woman than you'll ever get." That was the perfect summation of my gender at the time. I related to Angel's chameleonlike ability to morph into whatever he wanted to be, but I was still bound by a puritanical core of beliefs that demonized that ability.

I began to casually ask friends, "If I were to compete in the Beauty and the Beast Pageant, what would my name be?" The first name that came to mind was Jezebel, the *baddest* bitch in the Bible. My thinking was that at least starting with a name from scripture would somehow be pleasing to the Lord, and would somehow keep me closer to my comfort zone.

I brought my brainstorming to Art Garza, an Anytown friend and the student assistant of Gay, Lesbian, Bisexual, Transgender, and Ally (GLBTA) programs and services on campus. He and I had met as delegates during my first Anytown experience as a junior in high school. After culture night, an evening dedicated to bringing students' parents into the conversation and showing what we'd learned during the weekend at camp, Art disappeared. Word traveled fast that he had decided to come out to his father, who had then yanked him from camp in a fit of rage and kicked him out, leaving him homeless. Art and I had lost contact for some time, but I thought of him often as I remembered my granddad's anger and embarrassment when he caught me walking around in women's heels. I never understood how Granddad could watch the rampant gay sex on his favorite HBO show *Oz* with a straight face and then turn around and scold me for displaying feminine ways.

It was with great joy that Art and I reunited at UNL through the Queer Student Alliance. He quickly recruited me to be a part of the GLBTA Speakers Bureau on campus, where I began sharing publicly for the first time my struggle with being a person of faith and identifying as gay. I didn't have all the correct academic vernacular but was eager to share my story, especially on one particular panel, where many students of color asked a myriad of questions. There I met Dr. Amelia Montes, who invited me to take her Lesbian & Gay Literature course the following semester. I jumped at the opportunity to register.

When Art told me there was already a drag queen named Jezebel in the community, I immediately nixed the name from the list. With no better ideas or suggestions from friends, I finally decided to officially enter the competition without a name. All I knew was that if I was going to perform, it was going to be something special and memorable. Something unique. So I didn't let not having a name bother me.

Corey, Kenny, Michael, and Jarrett, my friends from Omaha, and many of my concert-choir peers were ecstatic, and their support meant the world to me. Jordan, a friend from concert choir, invited me to her dorm room one evening to look at a gown she had worn to a formal dance in high school. I fell in love as soon as I laid eyes on the silk chartreuse cocktail dress with spaghetti straps dangling from a hanger. It featured three tiers of ruffles down the asymmetrical skirt and a bow with rhinestones near the ruche on the side. When it fit perfectly, I knew I had found the right dress.

With every dress, one must have the perfect shoes, so I went to Dillard's to find a pair of heels. All my years of roaming the mall after school had created a database in my mind of where to find stylings suited exactly to my taste, so it didn't take me long to spot the gold heeled sandals with gold ankle chains and pink and green jewels cascading up the straps.

With my new glitzy heels and the dress in tow, I walked from campus over to the Q on the day of the competition. It was a Sunday evening about a week before Halloween, and walking into that bar, I felt timid, not knowing what to expect as the pulsating vibrations of electronic music filled the room. I was the first competitor to arrive, and I had a sense of déjà vu as I milled around the area in front of the stage wearing my favorite denim jacket. I recalled my picnic table performances when, as a young child, I imitated Whitney Houston and daydreamed about being Jessica Rabbit in her slinky performance from *Who Framed Roger Rabbit* and ran around saying, "Get out of here, get me some money too!" I'd wanted to be Tina Turner in her "Private Dancer" video. At every turn, I sang songs about being paid to dance sexually in a nightclub, and now, here I was about to make my debut.

I was living my dream! Before long I was surrounded by four guys holding plastic shopping bags filled with dresses and shoes, and the emcee began collecting music and drag names from each contestant. I panicked because my friend was still driving from Omaha, forty-five minutes away, with a burned CD of my music, and I was still undecided on what my drag name was going to be. I could see the emcee was irritated that I had arrived empty-handed. Fortunately, my friend Michael finally arrived, delivering the CD to me with a hug and a sweet kiss.

A troupe of drag queens sauntered in behind us to serve as our hair-and-makeup transformation captains. I looked around and hoped I wouldn't be paired with one of the ones who was garishly put together and didn't look "real." From a large clear plastic bowl, we all pulled numbers and were randomly matched. My number paired me with a tall, burly white queen, Susan Davis, who wore a floor-length frumpy white crushed-velvet gown with sparse feathers along the neckline. She had minimal makeup under her eyeglasses, and I breathed a sigh of relief. I found it to be a strange, ironic twist of fate that the person I wound up selecting to put me in drag also had the last name Davis.

In the brightly lit dressing room, Susan moved close to me. She breathed heavily as she clutched my jaw in her hands, turning my face from side to side, inspecting my skin as if it were a canvas. When she released her grasp, she looked at me through her glasses and said in a deep gruff voice, "Are you Negro?"

"What?" I stuttered. Another queen quickly threw her an appropriate shade of tan foundation. There was only one other queen of color in the competition, and the queen who painted her didn't care that the foundation didn't match her skin tone.

As Susan began applying the makeup to my face, I tried to process why I had just been asked if I was *Negro*. The emcee peeked back into the dressing room from the top of the stairs and asked me if I had come up with a name yet. "Ask me before I go onstage, and I'll know it," I said, even though I wasn't sure I would.

Susan continued painting my face, her stale breath lingering while she lavishly applied peach blush. I must've looked like a mix between being sunburned and being sun-kissed. She didn't boast much technique or skill as she pressed bubblegum-pink lipstick all around my mouth and applied fake eyelashes. Lastly, she threw me a pair of opaque tights to put on so that I wouldn't have to worry about using duct tape to constrict myself between the legs like the other new drags were being taught to do.

One by one, the announcer called each contestant to the stage to perform: *"Ashley Jordan!" "Nicky Fitz," "Bianka with a K," "Alyssa Monroe!"* Looking around, I decided that I was the prettiest of everyone. Susan lightly teased parts of my short textured strawberry-blond bob wig while adding spritzes of hairspray as she attempted to push all my curly hair up into it. I was giving off Whitney Houston circa "Heartbreak Hotel" vibes. Susan zipped me into the fitted charmeuse gown and clasped a rhinestone tassel necklace around my neck to highlight my décolletage. Then the emcee peeked his head in for a final time and said, "You're next! What's your drag name?"

I took a breath, walked over to the stairs that led up to the stage and announced, without hesitation: "Precious. Jewel." Never once in the deliberation process had that name ever consciously come to mind. Now it rolled off my tongue as if it had always been my name. Apparently my imitations of Bea's Sunday morning Southern hospitality at Eagle's Nest Sunday services had stuck with me. In high school and then college, I affectionately called anyone and everyone Glorious Jewel, Abundant Life, and Precious Jewel! Who would have guessed that when given the opportunity to name myself, I would choose the name Precious? Certainly not me. *Precious* meant something of great value. Priceless. Rare. Irreplaceable. Exquisite. I had never been called any of those things by my family. For my entire existence, I had been regarded as a nuisance at best, an abomination at worst.

As I pulled the heavy black door to the dressing room closed behind me, I was determined to leave that life behind. Everyone else's opinion, the pastors at Eagle's Nest, Ron and Valerie, Nina and Marshall—none of it mattered anymore. I didn't need anyone else's permission to be me.

The moment of truth had come; it was time to create a new me, on my own terms.

Backstage, an intense rush of adrenaline came over me as I glimpsed the faces of countless friends who had come out to see me and my first performance in drag. Kenny was there, along with my circle of pals from Iowa Western, and my friends from concert choir at UNL.

I walked out onstage delivering the slow first notes of Whitney's classic: "Whatever you want. Whatever you need. Anything you want done, baby, I'll do it natur-ally, cause I'm every woman! It's all in me-eeeee! It's all in me-eeee, eee-yah!" As the downbeat hit, I descended the stairs in front of the stage like I was Destiny's Child fiercely storming thirteen steep stairs at the Radio Music Awards in the 2004 performance of "Lose My Breath." I knew every syllable of Whitney Houston's "I'm Every Woman" and commanded the audience with my authoritative strut, swerving hips, and bodacious assets. I clutched onto the dollar bills flying at me from all directions and threw my head back in ecstasy, feeling a new kind of electricity moving throughout my body. I moved up and down the staircase to the stage at least twice. On my last ascension to the stage, one of my heels got caught in a divot on the staircase and snapped. Lunging forward but somehow keeping my balance, I whirled, throwing some movement into the train as the song ended. The crowd roared to a standing ovation as I left the stage.

Back in the dressing room, I felt as if I had just had an out-of-body experience and could barely remember what I had just done. But I knew I had served the children with my natural stage presence. I couldn't believe my heel broke in my first performance, but ultimately, I took it as a kind of break-a-leg good-luck sign, as it ended up showing the crowd that I was a natural performer through and through. I learned the most important rule of show business: if you mess up, *keep going.*

Thankfully, as the judges tabulated scores, a queen named Destiney slipped me a pair of clear slides before I left the dressing room since my heels were broken. We were all summoned back to the stage, and then the emcee announced the names of the top two into the microphone: *"Nicky Fitz and Precious Jewel."* As I stepped forward, I felt the weight of this moment, a moment that I had wanted for so long. Within seconds, the emcee announced, *"And the winner of this year's Beauty and the Beast Pageant is Precious Jewel!"* I looked across the audience, feeling as if I were Vanessa Williams in her crowning moment as Miss America in 1983. I was handed a cash prize in a white envelope, and Susan took her place standing behind me, beaming. I was so proud of my victory, and my friends joined me in photos that would serve as reminders of that night for years to come.

Winning the Beauty and the Beast Pageant would place me squarely in the Davis family legacy of working in the entertainment business. I began to receive invitation upon invitation to guest-perform in regular shows and benefits alongside veteran legends of Nebraska drag, including Faleasha Savage, Jessica Bower, Erica Joy, Ashley Simone, and Skylar. One of my first performances was with Destiney, who was Miss Q at the time and who invited me to appear as Janet Jackson beside her impersonation of Michael Jackson, to perform the 1995 duet "Scream." Once again, all my friends gathered to support me. To be perfectly honest, I didn't even know all the words, so I mimicked the sounds and overly pronounced the chorus. I just assumed that's what you did when you didn't know the words. Destiney recognized my natural talent despite this, and shortly thereafter she gifted me a light brown shoulder-length spiral curly wig that became a part of my signature look.

Susan had respiratory issues, and her public appearances were scant, besides the few times she randomly showed up with an oxygen machine strapped to her side and breathing tubes in her nose to watch me perform. We never had a personal relationship outside of the Q, and I never forgot that she asked me if I was Negro the first time I performed. I heard people mocking her because she considered herself a woman. I didn't fully process what that meant at the time but instead accepted the fact that I met Susan as Susan, and that was that.

Working in nightlife almost caused me to lose full sight of my academic obligations until the next semester when I became the first-ever volunteer at the LGBTQA Resource Center on campus. I oversaw book borrowing from the center's little library and held daily office hours with Art to direct students to queer campus resources. I retook several courses from the fall and watched as my grades improved across the board. I regained sight of my priorities and continued my involvement with the Anytown program, facilitating conversations on inclusivity for high school students in Omaha twice a year. With my whole self engaged, I started to feel affirmed in who I was and what I was doing. My Lesbian & Gay Literature class served to further expand my horizons.

～

Dr. Amelia Montes, the professor for LGBTQ lit, wore a pair of black ankle booties that gave her extra height as she facilitated a welcoming atmosphere. I usually arrived in the basement of Andrews Hall wearing a set of press-on nails from the previous evening's performance, paired with my Whitney Houston *Cinderella* "Impossible" wig, the swooping tendrils brushing gently across my face.

I often passionately weighed in during our contentious conversations on gender and sexuality from conservative, indigenous, international, black, white, gay, bi, lesbian, and queer perspectives. We broached the subject of transgender identity when we read Julie Anne Peter's novel *Luna*. I was introduced to the concept of the third gender via the glamorous *kathoey* ladyboy showgirls of Thailand and the outcast *hijra* of India in the HBO documentary *Middlesex*. I was anything but comfortable watching the full operating procedure of a sex change being performed in a backstreet clinic in the film. As the lights flickered back on at the end of our viewing, I clutched my pearls, and sitting upright, I said, "Altering one's body to me is playing God." Sindu, a Sri Lankan woman who was sitting on the other side of the room, was so offended by my opinion that she invited her partner, Cameron, to speak to our class about his trans experience. No one in our course identified that way, and the conversation was fraught, as many in the group, including myself, conflated transgender identity with physical surgery. This never came up when I was interacting with trans guys on campus; I simply perceived them as the gender they chose. But the thought of altering my own body was a step too far for me, even as I learned about gender fluidity in academic terms.

Anything medical has always caused me to become queasy, including having my blood drawn, watching medical-drama TV shows, walking the sterile hallways of a hospital, and even getting my teeth cleaned at the dentist. There, in that class, I recognized that I was imposing the same type of prejudice I had experienced from others, based on ignorance and lack of exposure. I decided then and there to expand my worldview. Several other classmates felt the same, and together we endeavored to educate ourselves and spread awareness on campus and in our local community. To that end, we created educational flyers with queer terminology and hung them on bulletin boards all over campus. I identified much more with the gender-bending drag-face performativity of Marsha P. Johnson and Sylvia Rivera, transgender activists, gay rights pioneers, and key figures in the Stonewall Riots. I first heard of Stonewall during a class viewing of *Outrage '69*. In my final paper for the semester, I wrote about *Luna*: "The strength it took for Liam to transition to Luna and keep her identity and then, at the right moment, walk away and start a new life—every person deserves that opportunity."

Even as I distanced myself from church, Christian theology remained a dominant source of the core of my moral principles. I had just begun to scratch the surface of how my sexual orientation and spirituality fit together, asking myself questions like *Are people born gay?* and *What does God think about homosexuality?* I fell hard for Pastor Mel White's memoir *Stranger at the Gate: To Be Gay and Christian in America*. White was a former ghostwriter for conservative fixtures Jerry Falwell, Billy Graham, and Pat Robertson. His memoir documents twenty-five years of conversion therapy, affiliation with the now defunct Exodus International ministry, and coming to terms with being gay after attending an LGBT civil rights march in 1987. As I grappled with whether choosing to identify as gay and perform in drag meant I was distancing myself from God, White's appointment as minister at the Cathedral of Hope United Church of Christ in Dallas, Texas, the largest LGBT congregation in the world, made me realize my faith. I still felt God's calling, and finally started to understand that my sexual orientation did not have to undermine my passion for service.

Standing outside the Nebraska Union Plaza, I asked passersby, "Are you an ally for LGBTQ rights?" Which I followed up by giving an ally button with a pink triangle and the phrase "Safety, dignity and respect for all." I had mostly positive interactions with folks as I pleaded our case, that LGBTQ folks deserve to be seen and treated with the same humanity and dignity as everyone else.

On an evening in April, I found myself pounding pavement with members of my class as we took a group trip to the Grand Movie Theatre near campus. Several class members and I had approached Dr. Montes with the idea of doing some kind of political social action in place of our final to honor the history of and carry on the fight for gay liberation and LGBTQ equality in America. We'd learned about the marches, celebrations, and protests of organizations like the Street Transvestite Action Revolutionaries, the Lavender Menace, and the Black Panthers, and we wanted to follow in their footsteps. Dr. Montes gave us her blessing, and when we told the theater manager of our intentions, she was very supportive too. Stepping away from our liberal bastion at the university in my cheetah-print high-heel boots, a rainbow flag tied around my neck like a superhero cloak, I didn't know what to expect.

At the theater, a group of people routinely gathered to hold up a tall white cross with the words "Lying," "Racism," "Murder," "Stealing," "Idolatry," and "Homosexuality" written across it in red paint. My pulse sped up, and my mouth went dry as we approached, but never for a second did I consider turning back. Bouncing a white sign with multicolored letters that read "Ignorance = Prejudice" we chanted, "Hey! Hey! Ho! Ho! Homophobia has got to go!" This was my very first civil protest.

"You're going to hell!" was the hateful response. The man holding the cross attempted to weaponize the scripture, but little did he know that I had been churched my whole life and knew the Bible cover to cover. The threat of eternal damnation no longer affected my psyche the way it had at the beginning of the semester. That, plus the allies driving by, including Dr. Montes, who honked in support of our activism, buoyed me.

"End hate!" and "Love all!" we cheered. A navy-blue van pulled up, and the driver rolled down his window. "Thanks for doing what you're doing," he said, passing us several large bags of chips and two twelve-packs of Diet Pepsi and Mountain Dew. "My daughter's gay."

LGBTQ people don't live only in metropolitan areas; they live in rural communities and often don't have the resources of cities like

Chicago, Los Angeles, or New York City. I believe that our organized protest ultimately increased awareness and started a community dialogue, and it will forever be one of my fondest memories of taking action to address hate in our world.

Each day I rushed to make it to LGBT lit on time, and I often saw a woman sauntering down the hall outside the classroom as I was storming in. With her curly salt-and-pepper hair, small stature, round face, and tan rosy complexion, she looked as if we could have been related. I guessed that she was a teacher, not a student, based on her swag and a seriously sassy shoe game. "I love your shoes!" I'd say as we passed each other.

"Jimmy Choo!" she'd blurt out without missing a beat before walking through the doorway of her classroom or continuing on down the hall.

One day I finally worked up the nerve to push beyond pleasantries. "What do you teach?" I asked. "I would love to take your class!" No matter her answer, I already knew that I was going to register for her course.

"African Americans in Film and Women in Popular Culture," she said nonchalantly, as if she were Phylicia Rashad herself.

An expansion of my knowledge of queer history in terms of pop culture and blackness in film felt like the next logical step in my exploration of identity in academia. That summer, as most students packed up and went home, I found myself moving my things into the Selleck dormitory on campus along with mostly international students. I missed Corey, who had returned to his family in Omaha for the summer. I felt totally isolated without him. I was still keeping myself at a distance from the Loves and my biological family, so I planned to survive on my own by serving tables, performing in drag, cashing student-loan refund checks, and using an education-and-training grant for individuals who had aged out of the foster care system.

I was excited to start Dr. Kwakiutl Dreher's Women in Popular Culture course. I'd long daydreamed of recreating Marilyn Monroe's "Diamonds Are a Girl's Best Friend" performance from *Gentlemen Prefer Blondes*, and Jack Lemmon and Tony Curtis in drag in *Some Like It Hot* showed me that drag was a valid vehicle for a career in performance. Now, in class, I learned that Marilyn Monroe had been a foster kid who was later adopted, and despite her difficult childhood and eventual ill fate, she'd ascended to everlasting iconic Hollywood prominence. I was further captivated by another woman featured in black-and-white archival footage: First Lady Jacqueline Kennedy. She had stood tall in the face of national and personal tragedy and was determined to honor the life of her husband, John F. Kennedy, the thirty-fifth president of the United States. She masterfully choreographed her interview with *LIFE Magazine*, demanding that her late husband be seen in the same honorable light as Camelot, despite his indiscretions. The lady knew how to craft a legacy.

Then there was Oprah Winfrey, whose talk show I watched as a kid after school. In the course, I learned that she had dealt with an abusive mother and had been raised by her grandmother in the Midwest, before building a media empire in Chicago. That gave me the idea that one day I, too, could make my own way in the Windy City, could pursue a life straight out of Kimora Lee Simmons's book *Fabulosity*—if I could just get there.

~

I was in love. The next semester, I registered for the African Americans in Film course and once again found a home in discourse on cinema and groundbreaking black actresses across the twentieth-century American film canon: Hattie McDaniel, who played Mammy in *Gone with the*

Wind and became the first African American to win an Academy Award; Dorothy Dandridge, who portrayed Carmen Jones opposite Harry Belafonte; Diahann Carroll, who embodied a working-class black mother struggling with oppressive social-welfare practices in *Claudine*; Pam Grier, who served as a kickass sexy assassin in *Coffy* during the era of blaxploitation; and Diana Ross, who played the fashionable Tracy Chambers in Berry Gordy's *Mahogany* in 1975 and whose line, "The men love me, the women love me, Mahogany" could have come straight out of my own mouth. I saw a bit of myself in each of their performances, and my awareness of black beauty, iconography, and history grew. I began to see the multitudes of blackness, the multitudes of experience and possibility, that contrasted with the narrow narrative I'd learned growing up.

Inspired by these classes, I started to visit the Ross Media Arts Center on campus, where Corey and I watched foreign films like *The Black Book*, queer films by Pedro Almodóvar, and independent features, including *Shortbus*, which prominently featured Justin Vivian Bond and other gender variant and sexual identities. I saw the documentary *Jesus Camp*, which took me back to my own teenage confusion. In my attempt to follow God's plan, I'd questioned my sexuality. "If I indulge my feelings," I asked, "am I going to hell? Or can someone like me get into heaven?"

EIGHT

A New Kind of Family

"You are beautiful," Joan Rivers told me.

I was standing in a lineup of local drag queens from Lincoln who had been invited to attend a reception in her honor after her performance. I was so eager for any opportunity to be onstage that I didn't do my research before accepting the invitation. I had recently been added to the entry-level cast for the show *The Girls of Desire*, and Jezebel, an aging white queen, had it out for me, since I stole her shine in the show in which she had been cast for years.

Erica Joy was there too. Erica was the reigning queen of the *N'Joy Show* cast at the Q. She was the former owner of the now defunct Joy Nightclub, which predated my young queer life, and she was an example of what I could become if I ascended to the upper echelons of drag. Erica had recently bid adieu to the Princess, who left Nebraska to work professionally at Play Dance Bar in Nashville.

Joan Rivers cackled at Erica's entire shtick and crowned her her favorite drag queen of the bunch.

Erica later added Roderick to the *N'Joy* cast, birthing Chanel Savage, who made her Lincoln drag debut as my solo background dancer. I was vying for the title of Miss City Sweetheart against Alexus

Rayeé, the dancing diva and winner of the other new queen pageant, Miss Gay Youth.

Alexus was a scrappy chain-smoker offstage and the kind of girl who would kick your ass if you looked at her wrong. Every now and then, she'd get herself banned from performing after her liquor got the best of her, and her temper flared. I watched her read someone their last rights after they disrespected her, and even though we couldn't have been more different, she always supported me, was always first in line to tip me.

Tipping drag queens is how you honor them and show appreciation for their work. Wigs, makeup, and costumes aren't cheap. I had never had any formal makeup lessons from the other queens; I got by on the generosity of those who took the time to put their faces on me and give me a touch-up here and there. One evening, Jessica Bower twisted six long bobby pins into my scalp and sprayed sections of my hair with black hairspray to create multiple looks for me after I'd worn my signature curly auburn wig. I preferred accentuations of my natural beauty with touches of MAC cream foundation, MAC blush and loose Coty powder, lashes, and french-tip press-on nails. I'd always stock up at Walgreens before a show. Back then the girls used to say, "If you aren't wearing nails, you aren't doing drag."

Weekend in and weekend out, we were booked together in the same shows. From the deejay booth overlooking the stage, I watched Alexus flip, dip, and sidewinder down the long runway in white heeled boots as only a former cheerleader could. Her take-no-prisoners style shined like the choreography in the music videos of Paul Oakenfold and Brittany Murphy's "Faster Kill Pussycat," Dead or Alive's "You Spin Me Round," and Uffie's "Pop the Glock."

With one win under each of our belts, the heat was on. Before her performance at Lincoln's longest-running pageant, Miss City Sweetheart, Alexus left the dressing room wearing a pink curly wig and holding a *Phantom of the Opera* mask in front of her face as P!nk's

"Get This Party Started" mixed into Eurythmics' "Sweet Dreams" and Marilyn Manson's cover of it. Midway through her number, the audience cheered like mad, and I knew that she had done something incredible. She returned to the dressing room without the pink wig, her bare-buzzed head spray-painted neon orange. I knew then and there the pageant was over as I prepared to perform a number from the Broadway musical *Aida*. Needless to say, Alexus, in a beaded lime-sherbet gown, was crowned the twenty-fourth Miss City Sweetheart, her new crown towering to the sky. She now held two crowns to my one.

She was adamant that I be her successor, however, as the next Miss City Sweetheart. After her win, she continued to tip me well. Clutching her hand with its corn-chip claws, I accepted the dollar bills and held on for several seconds, acknowledging her act of sisterhood.

At every show in their once-a-month review, a spotlight swirled over the audience as the curtain went up on Dominique, Jessica, and Alexus. Bouncing their hips in various dress styles made from the same lavender fabric, they opened each show performing "Dreamgirls." Former Beauty and the Beast Pageant winners Courtney Foxx, one of three black girls who performed at the bar, and Josalyn Summer, another white queen, were thrown into the rotation of the opening number but were never allowed to do lead.

Dominique, Jessica, and Alexus looked down on me for performing often, but we were in many of the same shows. Tipping around in drag month after month watching the Supremes-like choreography, I dreamed of leading the number in homage to Diana Ross, Sheryl Lee Ralph, and Beyoncé. I knew what the number called for as I watched their limp wrists moving in the air.

The director of the show always gave me a rambling list of critiques. He didn't even perform anymore, and the select times I saw him do his rendition of Lucille Ball's Vitameatavegamin commercial in the show, I found it to be boring and lifeless. He always left the stage empty-handed, and yet I still took his notes into consideration. I was trying to be respectful of my elders. "Hip pads." But I didn't pad my body. "More makeup." But I didn't want to look like a drag monster. "All of these girls are X, but you are Y." Even though I didn't agree with most of his "advice," I thought listening would help land me a coveted spot in the cast. It didn't.

It was foolish of me to try to appease all those other queens. I had my own shows every month and booked bigger crowds. I knew one day I could be a bigger fish in a bigger pond than Lincoln, but I kept my plans to myself.

One year after Alexus defeated me at Miss City Sweetheart, I looked up to see Faleasha entering the dressing room, carrying her massive silver makeup Caboodle and dragging her tall black suitcase. A few weeks before, at her house, she picked up a few clear bins next to her serger sewing machine and set them in front of me, then removed the lids to expose clusters of feathers, canisters of glitter, and bottles of tacky glue.

One of China Love's old dance costumes, which I'd gotten from a raid of her closet, served as an inspiration for my costumes for my second try competing in the Miss City Sweetheart Pageant. Back in high school, I used to buy China items I liked for myself from Wet Seal. Now my drag wardrobe consisted mostly of her old dance costumes, dresses I bought from vintage stores around Lincoln, and heels from Charlotte Russe, Wet Seal, and Deb, all of which I was proud to model at the mall. During most of my shows, I could look out at the audience and spot China's short, blunt-cut chestnut hair. She'd always be standing next to her hunky boyfriend of the moment. Her showing up meant the world to me, as did the occasional appearance of Ginger, Tanisha, and Granddad, who would record my early performances as I started to build a name for myself in the Lincoln drag scene.

From China's closet I selected a chocolate silk gown with a criss-crossed neckline to wear in the evening-gown competition; it fit my size-two body perfectly. I loved my black beauty—I was bronzed, naturally but in the most drag way possible, with subdued showgirl makeup applied by Faleasha. In a pageant, your outer beauty has to equal your inner beauty, brought out by whomever is helping you dress. Faleasha had shown up to serve as my dresser and stepped into the role of drag mother that evening, giving me her stamp of approval and stopping the other shady girls from getting to me. I could feel our unspoken camaraderie, the shared womanhood that separated us from the boys who were merely focused on an illusion. I was employing the tricks of the trade that I was learning, but on my own terms. I truly believed that I was Miss City Sweetheart, that I could embody the title in a way that was different from anyone who had been crowned before. I was Alexus's heir apparent, and my competition knew it too. Some drags collect crowns as validation, some are addicted to the art of competing—and some live, breathe, and embody the art form. The latter are my favorite queens.

Rocking back and forth on a swing, I was as close to the ceiling as I possibly could get. My legs dangled over the swing's edge, and I could barely resist leaping off as the driving disco beat and electric wah-wah of the guitar reverbed in the intro of "Lovin' Is Really My Game." With my springy Afro of curls and red velvet bodysuit that hugged my skin and showed off my bare sleek legs, I was a Foxxy Cleopatra goddess. I was ready.

The swing descended, and I stepped down onto the black tile of the stage in my five-inch stilettos with the barely there ankle straps. There was no other performer who could match me on the Q stage, who could wear the sexy, crazy-tall heels I wore to show off my self-proclaimed "ankles of excellence."

Looking into the eyes of the talent-competition judges, I twirled with fury and did a series of figure-skating hand tosses into the air. I whirled my right arm into what looked like a change-up softball pitch known as the windmill at the apex of the number, Dynamix and Inda Matrix's "Love Dominates" playing at top volume. Walking to the front of the stage, claiming it as my own, I declared: I will be the one who will dominate this love.

And I meant it.

I wasn't just the new showgirl whom everyone could boss around. I had found my sound as I ended the number with "I'm the diva, bitch." I walked offstage to thunderous applause. I'd shown every queen in that room that I was not to be messed with. I had dominated.

I melted to the floor when the emcee announced that I was the winner of the twenty-fifth Miss City Sweetheart Pageant.

The formers spun the crown a few times, a drag sign for good luck, before Alexus drove the first few long bobby pins into my hair, the other formers following suit to assist in securing the crown to my head. I performed my victory number, Jordin Sparks's "This Is My Now," through my tears.

Fresh off my Miss City Sweetheart triumph, I had decided to join up with six queer friends from campus to take a seventeen-hour drive from Lincoln, Nebraska, to Pensacola, Florida, for spring break. Our group resembled a *Real World* cast: a glossy gay, a more conservative-looking boyfriend, a lipstick lesbian, a butch softball-playing girlfriend named Katy, a thick Latino guy, and a gorgeous Latino brunette with hair for days. Corey and I rounded out the group with our Bert-and-Ernie "It's complicated" friendship, and of course I was the reigning black gay queen of the group. While planning our trip, Katy had told me that the Miss Pensacola Pageant would be happening while we were in town—and that she had signed me up. No questions asked.

I was confident I could win us some extra cash to spend on drinks for the week. The pageant was being held at a place called the Red Carpet Lounge. The girls did my makeup, playfully applying lipstick, blush, and eyeliner, while I looked around the beer garden that served as a makeshift dressing room. This, I realized, was a whole other barnyard. Ask any queen how glamorous dressing rooms are, and they rattle off a list of the worst places they have been forced to make work. Mine are a musty high school locker room, a disjointed gym teacher's office, a dank basement with a low ceiling, and a beer garden in Pensacola.

Once my makeup was done, I unzipped my suitcase and slipped into a strapless silver sequined dress I had borrowed from a former Miss City Sweetheart. All around me, queens were getting ready, and I noticed that they were painted drastically heavier than the style of my region, and their wigs were stacked so high it took the force of blow dryers to style them. Among the brawny bodies and chiseled faces, a Filipina goddess with amber hair and piercing eyes stepped through the space to a designated dressing area. I recognized her beauty from Myspace.

"Hi, Regine!" I called out, starstruck.

"Hi, darling," she said, looking at me as though we were old friends.

Most drag queens will respond with friendliness when greeted unless they're bitchy and only speak in quips and one-liners. To me, the best queens offer old-fashioned hospitality and kindness. But I've worked with some real bitches too, many of whom have run face-first into their bad karma, sometimes on television. I've seen more than one walk onto *RuPaul's Drag Race* with her head held high, only to leave in disgrace. Yes, that is a read.

Regine, along with legends like Maya Douglas, who worked at the Baton in Chicago, and the late Sahara Davenport and Britney Houston, who were regular fixtures on the New York nightlife scene, showed me that a full-time career as a performer was possible.

I knew I had the makings of a great queen, though I came in fourth place at the Miss Pensacola Pageant. There was no way they were going to let an unknown girl from out of town beat all the locals. You can be sure of that anywhere. As the winner was crowned, the queen standing next to me grabbed the microphone and shouted, "If you want to see a real pageant, come to Mobile, bitch!" With that, all hell broke loose. Folks in the audience stood and started throwing chairs.

I could see where this was headed, and I grabbed my suitcase and followed my crew out the door, managing to grab my score sheets in the midst of the chaos. Paging through them as we sped over the Pensacola Bay Bridge, I couldn't help but laugh. The head judge had written in all caps, "More makeup. This is drag!"

Trust and believe that the next day I called the pageant promoter to demand a refund of my entry fee. After witnessing the post-winner-announcement fiasco, she graciously complied. We continued on our vacation, watching dolphins, scaling the pier of Quietwater Beach and posing in front of a large conch, and consuming many buckets of crab legs. At night, I was the big spoon to Corey's little spoon, and I imagined what a future would look like if Corey and I were to end up as life partners. Corey was so on and off about his feelings for Kenny that Kenny had finally decided to move on. Our friendship, on the other hand, remained intact, and Corey and I promised each other that if it didn't work out with anyone else, we would end up together. Or our partners would just have to accept that we were in each other's lives.

"I can't believe they don't allow photography," Corey said as we passed a "No Photography Allowed" sign on the front door of the Emerald City, the gay club where we had ventured to see Regine perform the night after the fiasco at the Red Carpet Lounge.

"This is a military town," I told Corey. I appreciated the club's dedication to upholding its patrons' privacy, aware that not everyone has the privilege of being out in all spaces. I rolled my eyes as Corey continued his rant. We were in a town where "Don't ask, don't tell" was the law of the land, and people who were stationed at the naval base probably didn't want to be documented congregating at the local gay club. If they were outed, they would risk being dishonorably discharged from the military.

Corey soon forgot about his irritation as we made our way into the dark club. A few drinks in, and Regine took the stage, tossing her hair and lunging like she was JLo herself. Her legs were like jet engines, and her body was right and tight. I lifted some dollar bills to her, and she grasped the green with a grip as I took in, up close and personal, the big leagues of drag.

Weeks after we got back from spring break, Corey called me from an East Coast performance tour with his modern dance class. I missed him, but I could tell he was high, and that he was on what I considered a path that could destroy his perfect golden-boy image, his perfect life. Yet I vowed to myself I would not be left out of any self-exploratory experience.

I dreamed of New York, of dancing on the roofs of taxis like in *Fame* or attending the American Musical and Dramatic Academy like Roderick had. I longed for the beat of a city where I could play an instrument for change on a street corner like in *Raise your Voice*, or throw down in an epic dance battle in a massive club like in *Save the Last Dance*. A quick two-week visual-arts study-abroad trip to London and Paris served as a brief salve, but I knew I needed more. I knew the time had come to leave Nebraska, and that going to art school was my one-way ticket to Chicago, Philadelphia, or New York.

While I considered the University of the Arts in Philadelphia and the New School or NYU in New York City, I was daunted by the distance. Chicago seemed most feasible since it was the closest city to Omaha. I was only a couple of months into my reign as Miss City Sweetheart and began dropping hints about my desire to escape as I powdered my face in the dressing room.

Unsurprisingly, rumors of my pending exit began to swirl, so I called the owner of the pageant and one of Lincoln's oldest drag queens. "Could I still hold my title if I moved to Chicago but regularly came back to fulfill my obligations?" I asked.

"No," she said without beating around the bush.

I had a dilemma on my hands: either I could complete my reign in an unhappy drag dynasty situation, or follow my heart and move to a bigger city with more opportunity.

I chose the latter. Alexus and I performed in matching chocolate satin gowns at my goodbye show, relishing in the sisterhood we had built. Looking out across the crowded bar, my eyes grew misty. In my hands I clutched an overflow of dollar bills, each of which represented someone I had come to know, someone who had become second family. We were a congregation of sorts.

That night was one of the last times I would wear my crown before passing it on to my runner-up, who would take my place. I didn't care. I'd won the pageant, as history would show. Later, the retired queen would bring me a new crown as an attempt at reconciliation.

I knew I had to go and create the world I'd collaged on my wall from pictures pulled from *Vogue*, *Elle*, and *Harper's Bazaar*, with images of Naomi Campbell, Kate Moss, and models wearing Alexander McQueen and Manolo Blahnik. I had also placed a cluster of photos that included a headshot of Tara, my Eagle's Nest first love, with her hands atop a pink cashmere sweater, a photo I later recreated, plus a signed photo from the Punk Phunk Phairytale herself, the Princess, lying down with her feet up in the air, wearing a tall gray top hat, skintight gray tartan bodysuit, and a chunky red belt. She predated *RuPaul's Drag Race* and was one of Nebraska's native drag entertainers, performing in the *N'Joy Show* cast before placing in the top ten in the Entertainer of the Year competition and leaving to work five nights a week at Play Nashville. Her energy was dark and theatrical. I knew I possessed high-level performance chops just like her and could be the next drag queen who left Nebraska to work professionally.

But I was determined to get my college degree. To me, "female impersonation" was a performance art just like poetry, dance, and theater. I wrote as much in my admissions essay for Columbia College Chicago, to which there was a mass exodus of individuals from the University of Nebraska–Lincoln. After seeing video footage of students stomping runways at fashion shows and crowds packing into open-mic nights on the college website, I was sold. Drag should be taught on a collegiate level, I believed, and recognized as high art. To be a queen, you must cultivate specific skills, like acting, design, dance, public relations, and so much more.

I quickly mailed off my application, and Corey did too. Molly, a friend from Burke High School, was already at Columbia, and we felt comforted by knowing that we'd have a familiar face around. Even Kenny had mentioned that he was looking into CCC's creative writing program, though he ultimately decided against it as he felt like it would be completely starting over. I was willing to take that chance.

Corey and I didn't take a beat when we received our acceptance letters. We had only a matter of weeks to move.

∾

Chicago felt strangely familiar. Why, I wondered, did the swirling breeze fill me with so much emotion? Later, through Ancestry.com, I discovered that my great-grandfather was born in Cairo, Illinois, the southernmost city in the state. My grandfather never shared that detail with me, but he confirmed it and admitted that his father had later migrated to Detroit to be a foreman at Chrysler.

Darkness had fallen by the time we arrived at Midway Airport from Eppley Airfield in Omaha. A couple days after orientation, Molly invited Corey and me to her apartment to meet her roommate, named Korey, along with some other musical theater majors. As the party came into full swing, I stepped out onto the balcony. Beneath me, a rickety subway car left a trail of sparks and smoke along its track. In the distance, little clusters of light beamed in a navy-blue sky. Sears Tower loomed, like a fortress of Gotham City, or the tall LEGO structures I'd built as a child. I always stacked them too high, and inevitably they came tumbling down. That's what moving to Chicago felt like: an attempt to defy gravity. Yet it also felt like a reconnecting, a call from my lineage, like there was a presence from the past welcoming me home.

At the University of Nebraska, I had focused on a liberal arts curriculum, with a few vocal music classes sprinkled in. But after talking to Molly and her fellow majors from the theater department, I decided to go for the gusto and register for all musical-theater courses.

A few weeks later I found myself dragging my pink suitcase and a few less colorful ones, filled with all my life's belongings, underneath a bridge with rusting iron beams. Water from the previous night's downpour dripped onto the pavement. I'm sure I looked like a vagabond as I moved into the Buckingham, a high-rise student residence hall at 59 East Van Buren. Mismatched luggage or not, Corey and I had made it there in one piece. A mural of a large orb in what looked like a film reel cast in red paint sprawled across the side of the building, the perfect symbol of what my Chicago story could be. I felt grand walking through the revolving door, with its twenty-four-hour doorman, like I was entering the Mandarin Oriental or the St. Regis. But I couldn't really afford it. Other students had parental support that allowed them the luxury of not having to think about the cost of their college education, let alone housing or going out on the town for a deep-dish pizza and a movie. Not me.

I soon decided to downgrade to the University Center, where students who went to Columbia, DePaul, and Roosevelt lived. By doing so, I hoped to get a refund check like I had at Iowa Western and the University of Nebraska, but that didn't happen. Making ends meet was a struggle.

The other new students and I attended a welcome convocation in Grant Park, where balloons soared into the sky on a line flanked by pennants in what felt more like a mini Lollapalooza than a college gathering. It was an official introduction to the psyche of the institution that was named in honor of the 1893 World's Fair, a.k.a. the World's Columbian Exposition. I fit right in among the beatnik group, wearing a Rastafarian knit cap pushed back on my head, along with a green V-neck T-shirt and a hemp choker with glass beads.

I signed up for a tour of Chicago's gay neighborhoods, Andersonville and Boystown, and couldn't believe my *Queer as Folk* dream was about to come true.

The group exited the train in Andersonville and walked down North Clark Street to the feminist bookstore Women & Children First. "This is a predominately lesbian neighborhood," the tour guide told us. Next, we went to Boystown, nestled between the Belmont and Addison Chicago Transit Authority stations. We passed windows with mannequins wearing thin singlets, tiny colorful briefs, leather harnesses, and bulging jockstraps. I was somewhat shocked by both the suggestive and the overtly sexual nature of the displays—I certainly wasn't doing anything in the realm of kinky, at least not anything that I was willing to admit to at that point. I was still far too naive to appreciate sexual fluidity, and I wasn't yet comfortable in my body. I felt much more at home rummaging through the silver racks at the Brown Elephant, a thrift store benefiting Howard Brown Health Center. Its long show-room floor was filled with a plethora of couches in hideous shades of green and brown, as well as old hexagon dining tables for sale.

Across the street, on a tour, we passed a full-service kitchen, an expansive gym that hosted a weekly softball game, and a kids' play area, all at the Center on Halsted, a hub for the LGBTQ community, which also housed a local HIV hotline and HIV testing. I was daunted by the center, and I remember thinking it had nothing to offer me, that I had no reason to return. I was too proud to admit that I had needs.

Before leaving the neighborhood, I stepped into one of the adult stores and looked around. Sex toys, collars, and harnesses hung from the walls, and packages of edible underwear were prominently displayed on a table up front. I couldn't handle that either—I turned on my heel and walked out.

A huge audience had gathered at the Illinois Institute of Technology for the Intercollegiate Coming Out Ball, a grand event that rotated through local colleges and universities each year. I was so happy to be among friends, and I shrieked as, out of the darkness, a voluptuous diva emerged. Glorious ruffles adorned the shoulders of her floor-length red coat, and two rhinestone clips, set among her crown of blond satin fountain curls, sparkled in the spotlight. Her bangs swooped perfectly over one eye to frame her smooth face, and her long-lashed eyes seemed to pierce the crowd as she narrowed them, occasionally cracking a smile for high drama's sake. I was overwhelmed by her majesty. This diva, former Miss Continental Lady Tajma Hall (Taj), was the epitome of the might and caliber of the Chicago drag scene. She was the queen of Boystown and the host of the weekly Hydrag Revue, where anybody who was anybody performed, including legends Monica Munro and Mimi Marks.

Weeks later, as I was scouring the gay rags for a break into Boystown, I came across a contest for new performers: Chicago's Next Big Drag Queen. The prize was a booking in the Hydrag Revue at Hydrate Nightclub alongside Taj, Aurora Sexton, and Kelly Lauren— along with a cash prize of a hundred dollars. I surely needed the money and was chomping at the bit to step out and make my Chicago debut.

I'd planned to take the L to the event, not considering the fact that my gender presentation might put me at risk when traveling alone. I was feeling the fantasy, as the legendary children say, but my friends from my musical-theater history course were looking out for me that evening and refused to let me venture out by myself. They escorted me to the competition, though none of them were old enough to even get into the club. Kyle, a baby gay with acne-prone skin, short blond hair, and blue eyes, had been cast as the lead in the musical *Dames at Sea*—I was in the chorus—and on this outing, he dragged my pink suitcase down the long block of bars and restaurants on Halsted, giving me the space to lead the group with a fierce strut.

I was the de facto motha of the group in my short black wig of loose ringlet curls, a pink zebra-print wrap dress, and a french-tied chiffon scarf. I must have looked like I was a black Peggy Sawyer, suitcases and all. By the time we reached the venue, I was feeling more hesitant, especially after having to leave my entourage outside. I walked in, passed a large sunken bar, and proceeded to the back of the room in search of someone, anyone, some kind of lifeline. I took a seat at a large table with a long mirror behind it and, taking a breath, reminded myself once again that this was what moving to Chicago was all about.

I soon met Kaycee Ortiz, a transplant from South Dakota via Mobile, Alabama, who had also relocated for more show opportunities. She was open and inviting, tall with gams like a baobab tree, and her friendliness put me at ease.

The space was still mostly empty when the competition began, and for my first performance in a cropped Mary J. Blige asymmetrical bob, a periwinkle polka-dotted peplum dress, and a pair of silver curved-heel sandals, I felt like the sole entertainer. I used every inch of the stage to bop around, and soon enough the room started to fill. The pantheon of Chicago drag—Taj, Aurora, and Kelly—sat at the judges' table, reigning as trans goddesses who were being paid no matter how many people showed up.

I soon discovered that this was a world where the standard of performance was based on body enhancements, augmentation, fillers, and fantasy. Meeting Regine on spring break in Florida had provided a glimpse into this kind of pussycat drag, but I wasn't ready to perform alongside naked queens clad in pasties. Heightened sexuality was the center of the show. Except for Taj's performances—she was a gospel towel-throwing auntie who delivered Church of God in Christ and tributes to Jill Scott. I was in awe of her and set out to prove that a bright and bubbly church-raised girl next door from Nebraska could be an icon in the making too.

I felt liberated in this new city and often spent mornings getting ready for class by applying a full face of cosmetics, using the stage-makeup skills I was learning. I didn't have the words to completely describe what I was doing, but showing up to class in face was another attempt to further catapult myself into my soul's journey.

I'd signed up for ballet class, and holding my hands high above my head while classical music filled the air, I felt feminine, dainty, and limber. Corey was one of the principal dancers, along with Jaren, who is now internationally known as Shea Couleé and the winner of *RuPaul's Drag Race All Stars* five. They were pretty much neck and neck in terms of their ability to flawlessly execute any step, shuffle, or combo found in ballet, jazz, or tap. Our teacher, a Miss Sherman type, went around inspecting form, and I could hear her praise. "Excellent, Corey!" she'd say, followed by "Very good, Jaren" a minute later.

I usually received a correction or adjustment to my technique but otherwise was left alone. Until the day I was lying on the floor during one of our warm-ups.

"Can you please take your wig off?" the teacher said, a chill in her voice.

I looked up at the ceiling. I was taken aback but not surprised, and it took me a moment to collect myself. *My hair is pulled back out of my face,* I thought, *so what's the problem?* Ultimately, I had a Valentina moment and refused. My wig, my hair, my choice. Battle lines had been drawn, but the class carried on. I had won that fight.

While Corey succeeded in everything related to dance, he struggled with his singing. One afternoon, his vocal instructor berated him in front of the class, and at the end of the day, I met a defeated Corey who was all but ready to relinquish the fight. As I was in a similar battle with the ballet teacher, I would not let Corey be defeated by faculty whose job it was to weed out an overcrowded department.

Days later, on Halloween, Corey casually remarked that he was going to see the musical *Wicked* with a dancer from back home for whom I had the utmost disdain. I thought I'd heard the last of him when I'd left Lincoln, but now he was coming to Chicago for a mere twenty-four-hour escapade? Plus I had already made plans for our posse to go to the costume parade in Boystown. I was committed to making an appearance at all the right parties, and of course I had to have my best friend by my side. This grown-ass man, who was eighteen years our senior, was now infringing on *my* turf. I wouldn't stand for it. Corey was showing his Sagittarius centaur ass, and no doubt I would use my Scorpio tail to knock some sense into him.

No matter how deep I dug into my pockets, I could barely afford Subway's tuna special of the day, let alone *Wicked* tickets. The prize money I was winning at the Hydrate drag contest and the money I earned as a guest alongside the dolls didn't add up to much. I had applied for a server position at countless restaurants but couldn't even land an interview. Perhaps I was too gay for some people's taste.

My dream of sitting next to Corey, holding hands as we listened to Elphaba and Glinda singing "For Good" quickly faded. I couldn't put my finger on the dancer's intentions; he was openly HIV positive during a time when Corey was fully embracing the destruction of his golden-boy image, and I was worried that my best friend would make a decision he would later regret. I was also worried that he was going to get caught in a hit-it-and-quit-it situation, and I'd be the one left to pick up the pieces.

Now I can recognize how I had internalized and was perpetuating a stigma, and I am ashamed of my judgment of someone with HIV, someone who is part of the same already marginalized community to which I, too, belong. It's easy to fall back on bias and replicate patterns of oppression if you don't do the work to expand your awareness. Over the years I have apologized to this person, and they have always graciously accepted my apology.

Back then, however, Corey was busy flexing his independence, and the crack in our relationship deepened. We agreed to connect later at a party, after *Wicked* and the Halloween parade were over. I met up with Joe Carlson, an old friend I'd made while performing at Omaha Pride. He had just moved to Boystown with his then boyfriend, who ran an online gay radio station. They were both drag connoisseurs and lived in the heart of the neighborhood on Elaine Place. During my Chicago drag years, Joe would be my most ardent supporter.

With those two friends, the hours quickly passed. As the Halloween parade wound down, I ventured to the party where Corey and I had planned to meet up. I arrived before him and mingled while awaiting his appearance.

Minutes later, I saw him enter, a tall figure shuffling in behind him. I was instantly infuriated. I decided to ignore the dancer's presence completely, and Corey and the dancer took the hint and soon left the way they'd come. In the wee hours of the morning, Corey and I exchanged heated words outside our dorm. He was mad that I hadn't been welcoming, and I was upset that he'd brought that tagalong, that we didn't get to spend Halloween together.

"No, no, no, no!" I yelled, throwing my tiny purple Victoria's Secret purse to the ground. The sound of my camera smashing to pieces only made me angrier. We had never fought like that before.

I woke up with a humiliation-and-regret hangover. I was too upset to be proud, so I called Corey first thing, and he invited me to a coffee shop.

"I think I want to go home," he said, staring into the dark abyss of his coffee.

"Was . . . was it our fight?" I asked. I suspected that he felt broken down by the constant auditioning, that he was tired of being a small fish in a big pond.

"I just think that maybe city living isn't for me," he answered after a moment, avoiding my gaze.

"Obviously, I want you to stay," I told him, "but I will support you no matter what."

Utterly embarrassed, I called his family and apologized for losing my cool and to claim responsibility for my role in the saga.

"I know it's hard to believe now, but things will work out, and your friendship will probably grow stronger," his mom told me, saying exactly what I needed to hear. The pressures of the city weighed on me too, but her love and acceptance lightened the load.

I couldn't quite wrap my head around what life was going to be like without Corey. At the same time, optimism was in the air as we celebrated the election of Barack Obama, the first African American president, on November 4, 2008. I was filled with not just hope but the kind of joy that only the unexpected can bring. I would be alone in Chicago, but I'd have to buck up, rally a new confidence, be myself and more present than ever. I didn't have a choice. It was sink or swim.

NINE

Time for a Change

Recognizing the stigma about HIV that I had been holding on to, I vowed to further educate myself. My conscience still weighed on me for my ill will toward Corey's friend, the HIV-positive dancer. I spent a lot of time reflecting on the horrified expressions of people when they looked at me back in Nebraska, of the sanctimonious way people said, "I'm praying for you." I imagined what they were thinking: the next time they saw me it would be to say goodbye as I wasted away in a hospital bed, like the character Andrew Beckett, played by Tom Hanks in the movie *Philadelphia*. Maybe they would even get to claim that they had led me to Jesus Christ, or would bear witness to a final renunciation of my life labeled full of sin.

And here I was, judging someone else. Here I was, the ultimate hypocrite.

I signed up for the class Gay, Lesbian, Bisexual, and Transgender History in the United States and a Biology of AIDS course that counted as a science credit. For the first class, my professor, a truly empathetic educator, taught us the history of organizations like AIDS Coalition to Unleash Power (ACT UP), the activist group whose members put their lives on the line to demand effective treatment for AIDS. Their activism literally took flight in 1988 when ACT UP members scaled the FDA building to demand justice for the thousands of lives that had been lost. It was another piece of history that was entirely new to me, and which I now believe should always be included in the conversation about LGBTQ organizing and the quest for liberation. The need for a cure to this epidemic that has taken the lives of millions of people around the world remains urgent.

I remembered Pedro Zamora, an AIDS activist on the third season of *The Real World*, which aired in 1994, when I was just nine years old. I had been so inspired when I saw the episode in which he married his black partner. Although I didn't fully understand what that meant at the time, I tucked the image away in the folder of all things gay in my mind. They were proof that an interracial, gay, HIV-positive couple was worthy of love. That the LGBTQ community is worthy of love.

It was 2009 when I finally got my first paid booking on the Boystown strip from Miss Foozie, the pineapple queen. She wore only one wig, which looked like a piece of asparagus sprouting from the top of her head. She gallivanted around Boystown, usually with colorful rings on every finger and a baby-doll drop-waist dress made from funky bolts of fabric. Her variety show was held at Circuit, the biggest club on Halsted. It was a Latino nightclub that had the largest stage on the block and was across the street from the Kit Kat Lounge, where actress Angelica Ross worked several times a month.

I bounced around the room like a gazelle with my peach perched, performing Beyoncé's "Diva" in a pair of gold pumps that wrapped around my ankles. I felt dignified in that, for this paid gig, I didn't have to compete and try to figure out how much cash I was going home with based on audience applause. Joe Carlson brought several of his Nokia colleagues, and by coincidence, some folks from Nebraska were in town and came to watch the show. I was thrilled and hoped they'd run and tell the queens back home that I was working and turning it out. I knew they'd be asking questions and poking around for shade.

One paid booking wasn't enough of a big break, so I did also have to compete in the contest circuit at both Roscoe's Tavern and Spin Nightclub. I had started making a little money working on commission at the AKIRA clothing store in Wicker Park, Chicago's equivalent to Williamsburg in New York or Silver Lake in LA. I clicked around in heeled sandals all day, serving customers as one of the store's best salespeople. Working retail provided me quick access to the kind of cute, trendy clothes and shoes on discount that many of the real housewives on Bravo were wearing. I was hired to perform at store parties and at Pride in exchange for shoes. I was glad to have the opportunity to earn an extra Benjamin too, in drag, after working my shifts at the store.

Later that year, Miss Foozie and I met again when she hosted the Coming Out Ball at Columbia, and I was booked as the talent. I found myself standing in the same position from which I had watched Taj, except I wasn't regal in red like Taj; I wore only a tiny cheetah swimsuit from AKIRA with cutouts. I came out roaring, performing Kat DeLuna's "Animal." My bangles sounded like cymbals crashing when I clapped my hands in between spins and struts. That same evening, I filmed my second audition for *RuPaul's Drag Race*.

I had emailed Ru in my first weeks in Chicago, asking for her advice even before the creation of her show. She responded:

I don't give advice or tips anymore because it would undermine your own natural learning process, plus if you're anything like me, you're gonna have to take some chances and get knocked around a few times to make the lesson stick. I will say this, there is no set method for breaking into "the biz," but that's

really the good news because you can create your own unique success story. Just make
sure you're prepared by learning your craft
and knowing thy self. If you can dream it, you
can be it.

Good Luck,

RuPaul

I wish I would have printed RuPaul's email out and referred to it more often, as I think it would have saved me some heartache. She was right. The business was about to knock me around.

Spin Nightclub stood like a tank at the corner of Belmont and Halsted and served as the official entrance to the "gayborhood." Every year at Pride, a large rainbow flag was tacked across the entire building, which made it look like a fortress to anyone standing underneath. Robert Hoffman, the club manager, swooped me up after several contest victories, hiring me to work coat check in drag. There I met Dida Ritz, another new and immensely talented diva on the strip. She could hoist herself high into the air, moving like an Olympian, all while doing epic aerodynamic hair swings. Taj instantly claimed her as her drag daughter. Taj's blessing carried weight—Dida was soon added as a permanent cast member in the Hydrag Revue and worked with me, Saya Naomi, and Kaycee, the other young black performers on cast at Spin. That was my first regular paid gig on the strip.

It didn't feel like work to me. A "banjee" look best describes my drag at the time. My favorite outfit entailed jagged pink leg warmers from a Pebbles Flintstone Halloween costume, an oversized navy sweater I wore as a dress, a tie depicting various scenes of the Crucifixion paired with a cluster of Betsey Johnson pearls, and colorful bangles climbing my arms. We young black queens didn't take lightly the opportunity to walk around the bar in face, wielding clipboards to collect emails from revelers, since each of us had fought to get there. Up until that point, the unspoken rule was that there could only be one Latin queen and one black queen, but we broke it—we saw each other as friends, not competitors.

Dollar-drink night was the most diverse night on the strip; there was something for everyone. The Spin bartending staff consisted of several stud and high-femme lesbians, reality stars Shane Landrum from *Road Rules* and Dustin Erikstrup from *Big Brother*, and a rotating list of barbacks who ran around in tiny shorts and baseball socks. I was soon added as one of the rotating hosts of the Friday-night show, taking turns with Debbie Fox, Mercedes Tyler, Dida, Saya, and Phoenix (Phi Phi) O'Hara. Phi was a costume genius and could recreate anything Lady Gaga, Nicki Minaj, or any other pop diva did within a few days' time. And yes, her television persona definitely matched the girl I sat next to in the dressing room. Simply out of spite, she'd go out before me and perform the number I'd said I was going to do. Then, the next evening, she'd do my makeup exquisitely. I never knew which Phoenix would rise out of the ashes, but she is a legendary talent, like many Texas girls who came up in the pageantry tradition.

One evening after a midnight performance, a spontaneous show broke out. Dida traipsed upon the long wooden planks in alpaca heeled boots, her twisted braid strewn with hues of pink. Saya was out of face from her usual bad-girl nasty drag but was still moving her hands real sissy with it. Dida cracked her fan at her, cheering her on. I stood in the corner with my hair slicked up into a pompadour like an early Janelle Monáe, wearing a purple bodysuit, red fishnet tights, and purple heels. As "I Want to Dance with Somebody" came through the speakers, I leaped out from behind the tall metal racks, twirling and dancing. Saya and Dida looked on in delight, seeing a formerly quiet Precious come out of her shell. I was no longer Precious to them after that night; they started calling me Diamond.

Later, male dancers stood around, eyeing us while I waited for my payout from the booking manager, Robert. I had begun to notice that he attempted to pit the girls on cast against one another. He held bookings over our heads to try to get us to comply with his wishes. I vehemently refused to give in but can't say the same for every Ru girl who came through the club in those early seasons.

Instead of heading straight home that night, Saya invited me out to after hours at Berlin, an alternative dance club open until four in the morning. I tried to decline as usual, since I had class early, but ultimately decided to indulge.

At Berlin's after hours, people moved around with ease and danced to electronic music. At two in the morning, the crowd was lively and diverse: showgirls from the Baton, the club kids, men looking to take home a trans woman, and everyone in between. I was among industry people who actually went out after their shifts and enjoyed the nightlife. Saya whispered to me, "If you want to build your name in this scene, you gotta go out and meet people and support others' parties so they come to yours." I credit her with generously giving me that important piece of advice.

I thought dancing on top of the bars and getting paid to perform was my dream. But working for a man who routinely degraded me was taking its toll, and between school and my various jobs across town, I wasn't taking care of myself. I had completely stopped eating at school, since I found the food in the dining hall so unappetizing, instead grabbing the occasional Subway sandwich after a night of hosting and taking shots. I was just surviving, pure and simple.

A few months later, a coworker who liked to vogue began transitioning. As soon as I heard, I walked up to them and said, "I think I'm that too," letting the statement roll off my lips and, like a weight, fall to the ground. Saya told me that a manager, one who made the job bearable, was trans too. I was shocked, and though I didn't have the ability to label myself yet, I could cling to the fact that people I cared about could.

A new part of me was unfolding, but I was losing a part of myself too.

On my way to work at the club one evening, I was stomping the pavement in white pumps, white square sunglasses, and a small-brimmed white hat when I ran into a trio of homeless trans girls who usually milled near the Belmont train station, working as escorts late into the night. I stopped for hugs as usual and pulled out my phone to mark the moment. I could smell my perfume, which I'd lovingly applied before leaving the house, and I hoped it conveyed my love for them, just as I had felt breathing in the pastor's wife's perfume years ago. We gathered close, and the roughness of their lace front wigs gently brushed across my chest. I later uploaded the photos on Facebook and titled the album "a reminder to myself." Many in the neighborhood viewed those girls as a nuisance, though of course they were only doing what everyone does—working to support themselves, creating a community, making a home. The only difference between us was that I worked in the nightclub where men came to find me and tip me onstage, not on the street.

I was a lot more sheepish than many of the girls who went on "dates" as we called them. The cute boy with black curly hair and a charming smile who bartended down the street from Spin at Minibar was enough for me, and he accepted me as both genders.

One evening, as I ran up the large staircase from the basement to the Spin stage, I could see that the girls had gathered outside the large glass window on the corner, where they had a perfect view inside. I twirled for those girls alone, knowing that I could have easily been one of them. I had housing because I was a student, my student loans providing me an incredible view of Sears Tower from the twenty-seventh floor of my dorm, but really I was only one shake away from homelessness. I may not have been escorting, but I was traveling alone late at night, on empty subway trains from Boystown to the South Loop in full drag on dark streets. All it took was being in the wrong place at the wrong time with the wrong person, and I could very well get hurt, if not killed. Most of the time, however, I could ignore the fact that my life was in danger.

I often visited the office of Brian Shaw, the chair of the theater department, to discuss my interdisciplinary theater and cultural studies major. Every student was required to do an internship before graduation, and I had made it clear that I was interested in further study of representations of homosexual identity in performance. I watched *Paris Is Burning* and *The Boys in the Band* and was inspired by artists like Willi Ninja, Kevin Aviance, Candis Cayne, Tommie Ross, and Octavia St. Laurent. I was encouraged by a quote from queer performance artist Tim Miller, who said, "If you make work from autobiographical conceit, one has the notion that our lives matter." I noted the conundrum in Octavia St. Laurent's lifting her hand along a wall and pointing to the visage of the model Paulina in *Paris Is Burning*. She noted how unfair it was that the world didn't provide the same opportunities for the kind of Virginia Slims beauty she embodied.

On a Friday evening, I received an email from Brian: "I just came from a meeting with SK Kerastas from About Face Theatre. They would be happy to discuss a possible internship. Don't be shy. Enjoy your weekend, young sir."

Brian and I had a relationship that regularly included this kind of banter, so I'm not sure if the "young sir" was a clock or not. Regardless, About Face Theatre wound up being the perfect vehicle to bring me back into alignment with my Anytown roots and passion for education. I became their workshop intern, assisting the facilitation of Saturday workshops for LGBTQ youth, and helping to develop scripts around issues affecting young people with queer teaching artists Patrick Andrews, AJ Jennings, Armand Fields, and NIC Kay. We were all so different from one another, but SK empowered us to lead. They later shared with me that, during an initial meeting about bringing me on as an intern: "He told me, 'We have this kid we don't know what to do with,' and what they don't understand is you're queer." SK became a guide, a mentor, and later a friend as I ascended the ranks of the company from educational workshop intern to teaching artist to artistic associate, over the course of five years.

I was standing on the small stoop of Roscoe's six months after the fiasco that was the previous year's Miss Roscoe's Pageant when I spotted Taylor, a friend and trans woman of color whom I'd met through Kaycee and with whom I routinely flirted, standing across from the 7-Eleven. A trace of blond could be seen on the ends of her small 4c curly Afro. She truly served on days when she got Egyptian blowouts, and her healthy, moisturized strands lit up any room she walked into. I often scored invites to parties at her apartment across the street from Spin, where I met a wide community of trans folks from across Chicago. Her parties usually ended with me casually performing comedic routines, carrying on to the nth degree on her balcony as people walking on the street below became both subject and audience. Even though she was an introvert, she was a great connector for people like me.

That night, she invited me over to her friend's place, a beautiful three-story greystone home with long plank wood floors and an open floor plan, located near the Halsted strip. I sat on a long wraparound couch as a sly fellow in a button-down and jeans sized me up and a tall redhead with freshly moussed hair pranced out from one of the two bedrooms. Both were sex workers. They mentioned that they were looking for a summer roommate, which felt like a stroke of luck since I was in the midst of apartment hunting and nothing had yet materialized. I imagined not having to drag my suitcase from downtown on the train anymore or what it would feel like being able to walk home in face after my gigs. "I'll give it some serious consideration," I said nonchalantly before we left for the bar to watch the Tuesday-night drag contest.

I was thinking of the nights competing in the preliminaries to the Miss Roscoe's Pageant. I thought I was going to win.

The evening of the pageant, I felt tall and resplendent after having my face beat by two-time Miss Continental Pageant titleholder Victoria LePaige and that victory was certain. If anyone evoked Dominique Deveraux, it was her, and this was the closest I had gotten to perfecting such an illusion.

The Princess had briefly moved to Chicago and agreed to dress me for the pageant. Wearing a fur coat, sexy see-through black lace bodysuit, knee-high black stiletto boots, Dior sunglasses, a purple-and-blue cotton-candy wig, and several belts hanging off my waist, I served as a true hip-hop diva. I was a bad bitch, tossing my fur coat around as I performed to "How Many Licks" by Lil' Kim on the small stage, followed by *Glee*'s version of "Don't Stop Believin'" as my second talent number, hearkening back to my high school show-choir days. As three backup dancers in red-and-black costumes lifted and spun me in the air toward the end of the number, I looked out over the crowd and felt I was within minutes of cementing my name into legacy.

I knew it was going to be a battle between me and Kaycee, who had come out with twink boys on leashes and performed Rihanna's "Disturbia." For crowning, I wore an electric-blue eighties prom dress and stacked curls, looking like the oil painting *A Woman in Blue*, believed to be a portrait of the Duchess of Beaufort. Standing on the stage with four others, I waited for the other three girls to be dismissed so Kaycee and I could be announced as the finalists. Frida, the longtime host and another staple of the Boystown neighborhood, stood tall in a yellow gown to announce the rankings.

"In fifth place . . . Kaycee Ortiz!"

I was shocked. I kept my gaze straight ahead as she continued. "In fourth place . . . Precious Jewel!"

Now I was dumbfounded, gobsmacked, bewildered. But I put a smile on my face—they weren't going to see me crack. I knew what I had done, how loud the crowd had roared. Meanwhile, next to me stood someone who had attempted a flimsy recreation of Lady Gaga's metal-ring dress. I kept on smiling as she and two other mediocre white girls placed third, second, and first. In the end, Debbie Fox was crowned.

Kaycee went full Crystal LaBeija, telling everyone in the dressing room that the contest was fixed. I let her do all the talking and walked out with that same smile on my face, as put together as an airline stewardess.

The next day Taj publicly posted on my Facebook wall, "I wondered why things kept happening to prevent me from being there . . . NOW I KNOW!!! I have heard from numerous people how fabulous you were! Be proud and move on . . . this was not YOUR loss!"

I responded, "This was a lesson to me. I dipped my foot in the water for a trial run for something bigger, my eye is still on the prize, and I intend to cast my stone even further . . . as much shock as I'm in right now, a message coming from a true legend, a former Miss Continental and former Miss Gay USofA means the world to me!"

After that, I kept running into Debbie on the strip. Anytime there was a contest, I knew it was going to come down to me and her—and they were going to crown her. We were friends, but I knew I had been robbed, and I believed that, as a Latin American performer, Debbie benefited from white-passing privilege, along with the fact that she was a boy and open about it. Later that summer, Debbie stunned on the Roscoe's Pride float in a gorgeous pink ruffled dress, the crown glimmering on her head. She has gone on to be a celebrated queen in the neighborhood, and I have continued on my journey of being me. And that is no shade!

Still, after that debacle, I vowed to never put myself in that situation again. Never again would the neighborhood play me for a fool. Never again would I let my identity and my success get wrapped up in validation from just one block.

⁓

Diane Perry, the former administrative assistant at the National Conference for Community and Justice, joined Ron and Valerie Love and me on the morning of my graduation from Columbia College Chicago. Earlier that year, Diane had given me a loan for the remainder of my tuition for the semester, which my financial aid didn't quite cover, a common problem that I'd seen cause other students to leave school before graduation. After exchanging pleasantries, I raised the prospect of walking across the commencement stage as Precious. I felt it was actually she who was graduating, and she deserved to be celebrated. Valerie nudged against it, but Diane urged me to follow my instinct.

I debated about what I was going to do as I walked down the block to my dorm on the twenty-seventh floor. The easiest option was to wear my white button-up shirt. That's what I did—but I accessorized with a bright white-and-pink cheetah-print scarf.

I felt a deep sense of regret about my choice, however, during the ceremony. In the moment after I shook the dean's hand, I was disappointed that I hadn't followed my instinct. Two years later, I rewalked in the ceremony as Precious, wearing gold heels, a short AKIRA dress with planets and monsters on it, and large spiral earrings. My boss, Edwin, and his partner at the time, David, along with colleagues Rayna, Lex, and Kevin, joined me to celebrate. When the director of International Student Affairs, who had watched my journey from day one, read my name and shouted out, *"Precious Davis!"* I leaped forward for a hug, knowing that was how it should have been the first time around.

I accepted the invitation to move in for the summer with the two full-time sex workers on West Roscoe. One of my new roommates had a doctor for a sugar daddy and lived mostly in Dallas, while the other stayed in the room across the hall from mine—which meant I often had to disperse at a moment's notice. I was essentially appointed the social chair of the home and tasked with throwing large parties on their dime. In return, I had cheap rent and was mere steps away from the North Halsted strip; now that I was no longer a full-time college student, I could fully immerse myself in the scene and nightlife. I walked to my gigs and invited one and all to come to our epic after-hours house parties, where I finally mustered up the courage to start acting grown and lightly rendezvousing in the dark.

One morning after a late night hosting after hours, I put on some neon-green-and-black swim trunks and took a seat in the bright sunshine on the wooden stairs with their peeling black paint out front. The family directly next door usually appeared and disappeared to retrieve the newspaper, keeping their heads down, refusing to engage with me or my roommates or our many visitors to our house of misfits. A married couple—a hunky jock and a silver fox—had just moved in next door to them, and I could see the jock coming down the block, his two large dogs pulling him along. Walking by, he threw a quip in my direction. "OK, fish," he said. "I'm Steven." He was wearing a pair of basketball shorts without underwear and giving full swinging Richard.

Before he disappeared up the driveway, he extended an invite to his housewarming party.

I arrived to find a mostly upper-echelon crowd of elite gays gathered, along with a gaggle of cute-faced boys from around the neighborhood. I'd dressed for the party in drag, wearing a short taffeta black dress with a fabric flower tacked near the bottom of my torso. I sashayed past a black woman who haughtily stood near the gate clutching her small late-Speedy Louis Vuitton bag.

"Some people didn't know whose house they were going to tonight!" she said, insinuating that it was disrespectful that I had shown up in drag. As soon as Steven caught a glimpse of me, however, he yelled, "Yes, *ma'am*!" After that greeting, I was treated as an honored guest, and I paid that woman dust the rest of the evening. Eventually, the party moved outside and Dida, Saya, and I took turns jumping into a game of jump rope. We were the young black gays on the block and fought for every booking, the right to walk into bars and not pay cover, and respect. Steven felt at home, jumping in behind me, kicking off his flipflops, and squealing, *"Woo, woo!"*

I began to spend time on their stoop several nights a week. I soon found that Steven was a drag enthusiast, and our meeting was no ordinary encounter. It was a divine soul meeting. We talked about our family histories, our mutual interest in social issues, and our drive to find our life's purpose. He loved my youthful whimsy, and he openly expressed love for trans women. He was ahead of his time. I became like a daughter to him, and he always had a seat for me at their long dining table, where I enjoyed home-cooked meals of fried chicken, mashed potatoes, green beans, and flowing red wine. Sometimes there were even chocolate-chip cookies made from scratch, and he often played DVDs of the Miss Continental Pageant in the background.

~

I loved the life I was creating for myself in Chicago, but after a while, I decided to return to Nebraska to regroup. I call this my interlude.

Back in Nebraska, I moved in with a friend of a friend, a woman who smoked weed and burned incense every day, and who otherwise spent her time making large works of art out of tiny mirror pieces on canvas. Now that I was no longer living at a party house, I was able to do some self-reflection and focus on self-care. My roommate urged me to invest in simple tasks like making myself breakfast every day, and to massively scale back my large social circle. Of course, I was still a diva and performed in the local scene. I took a break from the performance character of Precious Jewel, but didn't go back to my birth name, Nathan, which I thought was disingenuous by that point. Instead, I became something in between: Nashon. I was reaching new conclusions about my gender fluidity and had started to identify as genderqueer. I no longer saw drag as the only way to express my feminine gender-nonconforming identity.

I was able to tap into my roots as a theater educator and taught after-school workshops for middle schoolers in Lincoln. The satisfaction I gained from those workshops reminded me how important it was to be connected to empowering young people, and with that clarity, I realized that my former hometown was no longer the right place for me.

After about six months, I returned to Chicago with a newfound confidence and a grander vision for myself that went beyond the nightlife scene. Though I continued to perform in Chicago, I didn't have the same need for accolades and validation. Despite my poor credit, I got my own apartment for the first time, scoring a place off the lake. I worked facilitating workshops that combined social justice and theater at About Face Theatre.

And for the first time, I began to truly feel like an independent adult.

Shortly after moving back to Chicago, I learned that Anytown, which I credit with providing me with my initial awakening to social justice, had a summer camp out of their St. Louis chapter and was seeking camp counselors. I jumped at the opportunity to work there. It was one of the best decisions I've ever made.

I felt like I had reconnected with my true self, my true passion and purpose. The camp allowed me to present as my authentic self, jumping in and out of "face" in between designing and leading strut workshops for the youth. In St. Louis, I met a core group of the queer community who were deeply engaged in social justice work. Working alongside them solidified my desire to lean into that work once I returned to Chicago.

~

After St. Louis, I went back to performing at Spin Nightclub in Boystown, the white gay enclave in Chicago. There were sex workers all over the neighborhood, and especially outside the club. It was right off Belmont, which was a major thoroughfare.

The LGBTQ center and the Broadway Youth Center were within a several-block radius along this strip, and because both places provided services and programming like free meals, HIV testing, and prevention resources for queer youth, lots of black and brown queer youths were often milling around. They tended to travel in groups, mostly for safety purposes, which made them extremely visible. Because they were too young to get into the club, they'd vogue outside on the sidewalk, and generally take up space. I connected with them very deeply and would frequently come outside and cheer them on. We'd hug and take pictures together and have a grand old time. I wanted to let them know that they were cherished, at least by me.

Around that time, the mostly white gay residents of that neighborhood created a local campaign to Take Back Boystown, which I learned about in the press and at a huge community meeting. The inherent racism of the endeavor was thinly veiled; its goal was to essentially remove the black and brown queer youths from the area. The campaign's official rationale was that a string of robberies in the area must be related to the Center on Halsted, and obviously the perpetrators were the youth, who just so happened to be people of color. I was shocked and horrified to hear firsthand at the meeting the onslaught of hateful comments like "We don't want those kids in the neighborhood" and "They're making it dangerous here." But I lived in the neighborhood myself and knew those kids, and I didn't for a second believe they were responsible for the crimes. By that time, I had witnessed all types of illegal activities, including rampant illicit drug dealing and use in the club scene, to which the meeting attendees seemed to turn a blind eye.

That meeting was a wake-up call for me, and in many ways, witnessing the darkness of that campaign led me to an epiphany: I needed to pursue a job working with the youths at the center they were pointing the finger at.

I applied for a vocational training job that had recently been posted, but at the interview, the executive director told me that he thought I'd be perfect for a different position. As it turned out, he wanted me to oversee outreach for HIV prevention as the center's youth coordinator. It was my first full-time, salaried job after college, and I wasn't making much, but I was so excited to be doing the work that I felt called to do—even though I was doing it as a boy.

I led a program called the Breakfast Club, a series of conversation sessions about social issues or whatever the youths wanted to talk about. The kids would be fresh off "night binges," doing sex work, or sleeping outdoors at Lake Michigan, where they tended to gather, and they'd come straight to the center in the morning for our sessions. They were an everyday example of what it means to live in your truth, especially the black trans girls! They became a constant source of inspiration.

Working in a professional office environment for which I had to dress up every day, combined with bearing witness to the trans teens who were living so courageously, confirmed for me once and for all the feeling that I wanted to present as a woman. After a few weeks on the job, I allowed myself to voice my wish to be sitting in that job as Precious. When I said this to my coworker, who was the manager for the Breakfast Club program, he responded, "And why can't you?"

The very next day, I went to work as Precious, rocking a 1980s-era power suit, complete with huge shoulder pads. After that, I began living as a trans woman. Initially, I was reluctant about using hormones to transition because I felt like altering my body was somehow a violation of the religious beliefs I still harbored. Once I realized that I was still dealing with some internalized stigma, I was able to let go in order to be the person that I truly was.

When I finally leaned into the hormones, I felt a cool fill my body, and an alignment clicked into place. As a proud member of the social media generation, I was publicly documenting my transition without even knowing it.

Shortly thereafter, I requested that my name be officially changed in the center's email system to Precious Davis. Precious Jewel was a known entity in the drag community, but now I wanted people to get to know me as Precious Davis. But the center refused. There was no official policy, but despite that, I was told that unless I legally changed my gender, I couldn't officially go by Precious Davis in their system. It was ridiculous, and I now understand that it was also classist, as it cost five hundred dollars to get a legal name change. I didn't have anywhere near that amount of money since most of my paycheck went to rent. It was a frustrating time for me because the very place where I felt I could do the most to support LGBTQ youths was the same place that was getting in the way of me living in my most authentic truth.

Despite their backward policy, I was living my full diva fantasy, clacking down the halls in my heels and power-suit skirts, and I was becoming something like a local celebrity. I received a lot of attention for being the center's first trans full-time employee, and I did photo spreads and interviews for local outlets, including the *Chicago Reader* and the *Chicago Tribune*.

Right around then, I revived my dream of being on *RuPaul's Drag Race*. Over my many years of performing, I had gotten so close to being on the show; most recently, they had even included my picture on an editing card that read Next On throughout the entire first episode of the season three casting special. I took it as a sign to keep auditioning, even though I had already started transitioning, and the show didn't cast people who were openly trans. I took a new picture of myself dressed as a boy for this final audition to conceal the fact that I was trans. I thought it would be worth it if I got on the show, since that kind of exposure had the potential to dramatically change my life, financially and otherwise. But I didn't make it again, and so I wrote a blog post about what I had learned from auditioning so many times. I finally learned that I had the power to create my own platform, that I didn't need Ru's platform to validate me or to be successful.

Two years later, Myles Brady walked into my office. I didn't know it then, but it would be a fateful day.

Myles worked for a black LGBTQ organization called Affinity, which focused on creating health and wellness services for queer folks who lived on the South Side of Chicago. Kim Hunt, the executive director of Affinity, had given him a list of people to get in touch with if he wanted to get involved in outreach for trans youth. My name was on that list.

"Are you interested in some kind of . . . research or study?" I asked. Countless people had come in seeking similar access, and I was very protective of my young people. Working with homeless youths every day had become a new form of ministry for me. It reminded me of my youth work at church, except now I was able to provide an atmosphere of unconditional acceptance. I felt such kinship with the people who walked through the center's doors every day, such compassion for them and their daily experiences.

"I want to work with trans youth," Myles said. Sensing my skepticism, he continued, "I'm trans too."

Honestly, I was shocked. I couldn't tell. He had passing privilege as a cisgender man.

After that first meeting, he pursued me romantically. He made his interest in me very clear. I'd see him around at community events like the Trans 100 reception, for which Laverne Cox came to town, and he'd always make his case for why we should go out on a date. I told him over and over that I wasn't interested, that I was focused on my job and had no time to date, that these young people were my life. I was so immersed in the work that I believed to be my calling. I wasn't simply dodging him for no reason!

He'd show up fairly often—he was persistent if nothing else! One Friday evening, he invited me out to a sushi dinner, and I finally gave in. I thought I would go out with him once, then ghost him, and that would be that. But that wasn't the case.

At that dinner, we learned that we were both scheduled to go to the Philadelphia Trans Wellness Conference for our respective jobs. I had attended the conference before, but it would be his first time. All of us trans girls who worked in prevention went every year, to kiki and hang out. Lots of other queer people of color went just to socialize, to be in community once a year. At that time it was *the* place where trans people in organizing gathered.

Right before I boarded the plane, Myles sent me an email that consisted of only the subject line: "I can't wait to see you in Philly."

That year, Janet Mock was the keynote speaker, and by the first afternoon, Myles had already connected with her, asking her to put a good word in for him with me. At the time, I was struggling with the notion of two trans people dating each other. How would it even work? It was one of my reasons for hesitating, even though I had messed around with one trans guy in the club scene. But this felt like it could be different. I was also very guarded after having a few romantic friendships that weren't holistically fulfilling. I was skeptical that I could have a fully realized romantic relationship, especially with another trans person.

When Janet Mock and I sat down for lunch, I shared my concerns about Myles with her, specifically about the prospect of two trans people being in a relationship together. She told me that it was important to see other trans people the same way we ask the world to see us. It was as if a cloak had been removed from my eyes. It was such a life-altering revelation for me, another moment in which I had to face my internalized stereotypes and prejudice against another member of the community head-on.

While I was having dinner later that night, Myles came in, looked at me, and said, "I think you're the most beautiful woman I've ever seen, and I want to take care of you for the rest of your life." My heart was aflutter. We went back to the room, there were fireworks, and the rest is history. We left Philly as a couple.

～

Back in Chicago, Myles and I started to date in earnest, like Dwayne and Whitley from *A Different World*. I was still performing as a showgirl and working at the center. I learned that he had been born and raised on the South Side of Chicago. His mom was a child psychologist, and his dad was a speech pathologist—his family represented black excellence in the Cosby-esque sense.

I was falling in love with this man from a completely different background. He had a notable sense of pride in being a black man, in the black man's strength, power, and potential, and his politics reflected his beliefs. He was a big proponent of transformative justice and prison abolition. Coming from a biracial family, having been a black man, and having had terrible experiences with black men, I harbored a lot of prejudice. Myles would simply say, "That's not all of us." He completely shattered my perceptions of black masculinity, and I'm forever grateful that he did.

He lived in this gorgeous condo in Hyde Park over the lake, and I'd go to his house after my gigs. Up until that point I had lived in Lakeview, a mostly white gay neighborhood, so I felt like I had come home in the diverse neighborhood in Hyde Park. Myles and I had a fully realized, passionate relationship; he loved all parts of me. Myles finally introduced me to the feeling of true unconditional love, and that finally allowed me to fully love and embrace all parts of myself, even my traumatic history.

We became a kind of power couple seemingly overnight. He began work at Howard Brown Health as their transgender outreach coordinator. We were essentially doing the same work while I was at the center, which wouldn't be for very much longer.

TEN

Work with Purpose

I had committed to spending three years at the center, and the end of that period was rapidly approaching. After experiencing increasing discrimination and tokenization and grappling with the fact that there was no room for me to advance professionally, I had grown eager to leave. Unfortunately, the center served as an example of an environment that I assumed would be ideal, but ultimately wasn't what it claimed to be. I would learn there that I needed to look out for myself and my own best interests with constant vigilance. Over my tenure there, I became all too familiar with the founding executive director's passive-aggressive leadership style. It created a culture of hostility for me, for other staff, and sadly, even for the youth patrons I worked with on a daily basis.

He enacted a no-sleeping rule for homeless youths who used the center as a drop-in space before programming during the day. Youth staff were regularly called upon to wake young people who had been out at the lakefront all night, or who were exhausted from a full evening of survival sex work and were simply looking for a safe space to sleep for a couple of hours. Senior leadership took the foolish and cruel stance that "we aren't a homeless shelter." They got rid of my beloved Breakfast Club programming that fed the homeless youths every morning—we'd lost our funding because our chief program officer "forgot" to renew the grant. That was my breaking point. Night after night, I came home and complained to Myles that I couldn't do it anymore. I felt unappreciated, undervalued, and underpaid, and to make matters worse, I was suffering from burnout from the institutional oppression and perpetual trauma of working with youths in crisis whom I felt were being mistreated.

To add insult to injury, the center chose to not prioritize trans-affirming healthcare. When they switched health providers, my hormone medication was no longer covered, and I was encouraged to seek it from another country. Thank goodness our local LGBTQ community health provider, Howard Brown Health, provided hormones at a discounted rate, so I was still able to access the hormones that were making me softer in the face day by day. I refused to give up and give in to forces that I felt were crushing me.

When I offered to step into a vacated director of public relations role, it didn't even go up for discussion. To his credit, our youth program director passed along my recommendation that an entirely new position be created for me as the director of transgender programs, which was ignored and denied. It became apparent that my name and talents would be used as a byline in a grant, and as a way to keep the young people "in order," which didn't resonate with my reasons for working at the Center on Halsted in the first place. I wanted to work at a place that had a more progressive work culture and that drew on my natural skills in public relations, communications, and facilitation.

On a lazy Independence Day weekend, I typed the word *diversity* into the search box on my laptop while Myles slouched next to me. Scrolling through the results, I came across two positions of interest: a senior admissions officer job and an assistant director of diversity recruitment initiatives role, both at Columbia College Chicago, my alma mater. I had seen other alumni working at the college while I was a student and had stayed relatively involved at Columbia during my time at the center.

After graduation, I had been invited several times to speak to Gay and Lesbian Studies classes about my activism as a trans woman and my work in HIV prevention. Later, I would use my position and influence at the center to collaborate with the Office of LGBTQ Culture & Community at Columbia in the creation of the tenth anniversary and annual celebration of gender and sexuality, Gender Fusions. Now, looking at those two options, I was excited at the prospect of doing something that wasn't solely LGBTQ-focused, as I was finding living, working, and playing in the gay neighborhood just as oppressive as living outside it.

I had no doubt that I could create change and lead initiatives that would make Columbia a more inclusive institution. It also paid nearly double the salary I was making at the center. I had found out that two of my colleagues who did far less work than I did were paid the same as me, and it infuriated me. I knew my worth, and I intended to let everyone else know it too. I updated my cover letter and résumé and applied for both positions, envisioning the serendipity of returning to the same campus that brought me to Chicago in the first place.

I ran through my Rolodex of contacts on campus, looking for those with whom I had established good rapport as a student and who were aware of my professional endeavors. Mark Kelly, the vice president for student success, had been the first booming voice I'd heard on campus when he addressed the new students at orientation. I'd hung on his every word and taken his charge to go forth and find our creative posse at Columbia to heart. I'd taken every opportunity to let Mark know I was indeed curating a creative posse with peers from the theater department, doing everything from appearing in the chorus of *Dames at Sea* in our musical-theater collective to participating in street photo shoots in drag with individuals from the University Center dorm. I had also circled back to Mark during my time working at the center when navigating how to pay off a balance on my student account that my financial-aid package would not cover. Mark and I ultimately discussed brokering a deal with financial aid for me to make payments in installments at a later date.

I emailed Mark to let him know I had applied for the assistant director of diversity recruitment initiatives position, with the hope that he might once again help me achieve something I so badly wanted. I attached my résumé and cover letter and wrote, "I feel my representation as an alumni and transgender woman of color could be a great asset to the Columbia community." I never heard back from him, but two and a half weeks after applying, the admissions project manager invited me for a phone interview with the hiring committee.

Dr. Kimberly Weatherly, director of multicultural and African American cultural affairs, encouraged us to eat before she introduced several diverse faculty and staff members. Among them, my eyes fixated on a tall, fine Tyson Beckfordish chocolate brotha with a gleaming smile and precise fade. I instantly knew that we spoke a "familiar" language of sorts—many queer people feel the energy shift when another queer person enters a space. Gemini Wadley stepped forward, waved hello, and introduced himself as the assistant director of diversity recruitment initiatives. I blushed, not knowing how I would manage to pull myself together in front of his fineness, but I managed to say hello with composure.

The day after I applied for the assistant director of diversity position, I saw on Twitter that Gemini was recruiting students at Essence Fest in New Orleans on behalf of Columbia. As a kid, I'd never gone on vacations; all my travel involved camping and horseback riding on church field trips. I had gotten a taste of the East Coast when I represented the Center on Halsted at a CDC Mpowerment facilitator training in

Providence, Rhode Island, and later in Philadelphia, Pennsylvania, for the Philly Trans Wellness Conference. Both trips piqued my interest in serving in a role that involved traveling. After submitting my application, I emailed Gemini and mentioned that I had always wanted to go to Essence Fest and let him know that I was applying for the assistant director of diversity recruitment initiatives position.

I didn't know if the reason his current position had been posted was because he was leaving the college, but I figured I might get some insight by starting a dialogue. Within twenty minutes of my sending the email, Gemini informed me that he was stepping into a senior admissions officer role, a role he previously occupied but that would now offer him more flexibility. He also let me know that the position he was vacating was being taken in a new direction and would focus more on training, though he wasn't sure of the specifics. When I heard "training," I knew I had an in, since once a month I offered safer-sex trainings to African American and Latino gay, bi, and trans youths across Chicagoland. That tidbit of information was priceless as I developed my strategy for navigating the interview process. With the knowledge that cultural competence was lacking across the board, I planned to rely on my personal knowledge of the institution as a former student, which positioned me as the perfect candidate to address Columbia's many blind spots.

I constantly refreshed my email on my T-Mobile Sidekick cell phone, flipping it up and down while I sat at my desk in the back of the youth-space cubicle I shared with three others. They must have been tired of hearing me declare daily that I planned on leaving the center as soon as I could. I just needed the email invitation to the next round of interviews.

Edwin, my supervisor, was one of my biggest cheerleaders and gladly agreed to serve as a reference. He considered me a top performer on his team and depended on me to coordinate large-scale projects, such as fashion shows and picnics, along with maintaining good community relations. Edwin often discreetly placed director-level job descriptions on my desk, highlighting the benchmarks I needed to meet in order to be competitive, which usually included getting a master's degree. I was thankful Edwin presented me with opportunities to grow professionally when the center at large wouldn't.

Being hired at Columbia would send a message loud and clear that it was possible for a trans woman to work and thrive in the "real" world. Far too many LGBTQ organizations treat trans people—and particularly trans folks of color—as entry-level cogs, instead of truly investing in our growth and development. Executive directors, I'm talking to you now: it is your job to work yourself out of an institution so that someone else can take over. The goal should be to train people so that they can flourish in multiple sectors, not just the nonprofit world.

Which is exactly what I did as I prepared to leave. I actively began advocating for Edwin to hire a young social drag queen from the community. I believed such a hire would benefit the young people, and the salary from the job could create some stability in the young queen's life so she might escape a cycle of homelessness.

When I started at the center, the careers of continental showgirls were the only examples within my orbit of what it meant to be a professional trans woman in the world. I could barely stomach nightlife and its many ills: the vicious gay men who presided over the dog and pony shows, the bar owners who profited by not paying their performers a living wage. I also felt that line of work ultimately wasn't the full extent of who I was called to be. Even back then, I told fellow queens that I was going to do something great with my life. They would all laugh and mock me, with an attitude of *Yeah, right.* Don't get me wrong, being born a showgirl or pageant girl is in fact a thing, but it's up to you to choose where you stand in the light and what you do with the platform you're given. Some girls are meant to be there; it's their calling, and it shows. I will forever marvel at the stage presence and beauty secrets on display in the drag scene, which have infiltrated the larger society. Contouring, exaggerated brows, long lashes and nails—that all came from drag queens, long before they were Instagram trends.

For me, wearing eighties power suits and *Dynasty* makeup by day made up for anything I might have missed by no longer being a showgirl full-time.

As I prepared for my exit from the center, I reflected on my three-year tenure. When I started there, I couldn't have imagined being a part of a national movement that *Time* magazine called the "transgender tipping point." Laverne Cox later recounted to Wendy Williams on *The Wendy Williams Show* that when I texted her the image that morning the magazine was released, it was the first time she saw herself on the cover. She was the first openly trans woman to grace their cover, after being the first trans woman to be nominated for an Emmy for her role in the Netflix series *Orange Is the New Black*. That same year, Janet Mock released her *New York Times* bestselling debut memoir *Redefining Realness*, and Ohio transgender teenager Leelah Alcorn committed suicide after her parents forced her to undergo Christian conversion therapy. That tragic news shook me because it reminded me of my own experience undergoing conversion therapy. It had taken me until the age of twenty-five for my own gender-nonconforming journey to lead me into full blossom as a trans woman.

I was officially interviewing on campus as a candidate for the assistant director of diversity recruitment initiatives position. With long ombre box braids cascading over my shoulders, I passed out the outline of my hour-long presentation to the hiring committee. I was confident yet slightly nervous, though I was able to keep my voice steady. If I got the job, I would make certain that no other student would ever have to deal with the hardships I'd faced.

I had been asked to present a workshop on a population of my choosing and to educate those in the room about that population. Naturally, I chose the trans population, laying out the various issues a trans student attending Columbia might experience on a daily basis. I touched on the importance of having gender-neutral bathrooms on campus, and I described the challenges of dealing with legal documents that didn't match one's gender identity. I covered the university's inclusive-housing practices, and how navigating health insurance coverage can be an obstacle for many LGBTQ students. Of course, many of the things I described were also personal issues, and I dreaded knowing that if hired I would have to actually out myself about not having legally changed my name or gender identity on official documents. I didn't know how Columbia would react. Based on the inquisitive nods and casual note jotting, I realized that, for some of the committee members, the information I was presenting was new.

I answered questions from each of the six panelists, keenly aware that they held my fate in their hands. I reiterated that the core of my diversity work was based on analyzing implicit bias in each of our everyday interactions, and that I believed in the institutional power of creating opportunity for marginalized communities. I'd intentionally demonstrated another form of diversity without explicitly talking about it by using a conversational style of speaking that was both informal and academic and therefore showing my ability to engage a wide range of people who might receive information in various ways. I was asked how I'd define the role, and I said, "I believe we must first have a shared vision of what diversity is. So many individuals think they understand what diversity is, and when you ask them, a long, rambling answer normally ensues. I would embark on ambitious training, community surveying, and social justice exercises, along with creating scholarships for LGBTQ students and other marginalized communities to create opportunity and access across the institution."

One of the women on the committee asked me what I thought about working at an institution that straddles the line between being both beneficial to and problematic for the population it serves. Without hesitation and without explicitly naming the center, I mentioned how my work as an activist gave me experience in creating change from the inside. "I think far too often individuals don't understand how their particular form of activism fits within social progress. I invite people who have not been traditionally present or invited to speak in rooms and spaces. I believe issues of gender, ability, race, socioeconomic status, and immigration status must all be included in social justice work. Working within institutions is my form of activism. I create change from the inside while pushing decision makers to be cognizant of the feet in the march and reimagine how improving systems can benefit people's lives." I was using code that meant *dismantle*.

I left the interview with a smile on my face and the promise that, if they hired me, I would run with the creative freedom on offer, and my work would be rooted in a foundation of social justice.

Not even a week later I received an email inviting me to move forward in the process in an interview with the director of admissions, Patrick Fahy, and the assistant vice president for enrollment management and admissions, Murphy Monroe.

After walking through the glass doors on the third floor of the admissions office, I was met by a short man with a scruffy beard, who led the way down the hall to his office. Patrick Fahy was the opposite of Murphy Monroe, who was tall and graying. I could see by looking at them that they were a sort of dream team. They seemed to welcome my authenticity, appearing pleased as I made my pitch about my life's work and my hopes for including Columbia in the next act. I was clear that if hired, my chief role would be as an advocate first. That aligned with

Murphy's vision. Over the course of our hour-long conversation, I was surprised by the feeling that my professional expertise was seen as valid by two white men. Gemini was right; Murphy and Patrick made it clear that they weren't looking for a carbon copy of Gemini. They explained that they wanted someone with strong skills in facilitation and training, and someone who could represent Columbia across the country. I knew I was a perfect fit for the job, and it seemed like they knew it too.

A few weeks later, I received a packet in the mail extending me an official offer to come aboard as the assistant director of diversity recruitment initiatives at Columbia. I immediately called Murphy to negotiate my salary, and it didn't take him long to get back to me to say, "Absolutely." I jumped up and down in my apartment, thrilled that I had just landed a new job. I couldn't believe it! I had wielded my backbone, found my voice, and refused to be treated as less than or given less than what I knew I deserved.

Every year on the Fourth of July, to commemorate this milestone, I ask myself: Am I happy personally and professionally? And if ever the answer is no, I will confidently update my cover letter and résumé and seek out a better opportunity. The name of the game is to forever grow and evolve into what I know is best for me.

I felt a weight lift off my shoulders as I typed and tendered my resignation to the center. Along with the jobs at Columbia, I had applied for another position at Public Allies Chicago, which was a second branch of the Public Allies organization and was launched with Michelle Obama as executive director. In that interview, the hiring manager, a sharp lawyer, asked me if I was burned-out, and I immediately burst into tears. Needless to say, I didn't get that job.

I couldn't help but think about the strength and broken pieces I had to pull together in order to land the job at Columbia. I decided to take a victory lap at the center, making my way to the other side of the building to the executive suites. Then I forcefully slipped the white envelope containing my two-week notice under the door of Human Resources.

The winds of change guided me back to my desk with glory, and with every stomp down the long hall of runway, I so badly wanted to scream out, *Checkmate, bitch,* but my first-lady instincts remained intact. I thought of all the colleagues, volunteers, and patrons I had grown to love so much: from the short senior man who volunteered at the center and greeted me in the mornings as I hit the top of the staircase, to the youths who called me Mama Precious. I received a trove of congratulatory flowers that piled up on my desk as my two weeks dwindled. It meant so much to me that the young people who had made an overwhelming impression on my heart took the time to wish me well. I had gone into that experience thinking I would be the one who would affect the youth, but in the end, it was many of those young people who experienced homelessness and other debilitating setbacks who changed me for the better. They were models of persistence and resilience, of making a way out of no way. I could hardly look at them as I thanked them for everything they gave me. I will forever cherish their faces. *Wicked*'s "For Good"—"Because I knew you, I have been changed for good"—sums it up perfectly.

I wrote in my goodbye email to all the staff, "If you are neutral in situations of injustice, you have chosen the side of the oppressor. If an elephant has its foot on the tail of a mouse, and you say that you are neutral, the mouse will not appreciate your neutrality." And with that, I hugged my fellow youth staff comrades, grabbed my box of office mementos, walked out of Jericho, and walked home in heels for the last time.

An overwhelming sense of gratitude came over me in my first days on campus, as I walked to meetings in towering black high heels. My lips were lacquered with bold mauve Kate Moss Rimmel London lipstick. I shifted my focus to the power and responsibility I now had to shape policy that would *actually* affect current students and future diverse populations on campus.

In my first few days on the job, I ran into John Green, a tall English fellow with a heavy accent who had been recently appointed as the new chair of the theater department. We exchanged pleasantries, and then I launched into my recommendations for extending current theater education curriculum to include queer performance. I told him it would be especially important to include the art of drag, considering the fact that my theater classmate Jaren Merrell (Shea Couleé), and later fellow Columbia alumni Tony Taylor (the Vixen), went on to become *RuPaul's Drag Race* royalty. They were fierce queens long before they ever paraded in pumps, although the Vixen did strut around the university dining hall in full-drag face makeup. It was comforting to know that I wasn't the only Columbia kid who dabbled in gender variance or queer performance and that I wouldn't be the last. In fact, Dale Calandra, my stage-makeup teacher, served as the second Edna Turnblad in the first national Broadway tour of *Hairspray* and later moonlighted as Aunt Lola Cabana, a drag persona that was a part of a national trend of drag queens making beaucoup bucks hosting and selling Tupperware at parties pre–*Drag Race*. I was surprised that John listened to my recommendations and assured me he would consider them.

I was faced with the important question of whether to use my legal name or my chosen name on the Human Resources paperwork. Unlike at the center, I went into this opportunity as Precious. I knew it was extremely obvious that I was trans, given my choice of presentation for the hiring committee, and that I had come from the center, but I was still daunted by the thought of having to fight another institutional battle. Murphy alleviated my fears immediately and didn't flinch for one second when I brought it to his attention. He looked me dead in the eye and said, "No problem," promising that I would be identified as Precious across the board, if he had any say in the matter. It took Murphy and Human Resources a single business day to ensure that I was treated with dignity from the start. It further confirmed that I had made the right decision to leave the center.

Now, when the sun crossed the concrete, I would lift my makeup-clad face to its shine, feeling like I was living the full Mary Tyler Moore fantasy. I'd travel from building to building with my skirts swaying among the throng of professionals working on Michigan Avenue and within its gleaming modern architecture, Chicago's most iconic street, Lake Shore Drive, buzzing in the distance. I often held back tears thinking of the gift of being a part of the grand downtown hustle and bustle, the urgency of the morning rush depicted in every opening movie scene set in a big city. I was even grateful for the opportunity to board the crowded bus and daily pass the Louis Vuitton and Tiffany stores on my way to the office for days filled with discussions on how to engage new diverse populations and push the administration to act on the requests and needs of existing students on campus.

Several weeks into my new job and a day before Myles's birthday, as I was power walking out of the admissions office at the top of the morning, I saw that Nate Samek, Steven Moore's fiancé, was calling me. I planned to call him back as soon as I reached the main landing of our office building. Steven often called me randomly and vice versa to discuss our latest bids on the Miss Continental pageant queens we loved and despised, but Nate calling gave me pause. I took a breath and called him back.

"Nate?" I said.

"Steven . . . was in a plane crash this morning and didn't make it," he said in a monotone.

I nearly stumbled in my gold platform heels before taking a few steps back from the elevator, and my vision got hazy. "Nate, I'm so sorry" was all I could say.

Months earlier, legendary Miss Continental queen and Halsted diva Tajma Hall had died from cardiac arrest after going into the hospital for back surgery. When I received the news of Taj's passing, I fell flat on the cement outside the center, narrowly missing hitting my head on the ground. I couldn't believe that Steven passed away several months after. Those two were best friends, and I often sat across from Taj when Steven hosted us for dinner, back when I lived next door to him. I had twirled many times in Taj's Hydrag Revue shows, and my name being put on the marquee as a special guest one evening was a badge of honor. The drag evangelist and mothering spirit of Tajma Hall would now be with one of her most adoring fans on the other side.

While the announcement of Taj's passing had caused me to collapse, word of Steven's death prompted me to dash down the stairs. Suddenly I was desperate to connect with the planet outside the building. Without thought, I walked back into the office, looked at the receptionist, and said, "Oh my god, one of my best friends just died in a plane crash," before running down the stairs in my strappy gold heels once more. I paused to gather myself, as I didn't want to create a scene at my new job. My mind ran through the memories: our sitting together on Steven's front stoop talking about sociology, our broken families, and how I was going to do something great with my life.

I appreciated Nate calling me, and I in turn called Chadwick, another one of my best friends who was also close friends with Steven. I demanded he meet me at the Buckingham Fountain best known for its appearance in the opening sequence of *Married . . . with Children*.

Chadwick and I sat in silence for a while, staring at the smooth cascading water of the giant fountain. The powerful geysers spouting upward felt too happy somehow, too exuberant. We finally talked a little, reflecting on how precious life was, though talk was unnecessary. I looked up at the cloudy mists drifting away on the backdrop of blue sky, the same sky under which Chadwick and I had sat with Steven. The loss we both felt was monumental.

Steven often mailed me notes on cards; on one particular card he wrote, "Feel your trans bitch!" a phrase we often said to each other as we were carrying on, going for ice cream, or sashaying into each other at the annual Pride reception he hosted at his house with his previous partner, Lee. Steven was a fierce lover of all trans who brought beauty to his eye. I often wonder why he didn't marry a trans person in this life, and I hope that in his reincarnation, he will come back as one fierce bitch. I will forever hold in my heart the sentiment expressed on the last card I received from him: "I hope I've been as beneficial to your life as you have to mine."

It didn't take long for me to roll out and introduce my first diversity initiatives, which included implementing cultural competency diversity training to all enrollment management staff, along with any campus faculty who requested it. Murphy and Patrick sat in the back of many of my training sessions, both taking notes. Sometimes I invited special guest speakers from organizations like the Center for Black Music Research or from the American Sign Language Department. I created a guide to help undocumented students navigate higher-education admissions and oversaw the adding of gender-pronoun identifiers and a preferred name option onto Columbia's admissions application.

I was certainly feeling my trans every day in Maggy London wrap dresses and houndstooth blazers. I could see my work happening in real time. I soon sat on staff hiring committees, and always demanded a more diverse talent pool be considered. I also introduced pronoun pin use for the first time at our open house, which I put on in collaboration with our event director, Ania.

Ania meticulously planned and executed all our admissions events with the highest degree of excellence. She later asked me to give the cold-open greeting at the Auditorium Theatre to nearly four thousand screaming and excited prospective students. I strutted right out across the pitch-black stage and into the spotlight after the college president, Dr. Kim, spoke; I could hardly believe that I was one of the first people whom thousands of high school seniors searching for colleges saw. Me. A proud black trans woman and a student who had struggled my way through college, finding myself bit by bit.

I later watched a dad's expression turn to one of confusion as he and his kid reviewed the various options for self-identification at registration. I could see the Choose Your Pronoun sign and the bins of colored pins blurring in the father's eyes. But within seconds, the young person walked around their dad and picked up a pronoun pin and said, "This is me: *they*." I was floored at the simplicity and beauty of that coming-out moment in which I got to play a small part. I smiled and lifted my head with pride as I quickly introduced myself and offered my card.

One afternoon, after our weekly management meeting—which was attended by our team of mostly women whom Murphy had hired and empowered, and from whom he solicited feedback weekly—Murphy asked me to stay back to discuss something. He looked distraught.

We stepped aside as the others cleared the room. Murphy took a breath and divulged, "I have a principal in Jacksonville, Florida, who has requested some training on LGBTQ issues and particularly transgender issues. The school board is having a conversation regarding whether they should accommodate a trans student's need to use the restroom that correlates with their gender identity. Will you go to Florida and meet with this trans student and give their school board an LGBTQ cultural competency training?" I leaped at the chance to offer my assistance, assuring Murphy that I would go, although I was slightly apprehensive about returning to Florida after my terrible experience in Orlando a few weeks earlier.

It had started out well. Checking into the Embassy Suites in downtown Orlando, I was downright gleeful to be escaping Chicago's frigid early-winter temperatures. I was shadowing Gemini and another veteran staffer who regularly presented our recruitment presentation, which I would later present across the country, in New Orleans, Cleveland, Seattle, and Pittsburgh. It was my first trip to the American South in some time, and it had been magical so far, with me relishing the humidity and the breeze and taking in the beauty of the Spanish moss trees that were everywhere. I had even decided to take a late flight out the next day so that I could visit Disney World, a place I had always wanted to visit as a child but could never afford. After the recruitment event, I wandered around downtown Orlando looking for a place to grab a bite and finally came across a posh restaurant with accents of red lamps and a long bar that looked inviting for a party of one.

Pulling up a seat at the bar, I ordered a dirty martini and the catch of the day. Just as my food was arriving, I couldn't help but overhear the conversation of the white couple seated right next to me. The woman, who was sitting closest to me, laughed at her partner's "jokes" about Michael Brown Jr., an African American youth who was fatally gunned down by a white police officer in Ferguson, Missouri, in 2014. I glared at them. I didn't know if I should walk out immediately or quash the mess by confronting those fools. Since I was the only person of color in the restaurant, I considered my safety, and after stewing for a few moments, I requested my check from the bartender, packed up my things, and prepared to leave. But before I left, I decided to address the couple.

"How sad that you find it humorous that a young man lost his life," I said. "I challenge you to think about that young man's family, his dreams, and the plight of being black in America."

"My husband was only being facetious," the woman responded.

Walking back to the hotel, I felt uneasy. I called Myles and, through tears, explained what had just happened. Being so insulated within my social justice circle, I had let my guard down and was completely blindsided by the display of such blatant racism. My Nebraska naivete was showing as the history of the South and slavery, segregation, and Jim Crow racism smacked me right in the face.

Despite that awful first experience, I forged on, making the trip to Jacksonville, Florida, the city of seven bridges. I spoke to a handful of LGBTQ youths who were a part of their performing arts school's one-hundred-member-strong Gay-Straight Alliance, which included a white trans girl with a bowl cut and thin-framed eyeglasses. I strived to support her advocating for the right to use the restroom that correlated with her gender identity at school. I was once again moved by how powerful it was to see a young person name themselves so clearly in high school. Over a burrito lunch, a supportive staff member informed me of other efforts around town to support LGBTQ youth. She mentioned the local LGBTQ youth center JASMYN and encouraged me to stop by after my training just to hug the young people who were living at the residential facility. And I did.

All throughout that experience, I couldn't help but think how incredible it would have been if someone had visited my school to talk about queer studies and LGBTQ history when I was a young queer person. I'm glad to see bills passing all over the country that ensure that young people learn about LGBTQ history. Before leaving Jacksonville, I met with the Duval County Public School Board and delivered a cultural competency training on the LGBTQ community. I felt like I was doing God's work.

ELEVEN

Settling in to Joy

C lad in a white cocktail dress and with rhinestone chandelier ear-rings dangling from my ears, I blew out candles on a large sheet cake patterned after the chinois navy floral wallpaper spread throughout the bar that I absolutely loved. It was 2014, and I was celebrating my twenty-eighth birthday at our monthly Pleasure Review at Wangs, a show I helped start with Pearl from *RuPaul's Drag Race*. That night, after performing the ballad "Here's Where I Stand" from the movie *Camp*, I decided to step away from my performance career. I thought I was saying goodbye to drag forever.

Shortly after the new year, however, I was invited to perform at the Turn It Up for Change event, hosted by the Human Rights Campaign and featuring Jennifer Hudson. I didn't identify as a drag queen then but eagerly wanted to work with my generation's Whitney Houston.

Years earlier, when I was just a junior in high school, I was furious when she was voted off *American Idol*. I suspected it had something to do with the fact that she was an unapologetic voluptuous black diva who didn't meet Simon Cowell's beauty standards.

The gig paid fifteen hundred dollars, which was a lot of money for me at the time, so I accepted the invitation. I thought it would be the crowning jewel of my nine-year run as a showgirl and would add to the list of celebrities with whom I had gotten the chance to work throughout my performance career, which included fellow *American Idol* alum Syesha Mercado, Jojo, and the legendary Joan Rivers.

I trounced on the treadmill for weeks, letting out whispers and sighs as I practiced lip-synching every intonation on the track. With each thud on the rolling conveyor, I inhabited "It's Your World," the song I'd chosen to perform. Days before the event, I noticed in the publicized PR materials that I was listed as Precious Jewel in between the names of two other Chicago drag entertainers. I was perturbed, as I had made it clear for over a year in various Facebook posts that I no longer wanted to be identified as Precious Jewel. Being listed as such felt like a slight and a disregard for my wishes.

I was now Precious Davis, the trans advocate and public speaker, *not* Precious Jewel, a character. Just because I went by Precious Davis now didn't mean my performing talent had left me. It didn't matter that I had been called to impersonate JHUD herself. At this moment, I only cared about my identity being respected. I was seething when I fired off an email to the promoter demanding that I be identified as Precious Davis in the promotional materials. He vowed to make the corrections, but they never materialized. I couldn't tell if it was shady showbiz antics or incompetence; from my experience working in bars, I was used to show directors treating me terribly while smiling in my face.

On the evening of the event, I confidently strode into the sleek corridors of the W Hotel, my face painted bitchin'ly for filth. With every step I took, my auburn blowout bob bounced. In our holding hotel room, I exchanged pleasantries with Shea Couleé and another queen, who were finishing their makeup.

Together, we rushed down to the red carpet with our respective entourages to do press. Cameras clicked and flashed in a frenzy. I nestled in right next to JHUD, ecstatic to be officially participating in my first legit red carpet with Getty photographers and all. Jennifer laid her hand atop my bare shoulder, which was peeking out of a sleeveless Eliza J silver sheath cocktail dress with clusters of rhinestones across the bodice. JHUD's lean frame was on full display in a black bodycon dress paired with thigh-high black stiletto boots and a piecey razored-style haircut. She was flanked by a tall queen with a flower crown on one side and Shea, who was channeling Egypt in blunt bangs and a black fitted dress with gold accessories on the other. The glory of the moment sank in as we pooched in front of rows of paparazzi.

"It's an honor to be working with you tonight," I said loudly to JHUD, who was used to talking to people without moving her head. She shouted, "Let's *serve!*"

Soon I returned to the room for a quick costume change before my performance. Myles bounced in and out of the room, asking, "Do you need anything?" He had found camaraderie with members of JHUD's security detail, and it seemed like they had scooped him up to be on duty too. I didn't blame him for not wanting to sit idle in the room while my makeup artist did the finishing touches. Then, just like that, I was whisked backstage. I could hear Shea, now in a floor-length cobalt satin ball gown, wrapping her performance of "And I Am Telling You I'm Not Going" in front of the packed ballroom.

I heard the emcee announce, "Give it up for Jennifer Hudson . . . plot twist!"

I felt like I had been launched out of a cannon. With a gridiron smile on my face, I took center stage, serving a dose of fierce face and beauty. Then I strutted down the catwalk in a black quilted jacket and fitted white classic shirt, the top few buttons unbuttoned, and my black bra peeking out. Myles burst out of the audience, and the crowd erupted—I didn't tell anyone we were going to perform a duet. With his open white tuxedo jacket, Myles knelt on the ground as "It's Your World" blared, proving chivalry certainly was not dead.

As the song ended, Jennifer came out and hugged me. She was ever gracious, saying, "It's the real JHUD," as Myles and I exited the stage on a high. It was a flawless performance we will never forget.

～

The morning of Tuesday, February 3, 2015, started off normally enough: Myles rode with me in an Uber to Columbia, since carpooling cut down his commute time of an hour and a half to his job at Howard Brown Health in Near North Side, Chicago. As soon as we hopped out the car, Myles pulled me in for a cuddle and a selfie. I didn't feel like I was at the height of my glamour, so I wasn't particularly interested in the photo, but I appreciated his random act of kindness to start my day.

Later that morning, I missed several calls from him while I was sitting in a meeting. I texted him, What's up? Myles replied, JHUD's dancers just texted me and said Beyoncé is at the Bean shooting a music video! Unceremoniously jumping out of my seat, I began telling everyone, "Beyoncé's at the Bean!" Folks on the floor of my office, folks on the third floor, and even Lex, the director of LGBTQ Culture and Community, whose office was in the building next door. Before I could process what was happening, I picked up Lex from their office, and we set out on foot to the Bean to glimpse the queen. If I was going to meet Beyoncé, I was going to bring someone to document the historic occasion, OK?

As we were walking past my office, Myles appeared as if he were an official tour guide. I was briefly bewildered, wondering how he had gotten there so quickly, but chalked it up to chance. We jumped into the back of the yellow cab and asked the driver to please hurry! I jumped out of the taxi so fast you would have thought I was scrambling to make first place at a pit stop on *The Amazing Race*. Running up the perimeter of Millennium Park, I was like a nighthawk capturing prey, scanning to and fro for a view of Queen Bey in the flesh. When I arrived at the silver fortress, however, all I could make out was drifts of melted snow. I squinted, fixing my gaze on the gaggle of folks milling around. Myles, trailing behind me, said, "Do you see her?"

I turned around to say no, but instead let out a rooster-like crow, *"Oh. My. God!"* with max vocal fry.

Myles was down on one knee! The mix of shock and sheer adrenaline made me take off running, my coat sliding down my arms, and my pink wool scarf brushing the pavement. I stopped. I couldn't take my eyes off him as he stood up and ran over to me.

"Is that a yes?" he asked.

He wrapped his large arms around me, and I nearly fainted like I had in the days of Pentecost as his love engulfed me. I held on to him, never wanting the moment to end. After a moment, I regained my composure, and he slipped a diamond ring with pink fluorescence on my finger and said, "You're my Beyoncé." Cheers erupted all around us as we kissed.

Myles and I were invited by Miley Cyrus's Happy Hippie Foundation, along with various other transgender activists from across the country, to participate in a photo-shoot project in collaboration with Instagram. I stared at the Twitter DM that asked if I'd work with an artist whose music I kept in full rotation, before running around my house, jumping up and down. I had recently been passed over by a casting agency overseeing a national ad campaign for Barneys, but oh how the tables had turned!

Myles and I nestled into each other on our Virgin Atlantic flight to Los Angeles. A sleek black car picked us up from the airport and dropped us off at the W Hotel in Hollywood, where a massive crystal chandelier lit up the lobby. A grand staircase overlooking gold and pink chairs made me feel as if we had arrived at Malibu Barbie's dreamhouse.

We were briefed—it would be a very low-key photo shoot, shot by Miley herself. But I knew that different people had different definitions of *low-key*, so I still wasn't sure what to expect.

I booked a hair and makeup appointment at the Blo Blow Dry Bar next door to our hotel. The stylist was blow-drying my short strands of candy-apple-yellow hair. I was reading a magazine when she whispered in my ear, "That's Elvira." I discreetly looked in the mirror. Next to me sat a woman with pale white skin and long damp red hair. I imagined her with her signature bouffant wig and black accoutrements, attempting to reconcile this person with the Mistress of the Dark. My gaze moved down to her bountiful cleavage on full display, and I could see that she was, in fact, Cassandra Peterson. I minded my own business, feeling it was best to let her enjoy her hair appointment without an interruption from a stranger. I was indeed in the heartland of Hollywood.

Miley Cyrus wore a yellow jumpsuit, her blond hair in knotted buns and various floral stickers on her round face. We were at Milk Studios for the photo shoot. She gave endless welcoming hugs, dispelling any nervousness we might have had, before presenting us with her vision for the day-long shoot. "Just have fun," she told us, then went over elements of our identities from memory. Other participants were the founders of Trans Lifeline, Greta Gustava Martela and Nina Chaubal; actor Leo Sheng; writer Tyler Ford; YouTube star Gigi Gorgeous; high school student A. J. Lehman; program manager for the Trans Wellness Center in Los Angeles, Mariana Marroquin; associate director for trans-gender representation at GLAAD, Alex Schmider; and viral sensation hand-performance artist extraordinaire, superstar Brendan Jordan.

Looking up at me, Miley said, "You're the classy one. I have seen all of your photos!" I truly felt seen; she had taken note of my first-lady tendencies.

I found pure allyship in Miley, who had transitioned from a teen Disney star to an unapologetically gender-fluid young adult in the public eye. I identified with her breaking away from everything she'd known in order to become the most authentic Miley she could be. Many criticisms of her aren't fair—her behavior throughout her early twenties didn't differ much from what college kids do every weekend. The only difference to me, it seemed, was that she was being paid to do it.

I dressed in a heavy yellow sequined gown specifically picked out for me. It wasn't long before Pati Dubroff, the legendary Hollywood makeup artist, transformed my look with pigmented yellow eyeshadow and bubblegum-pink lipstick. Pati regularly glammed stars like Priyanka Jonas, Margot Robbie, Kerry Washington, and Miley herself. Here I was the work of a master artist, who sculpted my face with ease, precision, and grace. Steph Stone, a renowned nail artist, painted a shellac of Funfetti-like multicolored glitter on my nails. Looking in the mirror, I gasped, much like Vida Boheme in *To Wong Foo*.

I never want to forget the radiant, proud feeling I had stepping out of the dressing room that day. There I was, at twenty-nine years old, standing beside my fiancé, being photographed by Miley Cyrus. I remembered myself as a sixteen-year-old kid, purchasing my first pair of high heels with the knowledge that one day I would wear them proudly. What would the young trans girl in me, the trans girl who longed to be free, have thought if she had seen me stepping into that gorgeous yellow gown and out into the spotlight?

I affectionately draped a yellow feather boa around me and Myles, as Miley snapped a couple Polaroids. We posed atop yellow paper that had been rolled out across the floor, while silver helium-balloon letters spelled out the word *love*. It felt like a family affair. When the shoot ended, Miley and I slow danced as I sang the epic lyrics to "Wrecking Ball." It was all very meta.

The next night, Myles and I strolled into MR CHOW for a dinner date in Beverly Hills. The kitchen staff were making egg noodles from scratch, occasionally stealing my attention from Myles, who kept lifting his head high and saying, "Who am I?" in a friendly imitation of the way I tilt my head in selfies. After dinner, I invited Rachel Lien, an actress friend from high school who lived in Los Angeles, to the W for cocktails. Myles kissed me adieu for the evening and returned to our room.

Jake Weinraub, another friend, whom I had met during my various vacation jaunts to Los Angeles, also joined us for drinks. Fringe shimmied on the sleeve of my black spandex cocktail dress each time I picked up my drink. Time flew by as I sipped gin and tonics in a mirrored alcove; I finally capped the evening with goodbye hugs before returning to my room. I peeled off my dress as quietly as I could, slipped my engagement ring into a side pocket on my purse, and joined Myles in bed.

The next morning, I couldn't find my mascara in my tote bag of cosmetics, so I decided to run out to the nearest Walgreens, which was about a block away. I groggily paid the cashier, still in a morning daze. Returning to the hotel, I walked past homes made out of cardboard boxes underneath the concrete towers of Hollywood Boulevard.

Homelessness had been at the forefront of my mind; addressing this issue was a core part of Miley's Happy Hippie Foundation's mission, and part of what inspired me to participate in the #instapride shoot in the first place. Within me I carried the stories of the homeless trans and gender-nonconforming young people I had met at the Center on Halsted. I passed a homeless man sitting on his sheet of cardboard, and without hesitation, I reached into the side pocket of my purse, pulled out a handful of loose change, and dropped it into his plastic cup.

I returned to the room to finish getting ready for a brunch reservation at Villa Blanca. Suddenly, my stomach dropped—*I had just given my engagement ring to a homeless man.* How would Myles react?

Just to be sure I hadn't misplaced the ring in the room, I ripped the sheets off the bed, flipped the mattress over, and rifled through every drawer.

"I think I just gave my ring to a homeless man on Hollywood Boulevard!" I told Myles. Completely unbothered, he said, "Things happen. We'll get you a new one." Classic Myles. Calm, cool, and collected. Pure patient love.

I couldn't help but think of myself as the young child who would have been punished for such a stupid mistake, who would have received a slap or a demeaning tirade about how inconsiderate and ungrateful I was or both. Myles had forgiven me right then and there, but I was still struggling to make sense of the fact that I had actually placed my diamond ring with loose change in the side pocket of my purse. What was I thinking?

I had a lunch scheduled with classical pianist and Hollywood writer Our Lady J, but I called to cancel because I was so distraught. After I told her what happened, she showed up at my hotel room to help me look for the ring. I was floored by her kindness. We had never actually met in person but were familiar with each other through our mutual friend Zackary Drucker and social media. We never found that ring, but I vowed to pay for half of the next one (and I did).

A couple of months later, I felt honored to be walking into the foyer of the White House. It was President Obama's LGBTQ Pride Month event. After Myles and I greeted countless advocates assembled in the East Room who were staking out the best places to get an up-close and personal view of President Obama, we went off on a self-executed tour of the Red Room. We paid a visit to the portraits of former first ladies Jacqueline Kennedy, Hillary Clinton, and Lady Bird Johnson. When we were walking down the hall to the East Room to hear the president's remarks, Aditi Hardikar, White House LGBT liaison, tapped Myles and me on the shoulder and said, "Meet me outside that door over there in about ten minutes. I have a surprise for you!" She pointed to what I now know is the White House Green Room, and my heart rate increased. We were going to meet the president!

Myles and I clutched each other's hands. Not only were we going to meet the president; we were going to meet the first black president of the United States, Barack Hussein Obama. Again I thought of myself as a kid. Fifteen years earlier, my life had been crammed into just a few trash bags. I had been seen as a rebellious teenager who was condemned to hell. Now, I strutted into the room serving First Lady in my floral turquoise dress and pearls.

I shook President Obama's hand, and Myles and I said in unison, "We're from Chicago!"

"Tell everyone I said hello!" President Obama responded.

We posed for the official White House photographer. I could see the height of the Washington Monument in the distance. We were then escorted down to the grand foyer near the East Room, which was approaching capacity. I didn't mind standing in the overflow, as I was riding a high. We had just met President Obama! We'd shaken hands with Vice President Biden! I wished I had also met First Lady Michelle Obama, but I certainly wasn't complaining.

There was a rush of excited whispering as President Obama appeared behind the lectern. He welcomed the attendees to the reception, and a voice from the crowd yelled out, "President Obama!" From where I was standing outside the reception hall I couldn't make out who it was that kept interrupting, but I did hear President Obama say, "You're in my house!" and "If you're eating the hors d'oeuvres and drinking the booze, then show some respect."

That was the blackest dad thing he could have said.

Shortly thereafter, the person was removed, and I later found out that it had been Jennicet Gutiérrez, a Latina trans woman who was calling for an end to deportation of LGBTQ immigrants.

When I said publicly that I was processing what happened in that moment, I was inundated with passive-aggressive social media posts criticizing me. I was dismayed by the activists who chalked that day up to just another photo op, invalidating my experience as a trans woman of color and what I had survived to even be able to walk through the gates of the White House that day. This moment will forever serve as a reminder that we must allow one another to have different perspectives and tough, tense conversations in order to bend the moral arc of the universe toward justice.

I perused hundreds of gowns hung in see-through garment bags while the gowns' designer, Lazaro, watched, and Lori and Monte, hosts of TLC's *Say Yes to the Dress: Atlanta*, stood across the room. I was in a state of shock. Here I was, a newly engaged woman working with an unlimited budget for my wedding dress.

"No . . . no . . . no . . . and no," I said, rejecting the first round of dresses. "I'm looking for something very ornate, mermaid cut, sweetheart fit, with a touch of costume, but very much like the queen!" I wanted a dress that felt like a cross between the bride's dress in *Coming to America* and Princess Diana's haute couture. I threw my right hand high into the air as if holding an invisible scepter and making a proclamation to my three fairy godmothers. The bridal attendant, Robin, reminded me in her cheery Southern drawl that I had made the right decision by choosing to shop at Bridals by Lori in Atlanta instead of Kleinfeld Bridal in New York City. Both iterations of the franchise welcomed my presence, but my visions of debutante balls, Scarlett O'Hara in *Gone with the Wind*, and Oscar de la Renta, Zuhair Murad, Michael

Cinco, and Lazaro cinched trumpet gowns from my Pinterest board made Atlanta the better option for me.

I was too busy to think about the fact that not one member from my biological family was present during my search. Or so I told myself. On the days leading up to the show, I had in fact thought about my biological mother, Tammy, and I'd surprised myself by finding new empathy and understanding. The dysfunction to which she subjected my brother, my sister, and me and from which she failed to protect us was real and wrong, but I also had to acknowledge that that dysfunction was an echo of what she must have experienced when she was young. Her father, Clyde, was either absent or cold and unloving when he was around. My grandfather is one of the most emotionally disconnected people I have ever met. While she denies any abuse, she described her dad as a womanizer with a penchant for girls who were freshly eighteen. Throughout her adolescence, Tammy was shipped off and shuffled between multiple juvenile rehabilitation centers, so at least some of her failures as a parent were inherited from her own lack of parents. I believe she was simply looking for love—in all the wrong places. Five kids with four different dads and a stream of boyfriends in and out of jail were all stand-ins for a father she never had. I, too, never had a father. Or a mother who stuck around, for that matter. But no matter how strong blood is, I vowed that, in my marriage to Myles, I would not let history repeat itself.

Partly out of anger that I have never fully excommunicated Clyde from my life and partly because they do not agree with what was once my homosexual and is now my transgender "lifestyle," Nina and Ethne continue to refuse to have any relationship with me. What would the day have been like if my sister Nina had been there? I considered her the model of the perfect bride. I wished she could have been there, making jokes and laughing about how I had walked around in her dyed ivory Payless pumps and beaming at how I was the bride now.

I didn't let that longing show on camera, as our estrangement was too deep a wound to expose to the world. Kandice and Chadwick, friends who had lovingly supported my transition, joined me on *Say Yes* instead of family. I flung myself into Lazaro's arms like he was my long-lost uncle. I carried on as if everything were normal. I thought of the little boy prancing around the house on Saturday mornings, a blanket tied around his waist. What would he have said if he could see me—himself—now? I remembered the Sunday after church when Myles drove us through his native Hyde Park to the most breathtaking cathedral I had ever seen. My Afro ponytail puff soaked up the sun as we stood in the front entrance of the chapel, and Myles said, "This is the church I'm gonna marry you in." That's when the entire fairy tale had come into view. I felt like Carrie Bradshaw in the *Sex and the City* movie.

I shook my head to wake myself up from my daydream just as Monte said, "Where's our beaded-top ball gown?"

"I'm *not* a ball-gown girl!" I quipped, trying to fight the expectations for a girl like me. Robin zipped me into a confection of blushing-rose organza and a bodice of lace intricately beaded with gleaming crystals. It was, in effect, a ball gown, and Monte couldn't help but point that out, saying, "Everything you're describing is opulence. Royalty. That says *ball gown!*"

Turning around, wearing an actual wedding dress for the first time, I admitted, "I thought I wouldn't want a ball gown, but I am the *princess!*" I laughed. I was indeed a ball-gown girl. I beamed at myself in the mirror.

Outside the dressing room, Kandice's face lit up, but Chadwick had on his resting bitch face. I posed like a black Mattel Holiday Barbie. "I can see myself marrying Myles in this," I told them.

Chadwick disapproved. "This is not that dress . . . at all. You don't have any shape," he said. Lori's jaw dropped at the sharp critique from the peanut gallery; I returned to the dressing room without even looking back.

"Look at your body!" Kandice and Chadwick yelled the moment I stepped up onto the circular wooden dais in my second choice, an ivory beaded fit-and-flare sweetheart mermaid gown. The fabric clung tight to my torso, putting my curves on full display, and it felt more appropriate for a gala than a wedding. "This is not it! This is in my closet fifteen times. I have this dress in purple. I would wear this on a Saturday night. It's not unique," I said, shaking my head, the regal ball gown still on my mind.

Monte, the saintly queen, spoke over my friends. "Wait! Listen to her; she's not feeling like a bride. What about putting the ball gown with the full skirt over this dress?"

I much preferred the beaded bodice over the lace corset and was in love with the grandness of the layered ombre organza skirt. I didn't know what to expect as Monte slipped the ball gown over the mermaid dress. Lazaro began pinning and draping the dress, and when he made the last alteration, a final cinch at the waist, I nearly swooned. I was speechless. I closed my eyes, not wanting my tears to flow on national TV, as it would surely ruin my makeup and leave me looking more like *Death Becomes Her* and less like Princess Tiana. As Monte twisted several bobby pins into place to secure the veil, Robin asked me the magical question.

I responded, *"I'm saying yes to the dress!"*

There was a cool breeze outside on Saturday, August 6, 2016. With its vaulted ceiling and Gothic architecture, the University of Chicago's Rockefeller Memorial Chapel felt more like a castle than a cathedral. Bryan, my bridal attendant, spread out my train, filling the vestibule like a cumulus cloud. When the wooden doors in the back of the chapel swung open, a massive wooden pipe organ began to play the wedding march from *Coming to America*. I'd chosen that song as an ode to black excellence, one of the pillars of our heads-of-state theme, which was reflected in everything, from our presidential invitations embossed with gold lettering to the reception venue, the South Shore Cultural Center, where Barack and Michelle Obama had held their reception years before.

I was ready for my Queen of Sheba entrance. My eyes locked onto the chocolate black prince waiting for me at the altar. He had a tight fade and was wearing an ivory sherwani, which we had picked out together to complement my dress. I held a bouquet of pink and white peonies that represented my absent biological siblings and Ethne and Nina. No matter how much our relationships had deteriorated, no matter their disapproval, I smelled the flowers' sweet fragrance and thought of a happier time on Sixty-Sixth Street, when I'd plucked a couple of flowers from the bushes at the side of our house. Every girl wants to remember something she did as a little girl to remind her of how far she has come to stand in her womanhood. I indulged in that delicate feeling and grounded myself in the sweet aroma as I embarked on the first steps to my new life.

The 250 guests now standing in the pews consisted of Myles's family, my biological grandparents, the Loves, members of my queer chosen family, respected colleagues from the Center on Halsted and Columbia College Chicago, along with the host of trans and gender-nonconforming folks in our bridal party. No single person had gotten me to that moment, so it felt right for me to be walking down the aisle alone, basking in the glory of my determination, resilience, and sacrifice.

When I reached the front of the church, Myles took my hand in his and guided me up the few short steps to the pulpit. We mouthed *I love you*, and I felt as if I'd just entered heaven's gates. Myles's father, Dr. Arnell Brady, was dressed in traditional African garb of blue-and-gold lamé made in Ghana, and he proudly served as the minister of our ceremonies, which included prayers to Jehovah from my foster brother, Alex, an invocation of the divine feminine from my beautiful Nigerian high school friend, Dr. Nkiru Nnawulezi, and a Native American blessing from our mutual friend, Holiday Simmons.

Syesha Mercado and her mother sang a soulful rendition of Whitney Houston's "I Look to You," another full-circle moment with someone from another period of my life. I was deeply moved by the lyrics that touched on surviving life's toughest challenges and highlighted the power of love to wash it all away and start anew. Every word of the melody described my overwhelming emotion of what Myles standing in front of me meant.

I declared my vows to Myles. "In you I find my strength, my confidence, and the ability to see the universe as God intended."

Overcome by the feeling of having everything I had ever longed for, a fire welled up in my belly. Like a young Pentecostal boy dancing with reckless abandon, I shed a lifetime of rejection. Myles whispered in my ear, "Go ahead!" I rocked back and forth, my eyes closed, shaking my head and thrusting my hands up in full surrender to the worship of the Almighty God, to the worship of the fullness of my truth as a black trans woman, to the worship of true love.

Myles and I each said "I do," and then we kissed. An old curse had been broken, and a new spell had been cast. We laughed, practically skipping down the aisle.

We found ourselves alone in the foyer, where we embraced, celebrating the promise that we would never let go of each other for the rest of our days.

Opulence was present in every detail of our reception, from the pink ornate ceiling and Wedgwood carvings to the flourishing white-and-pink rose bouquet centerpieces in gold rococo sticks to the silver Chiavari chairs. Applause greeted us, and our guests, like the true revelers they were, encouraged us to kiss as if we were the president and first lady of the United States dancing at an inaugural ball. Nestling to Sade's "Kiss of Life" as Mr. and Mrs. Brady-Davis for the first time, Myles looked even more like a king in his pink-and-gold sherwani. I'd changed into a sweetheart-cut metallic ruched mermaid gown pulled directly from Lazaro's spring and summer 2014 twentieth-anniversary runway collection. He whisked me off my feet, and I finally understood what Tina Turner must have felt like dancing on a checkered floor in high fashion in her "Private Dancer" video.

We managed to escape our reception before it ended, quickly saying our goodbyes to those near us on the dance floor. Holding my heels in one hand and Myles's hand in the other, I climbed into the back of our friend Joe Betancourt's car. At our hotel, we passed out from pure exhaustion, meaning my lace Victoria's Secret wares didn't even get touched!

With our real honeymoon several months away, we decided to enjoy a mini staycation in the days after our wedding. We ate at our favorite Italian eatery, Siena Tavern, and went to see *Bad Moms* at River East 21, the AMC Theatre that had served as our favorite date-night spot on countless evenings throughout our relationship.

Months later, we were preparing for our meticulously planned honeymoon excursion to Thailand and Cambodia. A few weeks before our trip, I sat at the end of a long conference table in the diversity, equity, and inclusion council meeting at Columbia. My phone was turned upside down and set to silent. It vibrated several times before I flipped it over to see I had several missed calls and a text from Myles's mom.

Myles was hit by a car.

I shouted, "Oh my God, my husband was just hit by a car."

I grabbed my purse, ran out of the room, and hailed a taxi on Michigan Avenue, on the same corner where Myles had kissed me the morning we got engaged.

I didn't know what shape I would find my husband in as I ran into the emergency room. At the nurses' station, I saw Myles out of the corner of my eye. He was slumped in a chair, completely out of it. I ran over and knelt in front of him. "Myles?" I said softly. He didn't respond. "Myles!" I yelled. I ran back to the nurses' station. "What is happening?" I asked, trying to keep my voice steady.

They told me in so many words that they had forgotten about him! Apparently, he had been hit by a young woman who ran a red light in her Ford Mustang, and the paramedics had simply dropped my disoriented husband off in the waiting room. Hearing this, my blood boiled, and I yelled at the desk attendant, "You *forgot* about my husband?" They quickly whisked us into a room as the threat of a lawsuit hung in the air. Myles became increasingly agitated and just wanted to go home. I was devastated.

The next morning, Myles threw up as soon as he woke up and then couldn't walk in a straight line, so we went back to the emergency room, where they declared he had a concussion. My lively, passionate husband was a mere shell of himself as painstaking migraines consumed him. I didn't know if the man I married would ever return to his normal self, but I was determined to stick by his side no matter what.

I continued my speaking engagements with a smile on my face, as well as my full-time job at Columbia. Only our closest friends knew what was going on, and a host of family and friends cared for him when I couldn't. Slowly but surely, he made a full recovery. Our faith and our relationship grew stronger, and though I didn't know what would come next for us, I knew we would be able to handle whatever was thrown our way.

That was the first pin in our love bubble. We had spent so much time celebrating and being celebrated that I'd almost forgotten the harsher realities of the world at large. Was my husband, a black trans man, being left alone in the corner of an emergency waiting room merely an oversight? Was that same neglect—neglect verging on medical malfeasance—likely to happen to anyone? Somehow, I doubted it.

I was sitting up in bed at around eleven p.m., watching the returns from the 2016 election and feeling a great sense of sorrow as the electoral count increasingly went for Donald Trump, and the map of the United States turned red. I pulled the covers up over my head, wishing that I wouldn't wake up to a Trump victory. At two a.m., Trump took the stage with his family, clapping and clenching his fists in victory. Two months later, I watched Trump's inaugural speech on "American carnage" and thought how much the tone resembled Scar's when addressing the hyenas as he plotted to kill Mufasa.

That's what living in Trump's America feels like, as he and his cronies try to obliterate the legacy of America's first African American president, kowtow to corporate interests, and remove vital environmental regulation of fossil fuels. Michelle Obama's face said it all for so many of us on that sad day: stone cold.

My heart, like so many hearts around the nation, was broken on that day in November of 2016. So many of us felt completely blindsided by our fellow Americans' decision to vote for a person with a long record of racism and misogyny, corruption and criminality. But I refused then and I refuse now to stay on the sidelines during this moment of history.

I went on to find a new position at the environmental nonprofit Sierra Club in the Beyond Coal Campaign. In my new work, I oversaw communications in Minnesota, Kansas, Oklahoma, and my home state of Nebraska. It was coal country that had decided the election, after all, and therefore my work there was a natural next step for effecting change and expanding my career in diversity work.

I will continue to give my whole self to the work of social justice, of living in my truth and helping others to do the same. Life goes on, and as they say, living well is the best revenge. No matter how many roadblocks the world puts up in front of us, we just keep on going, and looking good while doing it. For all of us who have been marginalized, who have been abandoned by those who are meant to love us, who have been damned by those who are meant to bless us, who have been looked at with disgust and told that we are wrong, that we are sinful, that we are abominations, now is the time to go forth and be fierce with clear intent while standing tall, showing that marginalized folks aren't going anywhere as we activate our power.

EPILOGUE

Three Years Later

I was in bed lulling in and out of sleep when Myles dropped a pregnancy test on top of the gold comforter. It took me a moment to come
fully awake and to understand the importance of the moment. I rolled
over, sat up, and rubbed my eyes. I wasn't fully familiar with how the
test worked, and I scanned the box to find out that one line meant a
negative result and two lines meant pregnant.

I picked up the plastic stick. I could see one strong pink line, but as
I watched, another faint pink line began to appear alongside the first. I
looked up at Myles. Could it be true?

We'd already been through one unsuccessful round of in vitro fer-
tilization (IVF), and though a failure to get pregnant is common, we
had still felt sad and discouraged. Now we refused to accept the reading
and waited a few days to take another test of the same kind. Two pink
lines. Still, not wanting to get our hopes up, we decided to switch to the
Clearblue test, which clearly states Not Pregnant or Pregnant.

I waited in the living room as Myles followed the instructions on
the package. Holding the blue-and-white stick in his hand, he walked
out of the bathroom. I rushed to follow him down the hall, and he

turned and handed the stick to me. We waited for what felt like an eternity.

Then the word *Pregnant* appeared.

We clung to each other and sank to our knees on the parquet floor. This was our final confirmation. *"We're pregnant!"* we said in unison as tears streamed down our faces. Laughing through my tears, I pulled Myles in for a kiss.

Two weeks later, our lab results confirmed that Myles was indeed pregnant. And so we embarked on bringing a child into the world.

Thirty-nine weeks later, we were just off of freshly celebrating our impending arrival with a New Orleans–themed baby shower with fifty of our closest family and friends, including the Loves and many of Myles's immediate family members. The calendar had just rolled over to a frosty December, which brought a fresh crisp chill to the air and strings of light on bare trees all over the city. Right after the stroke of midnight, he and I walked into Northwestern Memorial Hospital to check in.

"You're the smallest pregnant woman I've ever seen!" kikied one of the two receptionists of color who greeted us, looking at my mostly flat stomach underneath my designer jewel-embellished black sweater. They were unaware that it was actually Myles who had the pregnant belly underneath his wool peacoat. He had carried our child as a trans-masculine individual for nearly nine months.

I was grateful to our doctor for scheduling us to induce labor—this was the exact reason a controlled environment was better than a spontaneous scene in which Myles and I rushed to the hospital, only to be waylaid and forced to explain that yes, it was indeed my husband who was pregnant and not me. It was certainly not how it looks in the movies, when they cut from a scene of the water breaking to immediate pushing. I was in for a real surprise as I watched the hands on the clock circle, Myles catching stretches of sleep, nurses coming in and out to monitor him and the baby. They would check the wide strap contraption placed over his round cocoa stomach, which transmitted the thumping of the fetal heartbeat as an up and down frequency on a small screen next to the long bed. Cords and tubes from an IV wrapped around his arms. After his epidural, Myles lay in the bed, coming in and out of various states of consciousness. When he was awake, we bantered. He was even strong enough to joke about my fabulous sweater— eventually I went down to the gift shop to buy an inconspicuous pair of gray jersey pajamas to change into, with my long red stilettos, still serving my typical glamour.

Earlier that day, Myles and I had cozied up to each other as I gave him full creative control over our paternity photo shoot. The logistics of photo shoots are normally under my jurisdiction, but I felt this moment was his alone to curate. Leave it to us to schedule a photo shoot for the same day he was scheduled to give birth. Oh, and cameras were rolling for a TLC special on trans pregnancy. Not my idea. That was all his, as he wanted to document his journey, to publicly challenge his dysphoria, along with showing the world the experience of being a pregnant black man.

He encountered plenty of discrimination. On the day of our baby shower, he had gone out shopping for a new outfit, and a store employee had called the police after accusing him of stuffing his shirt with clothes. No, he wasn't stealing—that was his preggo bump. Every day, I worried about his safety, offering to call him an Uber so that he wouldn't have to take the bus and risk running into hostility. But there were so many beautiful moments too. I had watched with awe as his sweaters stretched more and more over his growing belly.

I didn't get to see Myles's outfit selections for the photo shoot until I walked up the stairs of the on-location studio site. I'd been paged repeatedly to wrap up my hair-and-makeup session, but I needed that extra thirty minutes to ensure my hair resembled Mariah Carey's. Inside the studio, I was rendered speechless. There the photographer was clicking away, capturing image after image of my barefoot, introvert husband in only a pair of black harem pants. On his bump was a tattoo with the words *GOD'S SON* in all-black lettering. His face stoic, he stood tall, leaning on an African walking staff, with a tallit with black and gold stripes and white tassels laid across his shoulders. A white kufi was cocked to the side on his head, and a silver ankh with beads of red, green, and black hung from his neck. It was a holy moment.

I took my place beside him. I was wearing an ornate pearl tiara and a crystal-beaded floor-length ivory farasha with a plunging neckline. I rested my head upon his shoulder as Beyoncé's "Spirit" played in the background, and we beamed black trans excellence, our owning and celebrating gender nonconformity, our defining what family meant to us, at the camera. We would be part of the mantle of our ancestors both known and unknown, staring into the face of our own lineage as we declared generations-old curses null and void. Still, I could not comprehend the fact that the title of mother would soon precede my name. I envisioned our child someday calling me Mama.

I had become more sympathetic to my own biological mother during the pregnancy. She had reached out to ask me what colors I would like for an afghan she planned to knit for our newborn. I requested pink and green, Alpha Kappa Alpha colors. Her taking that initiative was healing and opened a new line of communication between us.

Now I pressed the anesthesia button every time the green light on the lever lit up, just as the nurse instructed me to do. Myles's dad, wearing a small black top hat, leather vest, and printed dad shirt, tapped on the stretched leather of a small African djembe drum to the beat of our baby's heart, evoking the rhythms our ancestors used to celebrate their liberation. Our child would be brought into the world with drums and song.

I held Myles's hand throughout the labor, serving as a coach and yelling out, "You got this!" and "Push toward the ceiling!" as if I knew what giving birth felt like. His sister, an accomplished pharmacist and now med school resident, stood on the other side of the bed next to the silver railing, acting as the perfect motivational teammate. Over and over I wrung out a small white cloth, dipped it into a bucket of ice water, and placed it upon Myles's forehead, trying to bring some solace to his quaking body. Just as the doctor walked back into the room, Myles bore down, heeding a final contraction, and our little girl, with a head full of hair, twirled out of the womb after twenty-one hours of labor. That hair was the first sign and evidence that she was truly my child. I clutched onto Myles as her wailing matched my own tears of joy. I pressed my face to his and kissed him repeatedly; he was too exhausted to release his own tears.

"That's our baby," I said. "We did that." I could barely speak as they gently wiped her body.

"What's her name?" a nurse asked, wrapping her in a warm blanket and then placing her in a giraffe warmer.

"Zaaayynnn!" I said with pride, still crying.

Zayn Yemaya Echelle Brady-Davis.

Zayn is Arabic for *beauty*, Yemaya is Yoruban for *goddess of the ocean*, and Echelle is inspired by the Mayan goddess of the moon, Ixchel, which means *large rainbow*. Our beautiful goddess of the ocean, moon, and rainbow weighed in at 7lbs 6oz. I gently ran my hand across her head, taking in every part of her before the nurses placed her on top of Myles's chest. Zayn lifted her hand to cover her face like a true diva proclaiming no pictures as I snapped away, documenting her first minutes of life.

It all became truly real several days later as Myles and I left Northwestern Memorial Hospital with our little goddess. I had dressed her in her homegoing outfit, a pink polka-dotted onesie with ballerina slippers embroidered on it and frills on the sides and bows on the feet. My princess. We sat for a moment on a long bench outside, next to another couple and their baby embarking on the same life moment, congratulatory helium balloons swaying above.

At home, quiet greeted us. All the baby furniture we had arranged in the weeks before now had purpose. We transferred Zayn into the bassinet next to our bed and underneath a mobile of monkeys and elephants, Myles's and my favorite animals, which we'd chosen to fit with our gender-neutral safari nursery theme. We couldn't sleep those first few nights, often watching her just to make sure she was breathing. When she woke for feedings, I wrapped us in the pink-and-green afghan Tammy had made, rocking back and forth in the gray chair in our bedroom. Just down the hall, Christmas lights flickered on the tree in our living room. I experienced a kind of exhaustion I had never felt before; those first sleepless months were brutal, but I wouldn't have changed them for the world.

I'm grateful for the broken pieces I've picked up and put back together in order to become Zayn's mom. A new purpose.

Zayn, the world is yours. And as long as I have breath, and even from beyond, I will make sure of it. Myles, shall we discuss baby number two, before I explore running for a seat in the United States Congress?

ACKNOWLEDGMENTS

There are so many people who have enabled me to be who I am today and who made the writing of this book possible. Thank you to the folks who saw my light in every season of transition and provided guidance, support, and love.

Thank you first to Melissa Edwards, my literary agent, who first reached out and urged me to pen my story. I'm so glad I did.

Thank you to everyone at Topple and Amazon Publishing for bringing my words to the masses: Joey Soloway, Hafizah Geter, zakia henderson-brown, Carmen Johnson, Emily Freidenrich, Merideth Mulroney, and Emma Reh.

Thank you to Kan Seidel for serving as a confidant throughout this entire process.

To my best friends in this world: Kan, Nkiru, Lou, and Chadwick. Thank you for existing. Our conversations and times together sustain me.

To Dexter, Ginger, and Tanisha. Sixty-Sixth Street forever.

Nina, I love you even as we orbit on different planes. To Ethne, who bravely went as far as she could until the dam broke. To Tony, my favorite uncle, who has always gone along for the ride.

Thank you to Ron and Valerie for providing me a home when I needed it most.

To Alex, China, Chelci, Luke, Preston, and McKinzie. Love you all. We were always supposed to be siblings.

Burke High Music and Drama '05, forever.

Many thanks to Jamison Horton and Amy Negus for always holding me down.

Inclusive Communities (formerly known as the National Conference for Community and Justice).

Sandy McKenna, Gene, Corey, and Sean—you will always be another family to me.

The cast of *Ragtime*, Omaha Community Playhouse.

Thank you to Dr. Kwakiutl L. Dreher, Dr. Amelia Montes, and Dr. Pat Tetreault at the University of Nebraska–Lincoln for providing me a blueprint of the past and providing me references that laid the foundation for a fierce future.

Though it met its fate in flames and ashes, I will forever be grateful for the stage known as the Q, which provided the place and space for the birth of Precious Jewel. Much love to my Miss City Sweetheart 24 sister Alexus Rayeé. Shout out to Jon Beeck and crew. May the good times shake the table forever.

Thank you to SK Kerastas and Edwin Corbin-Gutiérrez for your professional mentorship and friendship.

Thank you to the youths at the center who shared with me dips, flips, and spins, and never ceased to make me laugh. I think of you often.

To Kaycee Ortiz, my first Chicago friend, you are the most hilarious person I know. Slay on.

To Janet Mock and Angelica Ross, you serve as a source of constant inspiration and beauty in this world. Thank you for convincing me to give Myles a chance; my life is enriched in a way I never thought possible. I am grateful for your sisterhood.

Much love to Pearl, Bryan, and Dylan. Grateful for so many memories where I could just be. I'll meet you on the dance floor anywhere.

Thank you to Murphy Monroe and Patrick Fahy for giving me one of the most rewarding opportunities of my professional life.

Thank you to Emily Gideon, Marta Stoepker, Jeff Shaw, and Maggie Kash for empowering a trans woman of color to lead at Sierra Club.

Thank you to Mallory Prucha and Cece Sickler for the gorgeous garments you created for this cover shoot and many thanks to Allison Kortokrax for capturing my life in motion with each snap. Thank you to Chad Stadt, Zac Coleman, Dee Desalu, Kan Seidel, and Arereal Strickland, who made this cover come to life. Arereal, you are a real one. Thanks for being a one-woman glam squad who always shows up and shows out!

To June, my therapist, thank you for always providing a reflecting pool for this project and beyond. It has changed my life.

To Grady and Essie, I'm proud to carry your name. You are the epitome of black excellence. Thank you for the continuous support you provided throughout this process. I love you.

Thank you to Tammy for giving birth to me, and I'm most proud that out of this process our relationship has blossomed.

Last but certainly not least, I will forever be grateful to my husband, Myles, who gave me unconditional support so that I could write this book. There were many days you ate alone and many nights you went to bed while I sojourned in my writing.

To my Zayn Zayn, I love you. Thank you for choosing me to be your mom.

ABOUT THE AUTHOR

Photo © 2018 Kan Seidel

Precious Brady-Davis is an award-winning diversity advocate, communications professional, and public speaker. She currently serves as the associate regional communications director at the Sierra Club. She served for three years as the assistant director of diversity recruitment initiatives at Columbia College Chicago, her alma mater, implementing the campus-wide diversity initiative and providing leadership and oversight of national diversity recruitment and inclusion policy initiatives. She also served as the youth outreach coordinator at the Center on Halsted, the largest LGBTQ community center in the Midwest. During Precious's tenure, she launched a $1.6 million CDC HIV prevention grant, which provided outreach, education, youth programming, and testing services to over three thousand young African American and Latinx gay, bi, and trans youth. Precious is married to Myles Brady and lives in Hyde Park on the South Side of Chicago, where they are raising their daughter, Zayn. In her free time, she enjoys online shoe shopping, travel, and fine dining with friends. For more information visit www.preciousbradydavis.com.